THE
PRICE OF
SILENCE

Hélène Pascal-Thomas

incorporating

THE PROMISE

℔

Tivoli Books

Tivoli Books
Copyright © Hélène Pascal 2021
First published in 2021 by Barnwolf Press
Revised, extended edition 2023 by Tivoli Books
helene.pascal@rocketmail.com

Distributed by Gardners Books, 1 Whittle Drive, Eastbourne, East
Sussex, BN23 6QH
Tel: +44(0)1323 521555 | Fax: +44(0)1323 521666

www.helenepascal-thomas.co.uk

British Library Cataloguing in Publication Data
A catalogue record for this book is available from the British Library.

ISBN 978-0-9567621-2-2

Typeset by Amolibros, Milverton, Somerset
Cover design by Jane F Tatam
www.amolibros.com
This book production has been managed by Amolibros
Printed and bound by T J Books Limited, Padstow, Cornwall, UK

For René-Jacques Baumer

Disclaimer

The author has recreated events, locales and conversations from correspondence, notes and memories. In order to maintain anonymity in some instances the author has changed the names of some individuals and places, identifying characteristics and details, such as physical properties, occupations and places of residence. The author does not assume and hereby disclaims any liability to any party for any loss, damage, or disruption caused by errors or omissions, whether such errors or omissions result from negligence, accident, or any other cause.

Contents

Prologue

Was it a leaf or a bird? They sometimes drop to the ground in the same fashion, the leaves barely turning at a slight slant. Leaves from the tall apple tree on the right litter the lawn in front of me like so many brass and copper coins in a fountain. No wind today, so they fall at long intervals, like reticent gifts. All is quiet. Apart from the bubbling of water on the top of the black egg-shaped fountain, there is no sound, unlike this morning when everything was a-flurry with squirrels and birds leaping about the place.

As if a squirrel had just jumped at my feet I am startled by an image of Odile standing next to me; I am eight years old and have found a role for myself: every Sunday morning I clean and shine my parents' and sister's shoes. Such a nice thing to do, left hand inside the soft leather, the right one busy in strong then gentle strokes with brushes and cloth, rubbing to a satisfying glow. I get approval, raise benevolent smiles – I have changed my life, I am mistress of that moment. Odile, all blond curls and three and a half years my junior, watches me finally polishing hers. She stands on my right and keeps still, looking at my face and hands

1

in turn, detached rather than involved, a spectator. I would like comment, preferably praise, as I am an older, kind sister, looking after her needs, but she stays silent.

"You see, Odile, I insist, I am polishing your pretty little shoes... What am I?"

"An idiot," she replies without hesitation – and doesn't even run away for she knows I was never allowed to hit her. I may not even feel like it as this was a time when she often made us laugh with jokes or playful tricks and so she could easily remain in this role that day, and my own role was to laugh along with it: what a funny little thing she was! Except that one day she just stopped laughing, and lived thereafter in unseen chaos.

Even though I didn't see much of Odile after childhood itself – our long internment in family life with its silences and moody rituals – my sister's image has obdurately followed me like a shadow visiting me in recent years and presenting me with a magnified and at times distorted image of my own life and hauntings. It is recognisable: we shared a childhood in *that* family, *that* small town with its peeling walls and narrow pavements; *that* society born of the war world where, the Germans having finally vacated our area of the South-West of France in 1945 after a two-year invasion, suspicions of collaboration and secret feuds would have grown and fermented around us as in a subterranean world: few words and half sentences spoke long and deep in people's hearts.

Like all children, Odile and I absorbed a great deal of the said, unsaid, denied and unexplained, storing the traumatic moments in our bodies for later examination, as they may choose to surface from their underground life through the pain they would later inflict, prodding us to dig ever deeper into that still-living soil. Childhood is a time when you don't know you know, but the scars, more visible as we grow, will one day be picked open and bleed the truth.

I was born in July 1939 in elegant and prosperous Bordeaux just two months before it was occupied by the German army, and Odile in January 1943 in a small dreary town in the Pyrenees when the region was still in the Free Zone and our father was finally able to find a lawyer's practice to buy with Mother's money. We lived temporarily in the house of some kind, local people until my parents found a large first-floor apartment to rent in a house that faced the Gendarmerie Nationale – the Army Barracks – on the main road to Toulouse. There in that grey and bleak little town we all lived until Odile and I, one a few years after the other and following what seemed an eternity, at long last left home to go to university.

As children, Odile and I shared a large bedroom, our beds at opposite ends for some reason, so we could see each other but seldom talk and confide, and I must assume this was of our choosing although Mother would usually decide on the best arrangement. Later, I was given the smaller bedroom between what remained Odile's bedroom and our parents' bedroom and this suited me fine: I liked my privacy and we often argued anyway.

Each bedroom had French windows opening onto a wooden-floored balcony that ran the whole length of the back of the house and overlooked a garden shared with the other tenants downstairs. The toilet was situated at our parents' bedroom end of the balcony so we all had to face the cold on winter days and the dark on winter nights when nature called. I remember, when little, carving with my nails into the soft plaster of the toilet walls the many haunting and hideous faces with large noses of 'the Man with Horns', (*l'Homme à Cornes*), who would come to get us if we weren't good.

Good or not, I dare say now that both Odile and I met him.

This is what is so difficult to say, and yet it is the purpose of this book: to tell the story of two little girls' early childhood abuse, emotional as well as sexual, in the veiled, alluded way it was recalled, mirroring the hidden and obscure ways it occurred, all of it in the 'comme-il-faut' silence of a middle-class family obsessed with propriety; how we struggled to grow up in our own different ways, suffering in ignorance the malignant after-effects of what happened to us in infancy and early childhood. This silence was sly, fog-like; penetrating of soul and limb, it put our voices to sleep, helped by Mother's ceaseless demands and her troubled, insistent and confusing exhortations to "forget, we must forget…"

It is only in later years that the obscurity became more clarified, illuminated at first through traumatic visions. These had an appearance of unreality, detached as they were from current situations: I hold my little girl in my arms, lulled in a motherly contentment that has been hard-earned after years of drama, and all of a sudden images appear in front of my eyes, superimposed on the room's furniture and objects, a shocking intrusion: a man in dishevelled clothes, panting, seems to be rubbing a small naked child against himself, oblivious, in a trance, and I want to scream because the man in front of my eyes is Jeremy himself, her father: I always felt his love for her to be his one redeeming quality and the reassurance that my baby would at least have a father, if not a conventional family. I recoil in horror, brutally struck by the odious presence of the images I am experiencing and immediately blame myself for allowing into my consciousness. They have invaded my mind like a blow, irrationally. I am going mad. It can't happen again, it mustn't.

4

– And who is the baby?

But it does, a few months later. I had consigned those odious images to near oblivion. My little child is five years old then, no longer a baby. She is in no danger, she is thriving. So who is the baby? I ask myself again much later, but at the time I curse myself in horror. The man this time is a new neighbour, an old man who has visited a little too often recently and I am overcome with panic, filled with rage and disgust at this invasion, this break-in.

This break-in: shall I say what rape is? I know what I am talking about: it is the unwanted *breaking and entering* of a body by another, a foreign body, an assailant of the integrity of your flesh as well as a life-long nightmare imposed upon your consciousness. It is always violent even if violence isn't apparently involved, as fright can freeze your healthy responses, making flight impossible. Besides, a small child cannot flee, and I realised several decades later when I was in my early fifties, that I must have been around two and a half years old at the time if not much earlier.

I am not just speaking of physical penetration as of all the adjacent events of being handled, positioned, prepared for the act, that are always accompanied by the sly traumas of sounds or words, body smells and touching, and the invisible intrusion of foreign breath, each leaving inescapable marks on the soul.

As a virus within a cell, the act has entered your nascent consciousness and directs from then on what reality is for your slowly developing mind. It is poison but you have no way of knowing its toxic ways and feral nature or differentiating it from overall familial affection.

It is also simply malware, conditioning your future thoughts and responses, your dreams, desires and choices. Your compass has been twisted, and actions which you think are your own, thoughts you assume to be yours, have been compromised, warped by unwanted and misunderstood knowledge. What should be normal perception and course of human experience of relationships is instantly altered. You are programmed to be confused, defective, easily acquiescent, often feeling paralysed, psychologically infected with false understanding. You are split. And you are damned. Because, more often than not you will in the future have no awareness of danger or safety, taking passing interest for life-changing opportunity, and you will tend to trust the wrong people since you have never been protected and are unable to tell the difference.

Having been exposed to sensations that your consciousness was too immature to process, your body's reactions falsified, you will tend to confuse sexual turmoil with desire and feelings, since the loneliness of abandonment has left you to be the prey of thoughtless and selfish others. And if you remain unlucky, you will ceaselessly look for love.

Trying for most of my life to find my way in this murky fog, I can attempt to report as I lived them the confused paths I took over the first fifty-odd years of my life, some of the wrong choices and judgements I made and those that were made for me. I can also describe many of the symptoms of post-traumatic stress syndrome, learned helplessness and dissociation in particular, which crippled me all my life without me realising it, hampering me in reaching my goals. In parallel with my efforts to understand the whys and wherefores of events I found hard to control, my younger sister Odile, equally damaged, chose a different path, but the harm done to us both had the most disastrous and long-lasting consequences.

> *"Something we were withholding made us weak*
> *Until we found it was ourselves."*
>
> *Robert Frost*

Chapter One

London, 15th July 2003

The small town in the French Pyrénées where Odile and I grew up looked for all the world to seem as if it was ashamed of itself: drab houses of grey and dirty brown, shutters and shop fronts unpainted for years if not decades – it might well have been. The war years cannot have helped, with eventual German occupation in 1942 when they finally crossed into the unoccupied zone and invaded the South of France.

I have often wondered what makes the spirit of a place, where the natural architecture of a landscape seems to predict, since it contains it, a future tragedy, a cataclysm: I think of Glencoe in Scotland, the Cathar region in France. Nothing as theatrical qualified our very provincial environment, but the very dullness and dinginess of the town leaked nevertheless into people's souls, with symptoms varying from ennui and depression to simple daily boredom. Mostly, I remember the hopelessness, the dead-insideness of the place. The silence.

Being a little child did not seem to help: Daddy was unresponsive and silent and Mum seemed sad and anxious. You couldn't run or you might fall, nor jump, you would get too hot, nor play since you would get dirty. I realised much later that I never knew how to play. Looking back, neither of my parents looked as if they had played much themselves or would have even known how to.

The seventh of nine children, my father was born in 1903 in Toulouse in a genteel and strict family of lawyers. He was a young boy when his father died, and an uncle helped him later to study law. Neither his education nor the spirit of the times encouraged him to complain, but I think he was aware of the sadness of his youth. I remember him whistling in the bathroom a tune – from *Madame Butterfly*? "*Toujours sourire, le coeur douloureux...*" and my mother raising her eyes to the ceiling in exasperated mockery with an air of saying: "What has he got to complain about? His suffering is nothing compared to mine..." and sighing, shaking her head.

His own mother, who remained small and slim despite bearing nine children, was a stern, strict but dignified woman who never complained and lived to the grand age of ninety-seven. I have no recollection of her smiling with joy, and she sent Odile and me 'to the corner' once for playing with water at the garden tap. I asked her when I was adolescent:

"Granny, did you want all these children?"

"One took them as they came, you know."

So it was possibly a good thing my grandfather died after number nine, I surmised, imagining her exhaustion.

My father as an adult was of average size and slim-built, his rather thin hair slicked back, a duller shade of blond in his grown-up years, with hazel eyes. Women friends – they told me so approvingly – thought him handsome and particularly distinguished; certainly his suits emphasised his distinction, all in different shades of grey with thin stripes of cream or Prince of Wales checks. '*L'élégance anglaise*' was much in favour then and suited his position in society: to him, being – having strived to become – a bourgeois, was an achievement.

He had no idea that my generation was growing up rejecting almost everything of the bourgeois culture, its self-satisfaction and self-serving narrowness of spirit. To him, his status was a reward for his hard work and had to show: he would almost always wear a grey felt hat with a trim adorned with the tiniest pheasant feather, a beige overcoat – later bought at Burberry's in Bordeaux – and fine leather gloves.

The car had to match his elegant but sober propriety and was usually black with a dark grey interior. Odile and I called it: *'the hearse'*. He wouldn't hear of a pale blue car, the only colour on offer in those days, having to look serious at all times, *'un Monsieur'*, betraying all his insecurities by looking stern in public, only allowing himself to relax and laugh with close friends.

It was a blessing that the French were free to enjoy good food and drink; indeed, if gluttony was mocked, the joys of eating were never proscribed by the Church. This particular pleasure of the flesh being reasonably sin-free allowed good cheer and made gatherings with friends pleasant occasions, but while Sunday lunches *'en famille'* were often sinister with my parents not talking to each other while expecting Odile and me to look happy, it was at least possible to rejoice at the wonderful meal of roast chicken and fine chips cooked to perfection, followed by sumptuous gâteaux my father went to buy at the best pâtisserie in town, putting a suit on again for the occasion. Odile and I having had to attend the eleven o'clock mass by ourselves, always a cheerless event, felt we deserved this weekly treat: we were good and obedient children, as our parents had had to be themselves; the gratification of good food gave us all a sense of existing at a most reassuring level.

Our mother strove to be the perfect housewife, aiming for a high standard of cleanliness in the home, elegance in her appearance and accomplishment as a cook. My father's comments, designed to humiliate her, could drive her to tears until their friends' high praise would silence him, so she loved entertaining, and on those occasions, out would come the silver, the crystal glasses, the little bunches of flowers in tiny individual vases, the fine embroidered tablecloths and napkins.

She was born in 1916 – thirteen years my father's junior – in Limoges, the daughter of an enterprising jewellery-maker and businessman who got rich not merely as a shopkeeper and entrepreneur, but casting gold bars for the State and wisely investing in property. He was of average height but imposing, dark-haired with a thick moustache, and it seems that he enjoyed elsewhere a jollier time than with his family. His wife, though, was beautiful with her smooth black hair and large blue eyes. They had three daughters.

My mother being the youngest and seemingly surplus to requirements was sent away after birth to a wet-nurse in the country: her mother wished to have an active life and running her husband's shop and looking after the two older girls gave her plenty to do. My mother adored her foster mother's family and was possibly rather spoilt while feeling abandoned by parents she visited rarely. She remembered her mother kissing her only once and was returned home when she reached school-age, sorely missing her foster mother's affection.

Both her parents died of strokes a year apart when she was in her early teens and she must have felt an orphan for the second time. Her older sister, recently married, was forced to take her in but made her life so intolerable my mother swore to marry the first man who asked for her hand. This she did, and she wept as she confided in me one afternoon, at great cost to herself both emotionally and financially as she had indeed become a very rich and therefore desirable young woman. I can only see, now that I have attained myself a degree of understanding and compassion, that being forced to have frequent sexual intercourse with a man she didn't love must have seemed to her as no less than repeated rape, conditioning her to life-long distaste if not hatred for the act. Exceptionally beautiful with her black hair and blue eyes, she was also needy and naive, a dangerous combination at all times.

The man she married, Louis, was a qualified lawyer without the fortune required in those days to buy an existing practice. Louis obviously thought my mother would provide but got side-tracked by his addiction to gambling and philandering. A visiting aunt found her in despair one day and rescued her, helping her to get a divorce as well as some basic qualifications at a secretarial college.

The first time my father set eyes on her was in Bordeaux where they both lived. Driving along one of the main streets full of smart shops and cafés, he got distracted by the gorgeous young woman walking on the pavement, and crashed his car into some road works ahead. She burst out laughing and they started chatting; "he was so distinguished..."

They lived together for a few years, marrying in January 1938, eighteen months before I was born. Odile and I never saw any photographs of their wedding, which puzzled me and remained unexplained for a long time. There was, in those stern Catholic times, a certain incompleteness and in this case shame associated with civil marriages – and she wouldn't have been wearing a white dress... Having been married and divorced before also meant that they were both excluded by the Church from receiving sacraments – including that of a religious marriage.

Free to find his fortune again and after some prevaricating which I couldn't explain to myself for a long time, my father decided he was making a perfect choice. For her, who had missed out so much on family love and care, this much older man offered a mirage of safety: a parental figure, he would protect her, while she would also raise her social status in her own eyes by marrying into a family of lawyers: coming from a shopkeeper's background wasn't quite respectable enough socially in those very conventional days: you served people... . She naturally offered to sell some of the property she had inherited from her parents to finance the purchase of a practice. In the middle of the war, he eventually found one for sale in that ugly little town in the Pyrénées. This is when, once Mother had paid for it, he put his sole name on the deeds, robbing her instantly. Having taken care to have their marriage contract subsequently drawn on the basis of separation of assets instead of putting them in common – as would have been at least grateful – she lost all recourse under the law.

Did it seem as if the past was repeating itself?

I can imagine her heart sinking at the sight of the dreary provincial town where father was taking us, and remember her frequent complaints about the dull and unsophisticated environment she was –we were – obliged to live in: it was a market town, all these peasant farmers... . He promised her to move his practice to Toulouse, a large and beautiful city not far away, once his situation improved, she would have to be patient, but they kept that dreary flat opposite the gendarmerie, much to her despair, until after Odile and I left home for university.

My father, who had little idea of how to be a father, furnished our lives lightly like a visitor who came for his meals, would occasionally smile and say: "I hope you are being good and obedient, huh?" but more often ignore us.

12

Good moods came more easily when friends arrived for a game of bridge or acquaintances visited, and you wouldn't have found anyone to believe my parents weren't a cheerful and happy couple, so strong were social pressures to present a good front. Besides, those moments took them out of their own wretchedness.

Mother, who hadn't had a real family life either, at least attempted to invent one, though it isn't surprising that it owed more to form than content; her insecurity was a constant strain, forcing her to reassure herself and the world that they were a respectable family by following society edicts tensely and to the letter. However, the marriage was unhappy and eventually, as it was believed in those days that a second child could steady a couple's bonds, Mother gave birth to Odile in the middle of the war, in January 1943. A few months later, one fine summer's day, the German army rolled its lorries and troops into the large courtyard of the imposing brick buildings of the Gendarmerie Nationale across the road. I was only three and a half years old but could feel her terror as she and I watched through the smallest gap between the wooden shutters of our dining room: how would the German soldiers deal with the population? Thank goodness it seems they were on orders to behave themselves so I now merely remember the pleasure of reaching out for my first wild cherries in a friend's garden where Mother rushed us for refuge that day.

If she aimed at beauty and elegance in the home, Mother did not leave the garden unattended, or at least the left side which belonged to us. It was mostly a working garden in those years of occupation and rations, but she had created a square rose and peony bed closer to the house where I had moments of wonder as I delicately separated their petals, working my fingers towards the stamens in the hope of finding a serendipitous and precious-looking beetle. I still see her, a town woman, growing vegetables, peas and beans as well as raspberries, redcurrants, strawberries. She made blocks of soap with saponaria plants that grew on the edge of the path and wove for herself lovely summer sandals out of raffia with soles of cork: women's magazines were always full of good advice and women were as always, closer to life, sensible and practical.

The Occupation, peaceful locally at least on the surface, presented my parents with daily fears: every morning we could watch enemy soldiers in their dull green uniforms (we called that colour *'caca d'oie'*: goose poo) marching towards some open fields beyond, singing fierce songs, and we trembled at the sight of the shaven heads of the Central Asian prisoners known as Mongols the Germans were using as guards, I learned later they had a fearful reputation for raping women and girls. I recall Father was at one point tempted to work for the enemy and Mother having to use all her arguments to prevent him doing so. I found myself once, a five-year-old near the end of the war, collecting our ration of sugar for the week from the grocery store two doors away, being watched by a young, blond-haired German soldier who tapped my cheek gently: he was supposed to be a dreadful man, never to be spoken to; I was so confused. Nothing, but nothing, was ever as it seemed. Maybe God knew what was truly going on? We were taught to pray to Him when little, and before going to sleep we would kneel by our beds and say with concentration, before jumping in:

– Baby Jesus, I give you my heart. Please bless daddy and mummy and all those I love. Amen.

We were taught that He cared, but why do we suffer so? Priests spoke of mysteries, leaving the field open, and Mother had prompted me a few times, when I was in tears for some reason:

– One must forget, one has to forget…

– Forget what?

I have forgotten.

Some Sundays differed from the housebound norm by family car trips to Luchon for lunch with Viktor and Maroussia, pleasant and talkative White Russians who I recall were very loud, Viktor being a little deaf. He was a barrister and spoke a spectacularly literary French; Maroussia had been a dancer before the war and looked very beautiful in the photographs I have left. Luchon, a grey town in a valley ensconced between the dark green mountain sides of the Pyrénées, with slate roofed chalets and damp gardens, seemed oppressive and claustrophobic, sunk in the winter mist which hid the view of peaks you would have had to climb very high to see.

After lunch, Odile and I were let loose in our buttoned-up coats in the streets of the sleepy town: 'You can just walk around,' Mother had said, so we did, trying to distract ourselves gazing at smart shop windows as Luchon was a spa with many summer visitors. On the few occasions I managed to see the mountain sides close to, I was awed by the stony and gritty slopes which didn't seem to invite climbing, so steep, dark and hostile did they look to me. I knew some people loved climbing mountains, attacked them joyfully with good cheer and optimism, anticipating the rewards of reaching the top, having gained the freedom of an unimpeded view on vast snowy peaks. It seemed to me such a fearsome enterprise, and an odd thing to want to do as if life wasn't hard enough already, since we would have to go back to school the next day.

School was a neutral sort of place – dull, strict, well-meaning – and I was a neutral sort of child – dull, obedient, well-meaning, with neat dresses and disciplined curls around my face. The playground, shaded by large plane trees, was noisy and I was quiet, sitting on the wall by the steps while others threw balls high up in the air, shouted and ran. A boy sometimes came to sit next to me. "You aren't playing?" I asked. "I don't know how to,'"he replied. "I know," I said, "I'm the same." In class, Madame Lupiac leant by my side, checking my work, and smiled at me sweetly, her bright lipstick shining like joy. I would apply myself for her, and for Mum, and, not knowing how to be without ties, I attached myself to another little girl, Marie-Claire, whom I did not let out of my sight. Naughty boys – we girls were mostly good – were sent to the corner and given lines, but threats at school were meaningful and infringements rare, while at home they were made tongue-in-cheek when we were little: "If you don't finish your greens, or are naughty, the Man with Horns will come and get you!" They later graduated to: "What would your father say!?" This worked for a long time. Carved with my fingernails on the bare plaster of the balcony toilet walls, a dozen worrying faces of men with horns and hooked noses observed me as I was sitting. They belonged to dark spaces, the foreign, the dreaded, the unsayable.

When there isn't enough affection to go around in families – genuine caring, unlike the casual currency lazily labelled 'love' – it is frequent for children to think it is because the other child is receiving it. Thus Odile and I felt equally and in turns deprived, unseen and unheard. I felt better when she wasn't there, getting closer to Mum, and she must have cherished the times she could spend alone with her. We both competed in giving her sweet loving notes and drawings: Mother showed these to a friend only a few years ago, to show that we used to adore her, what could have happened? It was incomprehensible.

As we grew up and learned to look at our parents with a certain distance, we were aghast: we must have been adopted, we couldn't possibly belong. We felt like props, not even actors, in an absurd play where appearances and manners were all that counted and where we had to show not merely that we were 'nice, well-brought-up girls', but a rung or two above many others, being middle-class of the professional variety: we should therefore not play or make friends with anyone whose background was 'not quite nice'. Apart from the example our family was meant to set for us, substance was supposed to be provided by school and religion since our parents showed no external signs of being religious themselves, dispatching Odile and me to mass without attending services and being mysterious about it. Odile and I were put 'on the rails', as was proper and good, and were supposed to come out of this traditional education as socially acceptable and marriageable young women.

In spite of the distance I have acquired, and the passing of so many years, I marvel still at the all-encompassing love Odile and I felt for Mother as children: she had such a beautiful face and gentle gaze that, like happy bunnies caught in her headlights, we could wish for nothing more than to be loved by our sweet goddess and meet with her approval. It is a fact that we tend to attribute goodness to beauty, but this can be a mirage as vast as our need to love: she was the sole object of our devotion, directing at all times that it should be so. This sad, beautiful woman who had suffered a childhood of terrible exclusion and loneliness would attempt to fill her enormous needs by turning Odile and me into her emotional slaves. The leitmotiv – it worked every time – was: "To please Mummy". "Do it to please Mummy". "Why would you do this since it would hurt Mummy?" Our own growing and needy selves were tortured by these constant demands often at odds with our own desires, and if they seemed not to be working, she came in with the master blow: "Well, in that case, I don't love you anymore." The cries, the tears of anguish, the protestations of love and submission: how to exist without her love?

The rumblings of adolescence which were beginning to affect me (I was *'looking at boys'*) did not seem to affect Odile in any obvious way when her time came, but maybe I wasn't paying attention since I was also beginning to find a voice, sufficiently at least to answer our father back; I cannot remember Odile getting angry at home; she seemed introverted, thoughtful and quiet. Mother told me much later Odile had secretly, in her early teens, fallen for my handsome sweetheart of our seaside holidays, René-Jacques. I had no idea of it at the time, as he ignored her almost completely. He and I wrote to each other for some years from the age of twelve or thirteen, when he came to visit me each August in our rented sea-side villa or we met in the scented pine forests that surround the Arcachon Bassin. I treasured his letters which were an event for me. Odile was a bland outsider to what I was living, she just tagged along, seemingly having no role of her own, and my own thirst for being allowed her no role in my life either.

I now see it already showed a pattern that would keep her from developing as she should; I was the older sister, the example to follow, the guide to admire and imitate – also the rival she would envy and hate. I was struggling to survive childhood, but I was animated by that struggle. Knowing I knew nothing and fragile in my sense of self, I was striving to understand: reading, questioning, at times daring to rebel. Odile, on the other hand, remained quiet and surly, developing a worrying passivity. When I think of her at that age, thirteen or fourteen to my seventeen, a chrysalis of a girl, unassuming and gentle if stubbornly closed, I see that we lived our lives separately most of the time, except on the few occasions when I was inviting school friends over and would be told to include her so she did not feel left out. Sibling rivalry being what it is, I wouldn't always have made her welcome and I can now imagine her need to belong and her pain at my occasional rejection.

Those were the early days of rock 'n roll ('Rock Around The Clock' was being played everywhere); my school friends and I were learning how to dance the right steps to the rhythm but I can't remember ever being thrown over any boy's shoulder, we were all fairly restrained if energetic. I loved dancing, a discovery for me, and have often thought my life might have been different if I had spent more of it on the dance floor. The joy of it took me out of the anxiety-filled fog I floated in most the time. My body had a voice and it was overwhelming, liberating, my feet wouldn't stop even when I was sitting, and I couldn't wait for a boy to ask me to dance.

Haunting me still, I have this tragic image of Odile 'dancing' the Rock, seemingly unable to move on her own initiative as her feet looked powerless to show free will or desire to bounce on the polished floor of our apartment as all our feet did ceaselessly. Like a rag doll, she actually had to be pulled – her partner had to *pull* her towards him almost by force, and then *push* her away, as she seemed incapable of sensing that her body could be a joyful and animated entity. I remember few things of my childhood but my mind's eyes are still wide-open in puzzlement and concern as I re-live those scenes. We had to explain to her that she had to do some of the pushing, pulling and bouncing herself, it was called dancing. Even now, after all my learning, training and a late career as a counsellor, I still feel aghast at it, it is too close to the bone.

My next salient memory of her is of an afternoon when we were walking on the pavement with a friend of mine, and we heard a crowd of rowdy young men behind us. It was customary at the time for boys of eighteen to undergo a medical to assess their suitability for military service and this was usually followed by a drunken binge. Those boys were loud and red-faced, linking arms and singing stupid songs. Two of them playfully got hold of Odile, pulling her into the entrance hall of a cinema. When I realized what was happening I fought the two who were trying to grab and kiss me, freed myself of one 'attacker', only to see her standing against the wall, her eyes closed and her arms along her body, limp. One boy was laughing, the other leaning against her. I rushed, pulled him off her and kicked him in the shins and they left smirking. She didn't move, opened her eyes, said nothing. I was very angry at her: what's wrong with fighting? Couldn't she fight?

And I thought much later: what happened to cause her to be so passive and resigned? So much a victim? Where had she learnt that this could possibly be a way to be? *The* way to be. It was pathetic, dreadful, and more than dangerous: it was insane. I didn't know yet that I could suffer from the very same affliction.

Chapter Two

If a bush starts behaving unreasonably on a still day, it has to be because of a squirrel, the birds are more discreet, but the squirrels are the hooligans in the trees, they clamber, tumble and leap extravagantly from branch to branch, crashing into the bushes. This garden is a playground, a comedy-theatre. I organise shows every morning at breakfast, when I throw pieces of bread and apple peel for them as a fast-food treat. Then I watch them from behind the glass of the orangery, a cup of lemon tea in my hand, laughing at their pranks.

This morning I slowly come to and remember dreaming my father wasn't dead. 'Am I going to have to kill him, then?' I thought wearily – that dreary, awful duty of mine. I struggle to emerge.

I see myself – was I thirteen or fourteen? – standing opposite him at one end of our dining table, clearing the dishes after a meal. I don't know what he had said, to Mother very likely, but I raise my hand and point my finger at him, I shout: "If you say one more word, one more, I will tell you what I think of you, I will!" and he stares at me astonished then looks away sheepishly without responding, slinks out of the dining room, pursing his lips. Mother has stood rigid. I sense they are both frightened. I have a strange awareness of a power I didn't know I had: what on earth did they think

I was going to say? And where did I get that courage, that daring? Why wasn't I punished for my insolence? Or was I acting upon something buried and forbidden? Something forgotten?

"I want to be shown respect!" he said vehemently on another occasion when we had argued. I remember retorting that I would respect him when I thought he deserved respect. These scenes, which I recall because they reflected my nascent and tentative coming of age, make me look strong and clear when I was none of those things at the time. I came to learn over many years that it is enough simply to *appear* stronger, clearer and slightly more aggressive than the enemy to be able to reclaim some territory: bluffing would do until I came true, and I was certainly not clear enough in myself to even bluff consciously at the time.

My anger came from deeper inside me, somewhere I didn't understand, while I would have explained it at the time by my duty – and my need – to protect Mother, which is nevertheless also true: all children protect their parents. And clearly Father wasn't strong, which on occasion gave me an advantage: he was shy, awkward, hesitant, and shifty, rarely looking you in the eyes, and when he did sometimes it seemed a 'not-quite-there' look that both doubted and withheld, often sad and self-conscious. His answers were usually evasive – "Yes, no, I don't know…" and gave me a sense of the fog he was in, which was contagious.

I came to notice the way he walked, disoriented, right foot and body to the right, left foot and body to the left, a yes-no of the body. Maybe the ground was not stable beneath his feet, and I grew to see that he had had no guidance, merely precepts, in childhood. On family outings, he would walk ahead of us on the pavement, separate. Odile and I followed behind, holding Mother's hand, and if she became aware of his aloneness – or a lack of symmetry –

she would push us ahead: "Go and walk with your father," and we would suddenly appear on each side of him, to his surprise, his two little daughters in identical coats and polite white socks.

"Go and kiss your father goodnight," Mother would also remind us when bedtime came. So we did as we were told and finally went to bed, me wiping my cheek.

Conscious of his own weakness, he would now and again attempt authority, but in daily matters Mother's reasoned judgment usually prevailed and his longed-for dominion over the household seldom materialised. He would on occasion announce a pronouncement by wagging his index finger for a while, then hector: "In Life..." followed by some warning or declaration, and would further delineate our world: "A meal is a ceremony!"; "A bourgeois house is a closed house!"

"Yes," I would counter later, "une maison close!" (a brothel) to his powerless indignation.

His authority a failure, he sometimes allowed himself to show his gentler feelings, indulging me with some extra pocket money – "but don't tell your mum" – or sweet talk, when he would express himself in baby speech which, as I grew up, irritated and offended me: "Don't talk to me as if I am still a child!" Most embarrassing was his question, uttered in private: "Who do you prefer, your mum or your dad?" I remained silent, unable to give him the answer he must have yearned for. But when he pointed at me the three monkey figurines sitting on a bookshelf, covering in turns their eyes, ears and mouths, illustrating some philosophy or other that he might have wished to impart to me, "A good philosophy for monkeys," I remember commenting.

I was puzzled the time he cried: coming into my room to kiss me goodnight (Mother would have checked: "Did you say goodnight to the girls?" if he had been in his study when we went to bed.), he kissed me, then burst into tears.

"What's the matter, Daddy?" I asked, embarrassed. "Nothing, it's nothing," he said, rubbing his eyes and composing himself, "It's only some work I haven't finished." I could relate to that. A little unnerved, I wiped my cheek as usual when he had gone and allowed myself to breathe again.

He had a friend who visited him on occasion during the war and also later, whose name I have never forgotten somehow, Bernard Michelot, or maybe Micheleau, whom I didn't think Mother liked because he hadn't been invited for a meal even though he brought a rabbit or a pheasant as a gift on occasion. I couldn't stand looking at him: he was a fat man with a red clammy face and hot breath, but he was supposed to have been in the Resistance, blowing up bridges or railway lines to frustrate the German invaders. Father said I should admire him, and sometimes went hunting with him so had to get himself a gun and some hunting clothes for the circumstance, which made Mother smile to herself, I noticed.

After lunch, Father always took a nap in his study, while Odile and I went back to school as we were day girls at the time. Then he left again for his office, or the Court of Law if he was pleading a case. At weekends, we would have to be quiet, whisper, tiptoe during his nap, then occupy ourselves as best we could until the day's end. Playing with dolls had its limits, as they were shy of role-play and slept a lot, ever silent in their frilly little cots as good children should be. I preferred reading, more and more.

When he drove to Toulouse to plead a more important case, I remember praying he wouldn't come back, there would be an accident: then life would be good, Mum would stop crying, there would be no more arguing and we would be safe, but he always came back. As usual, he would announce his arrival by whistling on three notes. Mother greeted him, dinner would soon be ready and it was always delicious even when it was a simple omelette. I admired without envying her the care she took over the meals. "I don't want him to be able to reproach me for anything!" she said at times, fretting with anxiety, as if defending herself. "Is it nice?" she couldn't help asking. "Umm, it was better last time," he condescended, and she winced.

His health often seemed to worry him although he was rarely ill, and then only with minor chest complaints. Red meat was de rigueur, this was a French household after all, so we ate steak regularly, because it was 'good for us'. There was implied a feeling that the blood-redness of the meat would transfuse into our veins, making us strong and healthy. When a chicken was killed – we had a small coop downstairs – the blood was kept for father who liked it fried in a pan like a pancake. I can still see the scene the first time I watched Mum cook one: it sizzled in the pan, the minute it met the oil, the heat, and spread to a dark full moon, with small volcanoes made by bubbles. A trembling in her hand, Mother pricked it with a fork, a little harshly, irritated as I stood watching, my head at her elbow, asking:

"Who is it for? What is it?"

"A blood pancake," she said, and shook it a little strongly, it nearly spilt. "Your father likes it," she added, an eyebrow up, tight-lipped, then complained: "To make him strong." And I could hear her silent prayer: "Let it not work, please God, let it not work."

Not knowing she was herself strong gave my mother other weapons; she would be the trembling victim, and her tears and cries would guarantee her daughters' adamant loyalty. In part because he was petty, also because he owed her what he had, Father took his revenge and assured his supremacy by both humiliating her and depriving her of money. Even the housekeeping was the subject of arguments that we heard through my father's study's door, Mother pleading that he hadn't given her any money that week, which he usually denied.

She would come out of his study wrecked, defeated, and would later kiss and hug Odile and me, saying we should be good and well-behaved, and polite with Daddy. We cried, kissed and promised. He would at times refuse to give her money to buy the clothes she needed, even though she had given him for safe-keeping the funds that remained to her after the purchase of his practice. At other times I recall Mother's voice shrill through the door: "No! No! You can ask me for anything but not that!" followed by more tears. I didn't dare to wonder what. It was just another of these mysterious things.

He had perfected a very subtle act at mealtimes: Mother would cook lunch, serve us all. He would watch her silently as she ate, focusing on her mouth as if she was eating noisily, playing 'gentry' to her 'shopkeeper's daughter'. She would wince again, feeling slapped. I would make mental notes, become little by little more radicalised: come the Revolution! He did, at the time, scornfully call me 'the rebel'.

Since he did not normally look at Odile's schoolbooks or mine, I cannot see that either of us received much comment or encouragement. Besides, he relied on our mother to take care of these things. She reminded us he came home tired after a long day's work. It seems true to say that work took up all his time as he had no interests outside. When I started secondary school, I naturally continued to go to the Lycée and I cried bitterly over Latin and Maths, was puzzled by chemistry, but showed liking and aptitude for French and languages.

Overall though, results were not brilliant. The social mix was unavoidable, and when I came home one lunch time and asked at the table what 'fucking' meant, my parents looked at each other with consternation and I didn't get an answer.

I was soon whisked off to a convent school nearby, run by nuns of the order of the Holy Family. Odile must have been moved as well, but I can't remember.

Looking back on it, the convent school didn't feel very different from home in atmosphere or style. There were, of course, do's and don'ts, duties. It was also fairly joyless, except that the other girls knew how to run and play ball games at break time and I didn't: almost a sin, not playing was a sign of 'bad attitude'; as if it were dangerous; conversation with a single friend was always broken up with remonstrations and exhortations to go and join a group. I much preferred to have a friend to chat with: there were secrets of sorts as we were all approaching puberty, and older or more precocious girls warned us about periods which spoke of a time at once dismal and vaguely exciting, when we would bleed every month, possibly feel a lot of pain, and have to wear between our legs folded pieces of towelling attached by safety pins to a cotton string tied around our hips.

What wisdom was imparted to us in religious education classes was based on the Bible, quotes from saints, addresses from the Pope. We sat and listened, tame, breathing an air of seriousness and piety without grace. I to-ed and fro-ed there daily in my own particular fog, a breathing automaton.

Why did my father go (with me, it was about me) for an appointment with the Mother Superior? He must have gone instead of Mother who was suffering terribly with arthritic pains at the time and couldn't walk. Was it about my work, in some subjects downright bad? Was it about not playing ball games?

Sister Marie de l'Annonciation greeted us with her usual – remarkable as it was – bounce in her step: she had a pretty face and a feminine silhouette alluding to a slim young body, and her leather belt always seemed tightly fastened. The memory strikes me, vivid – and with more unspoken lines than in a Pinter play Father stares at her body as we follow her into the Mother Superior's office, pursing his lips, twisting his mouth this way and that, a canine look in his eyes, insistent. And I can remember not a word of the conversation, but Sister Marie seeks shelter behind the masculine frame of the Mother Superior, putting her hands (these women who were never to touch) on the older nun's shoulders in a kind of affirmation...

Catechism was fed into us twice weekly and came out of us in a monotone: we mouthed words of prayers, promises, praises and appeals for mercy until, one day, processing in never-ending circles in the park of a local château, singing hymns in long white dresses and veils under the gaze of our approving parents.

In spite of the glamour of the occasion and supposedly resplendent in white, I knew I was a disappointment to my mother: physically, for a start, I left a lot to be desired: my hair was steadily going from blond to mousy; my eyes, blue and giving some hope for the future, were spoilt by my gaze which was thoughtful, but shy and hesitant; my body was a mutant entity with growing breasts I did not know what to do with – those awful first bras! – and I walked clumsily, particularly when Mother criticised and attempted to correct my posture, my walk, and the size of my hips (time for a girdle, or you had no idea how they would spread!). We pored over fashion magazines together in those pre-television days, when she attempted to guide and elevate my tastes, and I would stand afterwards in front of a mirror sucking my rounded cheeks in for a more sophisticated look. Her assessment of other people was often based on their appearance and clothes, which made what had become a task for me even more problematic.

At the same time, that beautiful woman was facing

middle-age with dread. Concerns for her health due to very severe crises of arthritis which made her almost weep with pain were a crucial argument in winning, after many years of quarrels with Father, the right to twin beds in their bedroom. "I just cannot sleep with him! I cannot get any sleep!" She sounded angry, as if his proximity and his touch were an imposition, even a threat of something awful, so she made herself 'absent' through sleeping tablets which had been in use for a great many years; it was something I couldn't understand although it troubled me.

I hated entering their bedroom on Sunday mornings to get a book, the cat, whatever: the smell of my father's breath filled the room, distinct to me in its hot, smoky and feverish staleness; it seems I was the only one who secretly objected to it as to something both intimate and unbearable, so I made my requests and left promptly, holding my breath. Being sensitive to all manner of things since childhood, I regularly felt nauseous, was sick easily and resented it as much for the disagreeable if minor incident it was as for the anguish that it seemed – as most things did – to cause Mother; she fretted, agitated, rushed for a wet cloth for my forehead, a hot-water bottle for my stomach. I made mental notes: if I had a child, I would never, ever, make a fuss if he or she was sick but would treat it as an ordinary thing and say: "Well done, darling, you will feel a lot better now!" instead of all this alarming drama. Suspicion would fall on possibly rich foods: was it the eggs? Did I eat two? Too many sweets? It was concluded I had a sensitive liver and should be careful what I ate; tablets were administered. The fact is that all my symptoms disappeared once I left home to go to university.

Meanwhile, there were the piano lessons, weekly plus lengthy practice, a harmless if tedious addition to my and Odile's education: noblesse oblige… Mother insisted on it despite our protests and I eventually got as far as playing 'The letter to Elise', although ploddingly and with clumsy feeling on the upright piano in my sister's bedroom. 'Is she gifted?' Mother asked on occasion. 'Oh, oui, Madame,' was the ineluctable reply. I knew this to be a lie but for my mother at least, the right words were uttered, as she felt reassured by formalities. The frightened and therefore conventional woman she was relied on propriety and conventions, and no more than the responses in a religious service were they for altering.

For my part, I was more and more putting my world into question, doubted received morality, pondered the nature of truth; reading helped a great deal, and Mother herself read quite a lot, later passing some of her books on to me, though seldom discussing them. Having had dreams in childhood of becoming a headmistress, she could have been a formidable one had she been able to continue to study, having plenty of authority in her temperament in spite of all her fears. I also now see her wish as a way of creating a large (and obedient) family for herself, perhaps also of looking after girls who had been sent away as she had. She might have been more enlightened with those girls, being less close to them than she was with Odile and me, since I realised later she was unable to see us as separate from her: "I am cold," she would say, "you must put a sweater on!"; or "you can't be thinking such a thing, I can't imagine it!"

In many ways she also spoilt Odile and me, making clothes for our dolls, but mostly by cooking the dishes she knew we loved; for me, pork kidneys with soggy chips, vol-au-vents with sweetbread and mushrooms, veal escalopes and petits pois, steak and frites, chocolate biscuits, meringues and clafoutis…and after school slices of bread and butter sprinkled with cocoa powder. This was a realm where all our dreams of pleasure and satisfaction merged without any chance of conflict, she creating and giving pleasures of her choosing, us receiving and enjoying those gifts and paying her back in praise and affection; we could then share a tangible and reassuring form of bonding. Indeed I often chose to meet her on her terms in that realm when in need of a safe place to exist under the gaze of her approving eyes.

Her beauty fed our adoration. Her large blue eyes with carefully plucked eyebrows accentuated the gentleness and often sadness of her gaze. Her thick black hair was cut fairly short, framing her high cheekbones with planned and docile curves; she had her hair done regularly, preferably in Toulouse where she claimed were the only good hairdressers. This was an opportunity for her to be in a large town where elegant living was on display in smart shops and lively streets, in contrast to the tatty shop-windows and dull styles on offer in our small town.

Many people would say: 'Oh, your mother is so beautiful, and always so elegant!' We were proud of her. Watching her was a more and more conscious occupation of mine, breathing in her feelings, her moods, being her almost. She smelled nice: Chanel No 5, her favourite perfume, was a regular present at birthdays; she used it when going out or when friends came to dinner, part of her offerings to herself and the world. When she felt in need of affection, it was blissful to be held in her arms for hugs and cuddles. Odile and I appeared to be the centre of her world, but were more often possessions to be administered, ruled over and processed: "To please Mummy".

Our obedience ensured her approval, as criticism always caused me to question, albeit unconsciously, who I was or wanted to become, and as I grew up defined me at times as an adversary in spite of my stubborn devotion. For although, when I was little, she 'won' at every turn, such was the depth of her need and her authority, as I became adolescent and required more freedom and time, or simply more of myself in me, her displeasure tore me apart in guilt and confusion. I have to be thankful to both my hormones and my books for once in a while standing my ground, but at those moments her face turned to deep sadness and disappointment, down came the long eyelids of disapproval, and a slight shaking of her head would point to her incomprehension; and depending on the nature of the infringement, she would react with:

"My little girl, you are hurting my feelings!"; "What a pain children are!"; "Children suck you dry!" and if I started to cry: "Oh, yes, we know, you are an abused child" (*une enfant martyre*), or quite simply: "Oh, stop all this play-acting, you are being a pain!" The tone was dismissive, contemptuous, resentful. In fact, she warned me often: "You'll see, when the time comes, if it's fun to have children!" She could not make it plainer that Odile and I were the disagreeable impositions in her life as well as to her freedom: "I stayed for you, I sacrificed myself for you!" We were humbled by that terrible gift.

Chapter Three

I am beginning to get used to the now regular morning thrill: living the day gazing at the garden – how lucky I am, this is peace with frills. I wake my face up with water, take my Euphoriac tablets most days, gauging my degree of silliness that morning, stash the unused ones away for a possibly different day in a different time. I laugh at myself, my pimpernel joy and soppy indulgence of all things around: how sweet the small wet leaves the cat brings in from the garden and drops all over my floor; how wonderful that today is Tuesday, or Wednesday.

– Hello squirrels, my little treasures, were you waiting for your morning treat? my fluffy babies... I show definite signs of an all embracing sugariness of the soul that I laugh at through a sickly pink fog. I must cut down, this is blinding goo. I need my brain back, the edge of clarity that means proper memory, and with it the pain, the coarseness, the dizziness of the edge, the ravines as well as the sky.

I make tea, take it to the orangery outside which are waiting, almost at my feet and as if in a song, three squirrels, two blackbirds, and one wood pigeon. The sun makes a late appearance and the light streams in gently.

I get some walnut and banana pieces, apple peel and core

and throw them onto the grass. They rush, pick the larger pieces first. I gaze and dissolve.

Later I sit there on the couch, and the wind is now going mad, in turn bullying, teasing and whipping all things on its anarchic course. Bad behaviour, outlandish, unwarranted; if this is punishment (I used to be a Catholic) it is undeserved, but just looking at it you feel de-stabilised, anchorless. The only antidote, for wind is pernicious if you let it, is deliberate indifference, turning away towards the domestic, the familiar, the comfortably material; a newspaper, perhaps; more tea. It's Saturday after all, a day for letting oneself be, and an article catches my eye. I start reading it with relish as if meeting an old friend because it is about France and a never-ending past, then discover it isn't really a friend at all, too crude, but captivating nevertheless: the yearly killing of the pig in my native South-West, la fête du cochon, which was a tradition for peasant farmers and their families, but for my sister and me, on that day, nothing short of an initiation.

I see Odile and me – two little girls in smocked dresses – alerted by the unearthly loud squeals of a pig dragged into the courtyard downstairs, and we rush to the balcony, lean over on tiptoes, and there it is, as if resisting arrest, stiffening its legs and digging its feet into the ground, shaking its enormous pink body in protest, and screaming, squealing.... Our neighbours are standing there, their country relatives and friends with them for the day, and they exchange jokes, noisy and raucous, animated by the thrill of the killing to come. The rest of the world has vanished, there is nothing but the squealing animal sensing its inevitable death. Women bring a wide tin bucket. The animal is then winched, shrieking, on a hook high up on the outbuilding wall, shaking and arching its body in anguish. A man waits for the bucket to be placed beneath the animal, then, knife in hand, deftly slits its throat. The squeals have stopped, the massive body convulses for a while before going limp, and the blood pours out of it like a horse pisses; people laugh and joke. Death is so natural, killing so easy. Odile and I are transfixed. A wooden table on trestles is brought out, the animal heaved upon it, and the carving carried out by two or three slick pairs of hands. The pig's body, upside-down, spills its bloody entrails. This reality is ill-mannered to us, rude even, but unquestionable. It is nevertheless alien: we lean over the balcony, ask each other, shaken:

– Did you see that?

It takes place well outside our world but survives in our memory to this day, at once incongruous and cautionary.

I had already been alerted to this other dimension by the endless night-time siren mewings of the downstairs black cat when she was on heat. 'They're fighting,' Mother had said, cutting speculation short. I loved the grace of the cat's slinky body as she rolled and stretched out in the courtyard below, dangerous, ready to jump and hiss at any approaching male, intent on scratching and scratching when she could, while letting the male get ever closer. She was laying a trap: look, I'm your friend – but I'm not – a pretend playground fight; it became other when the larger male would finally mount her, biting her neck fiercely in spite of her cries, after which she would lash out and abuse him again, hissing in open hatred.

Of course, like many children, I know about pain, physical, raw. My sessions at the dentist's in a region and at a time that hadn't heard of pain-killing injections must rank with some of the worst tortures, as he refuses to stop when I scream, and so I scream and scream as he drills and drills. Maybe it is too much for Mother, since she decides I will have to go on my own over the following weeks. She had been gentler when I had to have my tonsils out: as it was considered a simple and quick operation, they would dispense with anaesthetic. I was sat on a chair, a nurse holding my head back by pulling my hair; my throat was smeared with mercurochrome, and I immediately felt the surgeon's steel scissors cutting at the unwanted flesh inside, blood all over. Howling helped, keeping my mouth open. I recall being given as a present a pretty little red sewing box since I had been a good girl.

Books told me there was more, that real life's true landscape would be found beyond the valley, beyond the blue Pyrénées, away from this small town's walls – Elsewhere. I began to yearn to go there, wherever it was, whatever the journey, for I was living in a windowless house and would choke to death if I was not careful.

Only occasionally would the smoke screen dissolve, letting in dangerous light, before I was again retrieved, pacified: 'when you're older...' Alexander Dumas had solutions though: if caught, his hero had a way out, a magical sesame that opens the door to eternal release in the shape of a poison ring, and I shall often dream of acquiring one, just in case, because it is too hard sometimes.

Never having read Jack London, they thought he was safe, a boy's own adventure writer in a girl's hand; *The Call of the Wild*, *White Fang*, were classics. But he was, over the years, explosive, and fertilised my young brain with secret bravery, endurance, wildness, enthusiasm and heroism: I let him in at night and ran away with him to be taught about real life and how to live it. He became my mentor, my true father, pointing at injustice and suffering, courage and honour; he brought me up. I dreamt of wolves without fear, travelled on sleighs laden with the provisions needed for us and our clear-eyed dogs through our odyssey. We walked for miles in the blinding snow till we stopped for a meal by campfire. I should one day marry such a man...

Meanwhile, back at the flat, life was measured, metered,

rationed. One morning, there was blood on my sheets and my tummy hurt. Mother rushed about, came back with towelling strips, folded them; another chore ahead for these will have to be boiled clean in the washroom downstairs. She frowned, fretted, uttered: 'You know, if a man tries to touch you there, with his hand, or something else ... – well, don't, because you could have a child.'

– I know, Mum, I responded, ashamed. In fact, I knew so little. Only a year before my school friends were teasing me:

– You don't know?

– No...

– Well, look! and they drew with chalk on the courtyard floor two short vertical lines linked by a low horizontal one, the profile of a simple bed.

– You see?

– No, what is it?

– A bed!!!

I was puzzled. They progressed to electric plugs and sockets. I was stunned: how odd, how peculiar...I felt strangely numb and wrapped in fog, in spite of their sniggering. I mustn't go 'there'.

★

Mother read a lot, having won over her single beds, and furnished her evenings with ironing or rather good literature. She was now reading *Gone with the Wind*, and told me about the recent war, the terrifying void she felt plunged into once it ended, the vast and sudden silence; she had thought with anguish that nothing would ever happen again, what emptiness! But there were books, and I was growing up, nearly fifteen; Odile hardly existed for me, a small encumbrance in my life. All I know is that she was quiet, spending a long time on her homework. Mother, having finished her book, offered it to me:

"Here it is, she said, but I have pinned some pages together, promise me you will not read them, you are too young."

I was cross.

– Well, I don't want it then, I don't want to be censored. I had an inkling of what it was about: fine for me to read about the cruelties of war, the bloody massacres, the bodies torn apart, but I should know nothing about Rhett and Scarlett's married bliss, it is rude but joyful and therefore disallowed; besides, it has often been intimated that men do disgusting things. In any case, I was happy with Jack London, which meant I confronted my father more and more. I couldn't stand the smell of his breath, his hot touch even in passing. I always recoiled, as Mother did.

I was getting difficult, Mother got concerned and Father didn't know how to deal with me. Also, I seemed to be 'interested in boys' in spite of attending a religious school, it was therefore time for action. Mother had been receiving some brochures, and after talking it over with father decided that I should be sent to board outside Toulouse at a convent school run by Dominican nuns who were said by many to be the cream of the religious teaching orders. In spite of my protests – which I knew were useless – I was sent away to a pretty pink brick old château in large grounds, in the middle of a vast, flat and boring landscape.

Does it help to look at photographs? I had few, but my memories were parallel. I remembered Marie P and Mali A who shared my side of the dormitory, and that red-haired Mali used a lot of Nivea cream on her hands and face every night; fortunately – I am sensitive to smells – she slept on the far side of Marie; I was in a corner, probably alongside Madame Messal, (the nuns were called Madame during the war, and kept those titles) who slept in a small room on the other side of the wall to me. She would switch her light off before washing, not being even allowed to see her own naked body, and I recalled the irrepressible giggles that overcame us if we heard her drop the soap, imagining her large naked body fumbling on the floor in the dark.

Our long dormitory was divided into 'rooms' of six beds each by a flimsy curtain, open to the long corridor overlooking the main courtyard where newly traced rectangular beds awaited plants amid alleyways of gravel. There were still workmen on site, washrooms and showers barely finished and not yet painted. We were made to wear pale blue overalls over our own clothes, and the food was diabolical – not a word used freely in such a place. I was once kept behind after lunch by young Madame Lebrun for refusing to eat my carrots, but she was obliged to release me, carrots uneaten, for the afternoon classes. Madame Messal often prodded me awake in the morning with the sharp end of her knitting needles, but without ever drawing blood. Later, before class started – she taught Latin and French – she would read us some sermon from the Pope, or thoughts of saints (from the back of the class, I took a photograph of her, she had a moustache and wore large black-rimmed glasses). Maria Goretti, whose life in illustrated booklets we were encouraged to read, is much in favour: she had just been made a Saint by the Pope, and we were told with awe that she preferred to be stabbed to death rather than succumb to a man and lose her virginity. During outings, Madame Messal would wonder out loud who among us would make a good nun, inviting our comments and suggestions.

I had no close friends but some of the girls were rather nice; Bernadette C was lovely with her hearty laugh. Being quiet, I was sometimes regarded as sly, 'butter wouldn't melt…' I was, even to myself, a stowaway, my thoughts clandestine. True to say that I kept my feelings to myself, when I knew what they were; most of them were still sheltering, in the cocoon stage. We prepared for our exams, our Brevet, equivalent to GCSEs. One girl who worked all hours had lost a lot of weight and I looked upon her with envy, what a pity I couldn't be bothered to work that hard, I could lose some puppy fat (all those potatoes!).

I had brought with me as one of my personal treasures a scrapbook of postcard-size reproductions of paintings I admire, for I have been interested in art, mainly painting, for a few years and I love looking at them: Fra Angelico's *Annunciation*, some Nativities, *Adam and Eve* by Cranach, landscapes by Monet, portraits by Manet; wild fields and blossom by Van Gogh; a reclining nude by Velazquez; portraits and another nude by Titian; scenes by Murillo; chiaroscuro domestic scenes by de La Tour; then glorious dream scenes by Chagall, etc. It was confiscated one day, Madame Messal having glimpsed a naked body. I am told this was serious, grave even, my parents (ninety kilometres away) were alerted and summoned to a meeting with the Mother Superior from which I was excluded. Madame Messal returned the book to me later, thumbing through it, stopping at the Titian nude – luscious, mother-of-pearl flesh and wavy long red hair – to say:

"You must see this is not beautiful…"

I replied I liked it. She was displeased but I was not worried. It seemed my parents were this time, for once, entirely on my side as they told me later, adding they felt the nuns were 'just making a big fuss,' and it was all a storm in a teacup. They themselves owned a few art books, had visited museums. What the nuns hadn't realised was that art 'belonged' to the educated classes in those days, indeed it was one of their props and nudes were a given on a par with landscapes and portraits. My parents were hardly likely to criticise, even less renounce, what gave them, as part of that class, pleasure as well as status. They were also less obsessed by sin.

I felt stronger. Mother had also made me a rather nice pale blue dress, fitted at the waist, with a very modest V-neck that showed off the small gold cross I wore on a chain, but when the old priest who visited one day commented that my cross was standing on the Calvary, the nun who accompanied him made me wear a handkerchief in the opening afterwards. Such small breasts as I had seemed to cause a lot of concern, in spite of being God's creations.

When it rained, we sought refuge in the large barn that framed the courtyard at one end; no doors, just two wide openings and simple benches along the inside walls. If we were tired of playing ball-games – I was still not able to join in – we sat and sang some of the rather nice songs the nuns have taught us. One such stormy day – there was a terrific thunder and lightning show outside – we sang, sitting two or three on each other's laps for lack of room, when, dramatic as the storm and quick as lightning, Madame Lebrun rushed in and violently pulled us off each other's laps, screaming:

"Aren't you ashamed? Thirty girls alone in a barn!" The story competes for effect and educational merit with the scandal that erupted the day – the night, a Sunday night – when many of those who had been back home for the last two days needed time to confide in each other about such or such a boy met or even just glimpsed at the weekend, a regular episode in our young lives. Two girls were 'found' (in full view of the whole dormitory) in the same bed, whispering and giggling. Of course they were firmly separated and shamed. Their parents were called and they were expelled, such was the outrage of the nuns and their tragic fears. I learned that day about lesbians, although we weren't quite sure what they did. God, who had always been an unchallenged fixture in our lives, like houses, trees, parents and teachers, though invisible, started to be called in for more serious questioning as the effects of religion took their toll.

I didn't care too much since I had a nice friend, an older girl whose name might have been Nicole, I think. I could confide in her about René-Jacques, the beautiful young boy I had been meeting every summer on our seaside holidays in the pine and heather-scented woods around the Arcachon Bassin: God lived there in the sunshine.

"Gosh," she said, struck in awe at my boldness, "you have done more than me!"

And we looked at each other in wonder and excitement at all the thrills and delights to come, which we wouldn't have been able to describe to ourselves at that innocent time, let alone to another.

Chapter Four

René-Jacques. A dream of him, like a gift, lives in my head this early morning. I see him as he is – fourteen? – in the only photograph I have left of him, but alive, expressive. I see the texture of his young skin, the warmth of his hazel eyes, his generous smile, I want to touch him, I almost can. My heart goes out to him.

Pine trees were all around us in those days, owning more of the landscape than they do now, so many having given way to villas. There were roads, and holiday houses, but they were there courtesy of the woods, they did not presume too much as yet. Many pine trunks were slit on one side, a long wound weeping resin in small clay pots regularly collected for the manufacture of rubber and other substances. The stubborn scent of resin was everywhere, mixing with that of heather and those headily perfumed yellow flowers you only find by the sea. The Arcachon Bassin, a large lake open to the Ocean at one end, was a haven of lively blue water, tame tides, and typical long wooden boats with a spirited curve at the front, the 'pinasses'. The sandy beaches were not deep, but long, long, and merged with pure vast ocean sand where the ocean spread finally, by Le Pyla.

Those seaside holidays which started when I was twelve were a time of sensuous freedom. Odile and I were allowed to mix with neighbours' children, play in their gardens and the wilder territory of the woods that we invaded with thrill. Mother could relax – although she still has to shop and cook – father can read 'Le Figaro' outside on the terrace, sipping a Pernod or an orange juice. Their friends: my godfather, Lucien, a kind and witty man; my sweet godmother Josie and her husband, Daniel; my sister's godmother, Jeanette and her husband, Gérard, and others, came from Bordeaux to stay, as it is less than an hour's drive. The atmosphere was cheerful when they were there, and Odile and I had space to be. Even Odile looked happy.

With a group of friends, we explored the woods beyond the houses, also filled with young oaks and arbutus bushes among the scented heather; the long and sharp pine needles littering the ground were at times painful to our bare feet. One day, we happened (the second summer, I am pretty sure) on a group of children involved in a kissing competition. Their 'chief', called René-Jacques, was immersed in a feat of endurance and style, clasping in his young arms a girl with curly blond hair and kissing her breathlessly on, and on, and on, twisting his head right and left, miming screen passion. The others were counting, he won. He smiled broadly, engaging.

There were rumours of another gang who had collected ammunition, so we were under pressure to do the same in case we were 'attacked' and took turns gathering pinecones under the cover of darkness, just before bedtime. Mother, always prudent, sent our maid to accompany me, some humiliation for the soldier I was supposed to be. Odile was too young, she wasn't allowed. We built huts with young oak and hazel branches, sat inside and chattered, bickered, joked. The blond girl had disappeared and all of a sudden René-Jacques was mine, he had chosen me. We had our hut, where we kissed and kissed, holding our breath. He came to our villa to visit me and my parents liked him (his father was a surgeon in Tulle and they owned their villa), as he was a well-brought up, pleasant boy, from a 'good' family.

We all had bicycles except for Odile who stayed behind – again, she was too young – and we rode far and long on the quiet roads, sometimes as far as the Grande Dune du Pyla, the highest in Europe. We swam in the clear water – "Don't go out of your depth! Don't go out of your depth!" our panicking mother used to shout from the edge – ate a variety of tasty seafood, drank a little wine at mealtimes. My parents talked louder, laughed, we met them sometimes at the end of the afternoon in cafés by the beach, before returning to the villa for dinner.

René-Jacques wrote to me during the school year. I cherished his letters but Mother insisted on reading them first which enraged me, so I arranged for him to address them to our maid; however, his childish handwriting... and the postmark, betrayed him. Mother confiscated the letters, claimed I was too young; I cried, argued to no avail. I cannot remember how we kept in touch. I know he sometimes said sweet things to me in his letters (*"far from my eyes, close to my heart"*) and told me about his school. We just had to be patient until the next summer. Although my sister was around, I didn't always notice her; she had her friends and, being a quiet child, she was also my ghost I think, because I did not see her. I looked at other boys, but kept thinking of René-Jacques, his warmth, his soft hair so blond near his temples in the summer sun, the nape of his neck, his bold and joyous smile. I love him now as I write this.

We reached fifteen and liked each other still. I recall little except that one day we rode our bikes to the Grande Dune, then collapsed laughing, exhausted, as we reached the top. The heat weighed heavily above us, made of sea roar and scent, barely animated by tufts of reeds and the occasional screaming seagull. René-Jacques slid on top of me, took off my top, my bra, stroked and kissed me. He smelled so good.

"Do you want to?" he asked.

"No," I said shyly. He didn't seem to mind and we carried on kissing.

When I got home, I glowed.

★

After that there were no more summer holidays by the seaside; my father had decided renting a villa was too expensive, and I no longer saw René-Jacques. (It felt as if Mother was being punished, she was a beautiful woman in her element in Bordeaux and by the sea; Father preferred her sad and deprived as he himself was and our miserable little town was the right place to live such a life.)

I was now a boarder at the Lycée in Toulouse. I passed my exams after all, although, after the scrapbook incident, the nuns 'forgot' to put my name on the list of successful students on the board. Suspicious of their motives, Mother found out by ringing the Academy, and to my relief decided to remove me from the convent. For me, the Lycée had the added advantage of being in the centre of town, near the cathedral. If we joined the Ciné-Club or Les Jeunesses Musicales de France, we were taken on Wednesday evenings once a fortnight to hear concerts and watch the most important and beautiful films: Eisenstein's *The Battleship Potempkin*, and another on the Mexican peasant revolution; Carl Dreyer's *Joan of Arc*... I made friends, woke up to the world a little more. In the spring of 1956, I asked to be allowed to go into the senior girls' common room to follow on the radio the Russian invasion of Prague, and what emergent communist sympathies I may have had, dissolved.

On occasion, Mother came to take me out on a Saturday. She watched me walk, irritated as usual when she

46

disapproved of me: I had no idea how to walk when she was with me; I was also clumsy in my demeanour and facial expressions as she deplored the sorry fact that I did not meet her exacting standards: she found my nose a little too long, my legs a little short, and my hips will need disciplining. Even so, when she took me to her hairdresser, she insisted my haircut should be 'distinguished', when I dreamt of flattering.

"Jean-Louis," she asked him wearily, "do you think she'll be pretty?"

"Oh oui, Madame," he reassured her, "because her features are regular."

I felt absent, but at least there was now some hope of eventually finding grace in my mother's eyes, though my schoolwork was mediocre. I was dull inside, almost inanimate at times. Then one day, in the spring of my second year in Toulouse, Mother appeared at the end of the morning classes, unannounced:

"Get your things ready," she said with a smile, "I am taking you home."

Did she miss me, or had the danger passed? Puzzled but obedient, I went and packed my things without a chance to say goodbye to my friends.

Mother had arranged for me to finish my school year at the Lycée in our home town but my results were still not good and I had to repeat that year, with private lessons in Latin and Maths. I did do well in French and English though, and my parents decided – well, Mother, I mean, she was the decision-maker, only consulted Father for the form as far as Odile's and my education went – that I should spend a month in the summer in London with an English family chosen by a Franco-British organisation; morning classes would take place in a local school, and excursions in and around London were also provided. A well-respected couple in our town were known to have sent their children to England this way; so for the next three summers I would savour the true gift of freedom in a foreign country, not least the freedom to exist.

There were only two cinemas and an old swimming-pool in our small town; nowhere for young people to gather or be given a broader view on the world. I recall my mother taking me to a rare lecture at the Town Hall to hear Thor Heyerdal talk about his expedition on the 'Kon-Tiki', which filled me with wonder and fed into my yearnings for adventure and 'elsewhere'. However, a regular event took place once a year that we always attended; aware of a dearth of entertainment for their daughters, my parents always bought the best tickets to compensate, and I remember counting the days from the moment I caught sight of the first posters announcing the arrival of the Circus. Nothing like the sad, impoverished later shows contaminated with Music-Hall tricks and banter, these Circuses were world-famous in those days and dominated by three equally powerful and talented dynasties who toured our whole continent including Russia: Amar, Pinder and Bouglione. They each offered a menagerie that you could visit on the afternoon of the performance, exhibiting the animals that would be performing that night: horses, tigers, panthers, lions, monkeys, elephants. A noisy procession of drums, trombones and trumpets advertised the show through the town; they were all there, the artists in their finery, the horses decorated with plumes and ribbons, the somersaulting acrobats. No-one minded if the traffic was stopped, adults and children would crowd the street like the pavements and clap enthusiastically.

I was sixteen that year, and because nylon fabrics – think of it: drip-dry, no ironing – had just been invented, Mother had made me a green dress printed with small ochre lozenges, with an open neckline and a tie at the front, just what I could wear on that glorious evening at the circus as we would be sitting in the front row of the central and biggest ring, a special treat. Circuses in those days were vast, with three marquees, the big top in the middle and a compatible spectacle on each side. Even walking in the sawdust that attempted to deaden the coarse smell of the lions and tigers as well as horse manure was glamorous, announcing the feats of skills and daring to come.

I had long toyed with the idea – as an idea – of running away with a circus, sharing the travellers' freedom and discovering ever new horizons, living life on the road, living LIFE at last. My second-best role that night as a privileged spectator was still a terrific thrill, and I watched, starry-eyed, captivated, enthralled, clapping madly at every act, laughing at every clown's prank. And a moment of miraculous apotheosis materialised for me when, at the end of the show, in their final parade before the public, all the trapeze artists, jugglers, lion tamers, clowns, in turn stopped to pointedly salute… me, as I clapped louder still, beaming, in heaven.

After two girls in my class remarked with surprise on the event, it only dawned on me a few days later what an outlandish thing had happened to me that night, the Circus people's generous recognition of my enthusiasm making me for a brief moment a small part of them. That incident was never mentioned once by my parents. I now think it had crossed the boundaries of propriety and what should merely be expected – certainly not imagined. It was excessive, and we didn't do excess. Besides, I would have been in danger of thinking there was anything noticeable or special about me, opening the door to all kinds of worrying things, like dreams. Obviously, Mother hated it: was it fair I should be singled out at a time when her own life was sinking inexorably in the grey sands of our provincial world? This attempt at wiping out the incident also wiped me out of it. In the world of perpetual falsehood where I tried my best to function, my nose just above water level at times, I had little choice: either I kept making continuous adjustments, or I threw away the whole edifice. I was not yet equipped to be a free spirit and knew how to compromise so never dared to mention it myself, but without ever being able to forget it.

As nothing she did not mediate found favour in her eyes, finding her unprepared, my contacts with her were restricted to safe and lovely times when we would explore in her Citroen 2CV − a recent freedom − the villages in the surrounding hills in the hope of finding a bargain: my parents had recently bought an old and derelict farmhouse on such a hill facing the Pyrénées, and it would take a while to restore and furnish it.

There would be room for inexpensive but stylish objects found in bric-a-brac shops: a wine-press made a superb stand for an indoor plant, an old bird-bath became a gorgeous basin for the cloakroom... When I enthused, she could then approve of me, for in conflicts with others − my sister, school friends, a cantankerous teacher − it was easier if I could be blamed, solving the difficulty at a stroke, and it was all the more hurtful for being systematic. I always wanted to be 'good', indeed I was a 'goody-goody', at times irritating to others. However, I reasoned, you cannot be really 'good' if you are not also 'right', so I often fought my corner when I felt I had a just case, but she gave up the argument easily, if not the outcome:

− Oh, you are tiring me...

Otherwise, my resentments, disappointments, sadness were not tolerated easily, being cumbersome to her.

− One has to minimise, she would state, erasing me out of my feelings, another demand on me to surrender to her need for peace as well as supremacy; I would guess this was also an exercise in which she had long been well-versed herself, but I balked at every defeat.

Like love, education is a blunt instrument. You don't develop a child's brain without it representing a potentially explosive hazard. Studying Montaigne at school revealed in this favourite author of mine common sense and genuine kindness, setting standards for ordinary treatment of children that I hadn't seen put into practice too often. Only when you know you know nothing can you start to learn, and I knew that much. Indeed I saw that I had to follow an equally important and parallel process of unlearning most of what I had been taught, or at least examine without mercy the foundations of all so-called truths. But I was happy to learn with Montaigne, whose balanced view of the needs of humans made sense and were reassuring for that very reason. Montaigne could be trusted and at times of debate, used as a referee, even a reliable ally.

As we moved on to Pascal, a seventeenth century theologian and mathematician who later sided with Jansenism and whose 'Thoughts' (Pensées) were on the curriculum, I had serious difficulties when we came to the argument that we should place our bets – the mathematician was speaking there – on the existence of God, since we had everything to gain if He really existed (salvation, the possible rewards of paradise…) and if He didn't exist, we wouldn't have lost anything. I was outraged: what a crude deal, what contempt for truth seekers if he felt they should be swayed by his theory! – no better than a bribe! The arrogance! A seeker of Truth would have no such fears, and I was only too familiar with blackmail and pressure not to recognise them again here, oddly in one of my textbooks. Intellectually, I was on the alert. Emotionally, I was craving my own world. Would love be the solution, my Prince take me away?

One day, after probably three years' silence, I received a letter from René-Jacques, then another. I replied, of course. Our correspondence was that of friends, often querying our world, its rules and parameters. I told him my growing dislike of Catholicism and its hypocrisies; he wasn't so sure of his own Protestantism; our God hadn't yet been overturned, but we pondered, wondered as well as confided in each other.

After a few months, he announced his visit the following Sunday morning. I met him at the station, a tall, handsome young man with warm, smiling eyes. He was in time for lunch and my parents welcomed him. I remember exactly the moment he surreptitiously bent forward to kiss my hand during the meal as I removed his plate. We went for a walk later, on the Promenade – where else? – facing the mountains, hand in hand, stopping on benches and no doubt kissing too. It was a lot for me to take in, as I wasn't used to getting what I needed, let alone what I wanted. Part of me was outside, looking at us dreamily. I walked him back to his train later and we continued writing.

Then, one month later to the day, a telegram arrived for me at the house. My mother was handed it, and, having caught sight, she claimed later, of the word 'deceased', opened it without hesitation.

"There is a telegram about René-Jacques, he's been seriously injured in an accident," she said.

"Take me to church," I begged urgently, full of fear, and she waited for me outside on the square. Inside the church, kneeling, I prayed, bargained as one does: one year of my life, five years even, if You spare him, please God, spare him, he wants his life…

In the evening, at home, she told me he had died. Inside, I felt blank, the sweetest part of my life having suddenly been erased. I was mourning René-Jacques. Later, I would mourn God.

A few weeks later, my sister and I were in my bedroom with the eight-year-old daughter of people who lived further along the street. I was playing my record of Schubert's

Unfinished Symphony that René--Jacques and I listened to after lunch on the day he visited.

"How sad," said the little girl, "it sounds like a young man's death."

Odile and I looked at each other, awed, and I switched the music off.

Chapter Five

Life went on, I am not sure how and there may not be that much worth remembering. It cannot have been very different from the life between day and night that went on before, living indoors, looking out.

Mother took over, since I was not yet and would not for a long time be the agent of my own life. She wrote her condolences to René-Jacques' parents, telling them of his visit one month previously (he had told them he was going skiing for the day and put his equipment in the garden shed). She had felt, she said, that "tender feelings were growing between us". I took no part, both numb and once again sidelined. Giving me the initiative to do it myself would have been a recognition of my feelings. Why did she not think I could go to the funeral? Although this did not cross my own mind at the time, it left me once again outside the very events that concerned me, feeling more deprived of hope and a possible future than I had been of a living relationship as only recent letters remained. René-Jacques' visit had been fleetingly magical and magic wasn't a feature of my existence. I had yet to learn that I must recognise it before letting it in, otherwise I would remain exiled forever inside the narrow confines of my world.

I cried a lot at times, then less. Mourning receded, took its place in a life of ordinary moments mainly made of waiting, in a structured timetable.

For many years, in order to make myself acceptable – lacking truer means – I had chosen to appear sweet and pleasant: smiling easily, being attentive to others, well-mannered. The role suited me since I had a gentle nature. Adults around me loved it and I earned a lot of praise, though it worked less well with my peers, most of whom were a little younger than me and seemed unencumbered by such need for approval. Besides, they weren't real friends; we saw each other because we were in the same year at school and on the same level socially, but I had only one real friend: Andrée, a very bright and subtle brunette, and the only one with whom I could truly talk.

All of us would party in the large room where we could also play ping-pong in the attic above the flat, dancing rock for the most part – 'Rock around the Clock' could be heard everywhere and 'slows', when we became aware of each other's body smells and touch. Catherine and Jean-Pierre were an item although they often broke up and Catherine cried. Eric, her brother, danced quite well but sweated profusely which to me forbade close proximity. The rest of us, Françoise, Serge and Odile, were joined by one or two others on occasion, like the very stiff boys of the opticians on the town square. There wasn't much choice. Then Serge stopped coming and the brothers left, maybe feeling ill-at-ease as add-ons. Maybe like us they were bored.

The younger Niklaus boy, Francois, who was about our age and a boarder, joined us on his holiday and one Sunday afternoon sat between Odile and me during a film, when I saw him, out of the blue and without any preamble, turn Odile's face towards him and kiss her on the lips. She just let him. She hadn't met him before, and we were all aware that he had a girl-friend called Louise who was arriving the next day. I got very cross with her when we got home, asking her why she let him, didn't she know about Louise? It was a terrible thing to do. She didn't argue, merely cried.

Twice that year I have been pushed into Jean-Pierre's car, he at the wheel and the most virulent, with Eric at the back trying to emulate him, and they interrogated and accused me of breaking Serge's heart, therefore I was a slut. Serge and I had briefly kissed once during a dance, out of curiosity I thought, but apparently he broke down one day and had to be helped home crying. I was the lowest of the low, even though, or maybe because I replied I had no idea he was in love with me, he never talked or did anything. I argued back, defending myself, but I remember the wildly hostile expressions on their faces. I told myself they must have been watching violent thrillers, they were playing gangsters, they were idiotic boys.

Only the second time it happened ("Get into the car," they said, and pushed me inside.) did I experience danger because they were driving me to the hills this time and shouting at me: apparently there were rumours going round the town about me, people were saying that I was taken to some fields and raped by seventeen men, no less, therefore I was a slut again. I fought back angrily because it was all so stupid, but I don't recall even asking them why they were behaving like this. It was just too shocking and best forgotten.

Having somehow passed the first part of the Baccalaureat exam, I found myself in the Upper Sixth form, which gave me the choice of more Philosophy classes as against more Sciences or Maths. That option appealed to my reflective and argumentative side as much as it protected me from the other two. I was also very lucky to have as my teacher the gentle and tolerant Monsieur Coutant, a friendly and egalitarian man who actually liked young people without cultivating too many illusions. My first essay title was '*Who are you?*' I described myself as a passionate person without any passions, disconnected, an observer, a doubter.

'*Order and disorder,*' he requested the second time.

'*Discuss.*' I pointed out that order had more appeal for its reassuring qualities than for the possibly restricting demands it might make, while disorder, albeit suggesting freedom, was decidedly worrisome. It was wonderful that my thoughts and feelings mattered, if only on paper. And after all, he had asked.

I look at photographs of my parents at that time, for the most part a theatre of make-believe. People will look at her smiling and say: 'Just like her, a charming woman, wonderful cook, adored her children.' They won't know what it cost to make it seem that way. In one, father sits under a lamp, seems authoritative – he could not bear not to appear that way, put a suit on to buy cakes on Sundays, worried people would think he had no dignity. She, going out with him, would place her arm under his arm, to show that she possessed what she was most lacking: closeness, belonging, so stole it for herself at times like these when she could feel what it felt like, and wonder, and mourn. Since I was not allowed my own emotions, I had nothing to falsify yet, but knew that I must smile and smile, so play a part in that confusing world of confused notions. Only later would I learn how difficult simply being would be.

Underneath, my world was pared down to the essentials: where is God? Who am I? How does one live? (*Not like my parents!*) What is the Truth? Reading mattered more than ever. We never talked of serious things at home, trivialities being far safer. Certainly nothing would 'pass' that hadn't been through the sieve of Mother's judgement, and if the topic went beyond her knowledge or her liking she would promptly change the conversation. My parents knew that Monsieur Coutant had spoken to me after school recently: he wished to present me as a candidate – his first ever – for the National Philosophy Competition, the Concours Général, a few months hence, was I interested? I was. He gave me book after book to read, some Kierkegaard, Bergson, a lot of Kant whose *Critique of Pure Reason* I loved.

Descartes, of course, Plato, Aristotle... For even more pleasure, I added Gaston Bachelard.

My parents were proud of my extra-curricular activities and hoped they might take me away from too much listening to new and disturbing modern music, and particularly 'looking at boys'.

Since I looked.

The tension of looking and being looked at, the way Paolo did, was sometimes acute to the point of being unbearable so much was I aching to touch and kiss him. His full lips on good hungry teeth gave him a sensual and rebellious look, and his square jaw was very male in a daring way. My young legs went weak at the thought of him.

He had left school at sixteen and we met outside school hours in the country lanes among the fields that surrounded our town. The scent of grass and trees reached us straight after the last houses, and his own smell I thought heady, that of a young male body soaked in hay: not a polite town-boy smell. He sent me messages at school through a little boy who lived near his house and would pass them on to me at break time. There would be small presents on occasion: a watercolour he had painted of a singing wren, an image of a stained-glass window made of painted pieces of eggshell stuck on wood which I still have.

We walked across fields, my nice-girl shoes getting muddy, startling hares, observing birds. We sang Paul Anka songs ('Diana'!) and teased one another. We pressed our bodies against each other, kissing endlessly, almost fainting with desire. I think I would recognise his smell today, such was the headiness of those moments. And yet we were chaste. A glass barrier held me in somehow, made of fears, a learnt code; I knew he was 'the wrong sort', was aware of consequences. I was no Maria Goretti who had fought and died for her virtue: mostly, I could not afford to lose my head.

Being not just noticed but 'godfathered' by my favourite teacher was a timely happening: it said I existed, I was on a map, I could get somewhere. I worked happily, feeling rewarded merely by the attention I was getting. Being a child had seemed like feeling very cold in a large room. There were now occasionally some warm faces around, not just friends of my own but my parents' Jewish friends from Paris who enjoyed talking about events, politics, values, relationships, as much as gossip, food and fun. I liked them for their intelligence and generosity. They had suffered and knew what mattered. I stayed with them in Paris when I came back from my London holidays. They took me out, asked questions, endlessly curious and caring. And eventually, University loomed.

The choice of university, which seemed to be mine as my parents were not aware of different criteria and there was no independent information available, was limited by geography and a duty of relative proximity. Having learnt to be devious, I told my parents that the University of Toulouse — too close for comfort, it would impose on me to go back home at week-ends — wasn't thought to be as good as Bordeaux University which had a high reputation. Knowing that I would be well surrounded by a number of uncles and aunts as well as godmother and godfather, my parents agreed. I would only have Christmas, Easter and summer holidays with them and we had that lovely country house now, gifted with charm, large fields, an orchard, and impregnable views on the Garonne valley beyond, the foothills and the chain of the Pyrénées.

In my new town bedroom next to the attic which used to be our maid's – we only had a daily help now – I floated above the shufflings and doings of daily life, but I could open the window that sat among the roof tiles and see the mountains, with the plain below where the river gently ran. I could see the suburbs at the foot of the town where Paolo lived and on occasion, at an agreed time, he and I made contact by waving our pillowcases. I imagined there was also the hope in my mother's mind that my going to Bordeaux would finally separate me from Paolo, whom she knew about and disapproved of:

– What does this boy do with his time? Is he clean? What do his parents do?

The occasion I wore a scarf around my neck to hide a kiss printed by Paolo's lips ended in a row loud with her fears and my stubbornness.

And I started writing. Just sentences, paragraphs, about being, about trying to feel what it is like to be. It started as a journal but I let it go. I wanted to write but didn't know how, or what. I should be revising as my exams were near and would be followed by that awesome Philosophy competition. In the spring, Monsieur Coutant received a letter from the Academy which disappointed us both sorely: I was three months too old to enter it.

'Still,' he said, 'it will have been a good year.' I agreed.

As we said goodbye at the end of the term and he wished me well, he asked if I would keep in touch. And so we started writing to each other, intermittently, for nearly thirty years.

The summer before university was sunny with the promise of freedom under an implacable sun that we shied away from in the middle hours of the day, pulling the wooden shutters to, creating time for a siesta with or without a book. Odile was around of course, and, hungry for the sun, defied caution and warnings, getting burnt. We did not mix much, she had her own friends and didn't seek my company, which was a relief as she was aggressive and caustic with me. I let her be. All that green space around us seemed to loosen the very tight knots and tensions so closely woven in our town flat. Father was happy cutting the grass, he had his work cut out. Mother tended her flower beds, read gardening magazines, and we often visited markets for more plants. It all looked very pretty.

Friends of my parents, the Niklaus, sometimes came for Sunday lunches at our country house with their sons and as usual with a book for Odile's and my spiritual education. Madame Niklaus, a thin and ascetic-looking woman, was on a mission with us: she knew Odile and I no longer went to church and it saddened her so she always made sure to stress the salient, admirable points of the latest sermon of the week. I tactfully turned the book down – I had so much to read – but Odile, famished for adult attention, gratefully took it, and from this moment another step of her tragic future was drawn, in the guise of a promise of meaning as well as safety.

One Sunday after lunch the older Niklaus son made discreet approaches to me. Pleased to be noticed, I accepted to go for a drink in a village nearby and my mother consented – she must think him a future possibility. Not unattractive but given to sneering and much older than me, he was apparently knowledgeable and asked about my plans for the future. On the way back, he stopped his car on the side of the road and looked at me with intent. When he kissed me, I felt cold but troubled. When he slid his hand under my skirt, I squirmed.

"Don't you like it?"

"Er, yes," I lied politely.

"Well, let me, then."

I did, but immediately pushed him away because I really did not want what he was doing.

"Well, my dear," he sneered, giving me his card, "when you are in Bordeaux, give me a call when you are ready."

Bordeaux is a most beautiful, classical city with well-preserved vestiges of Roman times. The town centre luckily escaped American bombings aimed at the German ships that were stationed in the port during the war, and stands elegant and proud. The classical tree-lined avenues designed by Baron Haussman, who went on to build the Etoile avenues in Paris, house some prestigious apartments above exquisite and tasteful shops and boutiques and one can also stroll or sit on benches on the Allées d'Etigny that lead to the majestic Grand Théâtre.

My parents and I found me a ground-floor bedsitter in the house of a kind lady Rue Mondenard. Straight off a cool hallway, my room looked out onto a narrow street, giving me the independence I sought; the landlady's apartment proper was at the back, lucky to overlook a tiny town garden.

I was to study for a Literature degree: I was good in French and couldn't think of anything else to do. My quandary was that I did *not* want to become a teacher and it didn't seem to be leading to anything else. Not for me standing on a platform pontificating at students as so many of my teachers had done, hardly ever addressing them as individuals. I had thought of studying Psychology, but needed much better Maths than I had (all those statistics!). Very tempted by an Art degree since I adored painting and was not too clumsy, I was horrified to hear of the new students' initiation practices, when once a boy and a girl, plastered face to face naked, were left on one of the city's bridges, to be found at dawn, traumatised. I could not bear to risk facing anything of the kind.

I soon realised that none of my tutors, if they knew who we were, showed the least interest in our opinions and ideas about authors: you only ever got a good grade if you regurgitated the lecturer's course faithfully. At times I failed to do so, exasperated at being on a leash still, almost defeated at the start of a new campaign, lacking not just weapons but armour, while raising a small and often invisible flag.

I had friends though, bright sparks, and we often listened to Miles Davis into the small pale hours, when I walked back to my room while the town was still asleep and there was no-one in the streets but dustmen carts doing their daily rounds. I was fascinated by a multitude of things but incapable to do more than scribble odd thoughts, my attempts at being. Left on my own, I sat and stared. I was aware of everything but unable to reach out, as if dissociated. Paralysed and useless as well as invisible, I came to life only under someone's gaze. I felt mostly helpless, often on the verge of tears, my head pregnant with a monstrous child.

Chapter Six

I started reading all kinds of poetry in those university days; the Surrealists, Andre Breton and his novel *Nadja*, wondering how I could live life on the level of poetry. Parallel to the Existential certainties of Sartre, they left me attracted to a dreamy and fantastic reality that I could slip into easily in my unsettled states of mind. The constructs of Existentialism talk no such nonsense, merely describe the world as it is after the death of God: we are free, alone, and responsible, get over it. I was, though, in mourning for God, and somewhat angry in my grief, feeling let down and unheard yet again: father, why have you abandoned me?

I write and write; about what it's like to be me and broken. I write about what I see, discover, doubt. I write about what I now know are lies, about how to know; how to be me, which I am unsure of, because it seems like being new-born to the world blind and mute, barely discovering thought and speech. I write pages, heaps. Then I read what I have written and feel better. Maybe I exist: would Mother agree?

My girlfriends and I talk about how to live, and Anne, a charming brunette who will become a lawyer, declares she wants to be a Great Romantic Lover. The others merely wish to make minor adjustments to their lives, declare satisfaction, but that is the bourgeois life.

My own aim is not personal happiness which I deem a selfish, short-sighted, narrow and often materialistic pursuit, yet it seems that's what is on offer. I had seen some of my school friends, brought up in decent, fairly harmonious families, their minds ever untroubled by complex thoughts or questions, and I despised, in my youthful absolutism, their passive and complacent lives. My aim is to get at the Truth of existence, since a childhood full of fallacies was bound to lead my thoughts towards the metaphysical.

I know I must change, I am unhappy in my own skin, having little sense of my own reality, feeling only half alive a lot of the time. I need a milestone to effect transformation, a rite of passage of sorts: what if I became a woman, experienced the loss of my virginity as a gain (a door opened?), would I be different? For I need no less than metamorphosis. Losing my virginity might 'do the job' but was problematic in other ways: I was just twenty. In the late fifties one was supposed to wait until the legal age of twenty-one and preferably for marriage; besides, there was no contraception since the Catholic Church, all-powerful in matters of sexual conduct, disallowed it, so one had to rely on uncertain biological calendars based on our menstrual cycle. I discussed my plan with my girlfriends who thought me daring, but were also puzzled:

– Are you in love with him?

– No, that's not what it is about.

Outside of its mechanism, the act of sex was still mysterious to me, despite the dizzying sensations of desire I had experienced with Paolo. If I had given in to these, I would have lost myself in a way that I couldn't bear to think about. Sex, or sexual relations as we termed it more usually at the time, seemed to be of such importance in the story of people's lives as in literature and history, that it obviously held some insidious transforming power or spell of a kind. It had such unspoken grip on the relationships I occasionally observed, such disturbing dominance, that I knew I was still too vulnerable to open myself to its perilous magic. I wanted to keep my strength while acquiring the 'knowledge' and be changed into 'a woman', a being imbued with strength and purpose. Maybe.

It was therefore vital that I should go into such an adventure with indifference and cool, so having no particular physical attraction for my intended initiator suited my purpose. I knew I wouldn't lose my head. I picked up the telephone, rang Arnaud Niklaus and we fixed a date for my coming to Paris.

To celebrate the event in a gentlemanly fashion, he had booked a room in a pleasant hotel on the Ile Saint-Louis, a superior location, and I arrived before him as he hadn't yet left work. The river Seine, shimmering behind the net curtains, left me unaffected; I didn't feel romantic. I had a job to do.

"Hello, my dear," he said with a faint smile as I opened the door.

"Hello," I said shyly, and waited.

He lay down on a small couch by the window, declaring he was exhausted but would be fine in ten minutes. I thought I should bend towards him for a kiss, but kisses not being forthcoming I withdrew and sat down.

I cannot remember a meal, but there must have been one: after all, one has to eat. He took me to a play, an excellent comedy (*Gog and Magog*) which had me and the audience in peals of laughter while he remained impassive, explaining pompously afterwards that it was raising some extremely serious philosophical questions.

When we got back to our hotel, I got into bed and he rolled on top of me. There was no ceremonial, no kissing that I can remember, no gentleness, no whispers, no play or foreplay. He rammed into me three times that night, leaving me both chafed and numb. There was no blood. In the morning, he grinned, gratified:

– Well, well, my dear!

Then took me to the train station for my journey back to Bordeaux since he had a lot of work to do. His parting words were delivered with glowing self-satisfaction:

"Why don't you come and live in Paris? I'll have you study oriental languages, I think."

"No thank you, I like it in Bordeaux and shall study what I want."

"Well, my dear, go, go and sleep with some young men, and let me know if they are better than me!"

Taken aback by such arrogance, I assured him I would.

Later looking back on that particular adventure, I couldn't be sure it had altered me in any vital aspect, except that for the first time, and this was surely a major step, it was the result of my taking an initiative designed to effect change. Whatever my battles, it wouldn't be the last.

As long as one has strength, it is good to be able to test it on some adversary, if not an out-and-out enemy: your instincts are awake, your mind alert, you know what emotions fill you; but remove the battlefield, take away the enemy, and the internal fight that animated you and gave you courage disintegrates, melts away, and you are left with very little inside to sustain and define you: you are an empty vessel, an aimless and pointless soul without any reason left for being. Removed from home, I had no fuel for my striving and anger, and as they vanished I myself vanished, became meaningless, like an ectoplasm. Shop windows, endlessly tested, assured me I had a reflection; my shadow met me at my feet, proof that the sun saw me, and if I cut myself, blood flowed; screened at the hospital, I gasped at seeing my heart pumping away, such an orderly feat; my footsteps in the snow; a mist on the mirror, my breath curious at my image...

The essay title of the National Philosophy competition that I had turned out to be too old to sit would have been way beyond my means: *'There is a long way,'* it asserted, *'between whim and wish, wish and desire, desire and will, will and decision, decision and action.' Discuss.'* The A to Z of living, of being, is there. But in those days wishing was daring to my poverty, desire and will belonged to a faraway country, and decision and action were demonstrated daily, by others: how do they do it? What is it like? Is there a learned way, or are you born with it?

I felt like a mummy not quite dead under many bandages, breathing somewhat clumsily. Through her insatiable needs and fears, Mother had willed it that way: she was good at stifling cries; hers I heard though, always, in a passing glance, a clasping of the hand, a choking of the throat, a restrained sigh; they were all mine. But when it came to me, when my tears from my grief burst uncalled for on her life, the threat was too much to take – another life when only hers mattered, and should fill mine. "Stop playing martyrs," she would say, and there would be less of me that day.

Indoors, life was subdued, as if sounds forbidden (you listened to your heart beats for reassurance, relieved they were quiet, and yours). Her voice, her thoughts, were yours to breathe, to own and to follow, guiding your steps. Your conscience was in her hands, and your will a mere convulsion of your heart. The future was a mist, improbable for she did not envisage hope or lack of fear. She dealt you those cards, too, the only ones she knew, placed them in your hands, watching you go to sea without a buoy, a sail – since you must drown too, or life would be too unfair.

So I drowned, time and time again. Increasingly consciously, death had its fascination. I would cut out and keep newspaper articles, the small ones from the side of the page: an English gardener who destroyed all the flowers in his care in the park had looked at himself in the mirror and found his own ugliness unbearable. An old soldier, a lover of the East, having made his way home found his home too foreign and set himself alight in protest at the impossibility of living in an ideal way. So many things happened, mirrors facing my way, like that actor obsessed with battle scenes, endlessly, like a mechanical puppet, reproducing his own death, dissolving in the giddy gestures.

Meanwhile, in my small town, the town hall siren would howl at noon, cutting the day in half, and along streets leading nowhere little children would learn to live a certain way. In summer, the swallows dizzily raced around the church square, screaming shrill dizzy screams, setting an incomprehensible standard for joy, ever unmatched by dreams. Winter, a safer season, would come, freezing desires as surely as ponds, keeping life still. A spider lost on her own web, I couldn't tell North from South and fell through my grid of longings along a thread leading nowhere.

No-one knew of my state of mind, or that I would lie on my bed for hours, paralysed, aimless, destitute almost, and that I cried like a child, calling for a mother who could neither understand nor help. I cursed the morning light, wishing I were dead, having to go through the motions of yet another day. And I could do it, I could 'do' normal, I had been brought up to present it as my reality, to please, to reassure, and to hopefully convince myself that my life was real enough or at least bearable. I must have often seemed gauche to others, self-conscious, unconnected.

I had friends, university friends, among whom the owner of an unconventional bookshop, L'Alittérature, through whom I met writers and artists. I even bought an oil painting representing Ophelia by a fairly successful local artist called Georges Braem with money borrowed from my godfather, repaying him monthly out of my allowance: it depicted the face of a very young-looking Ophelia *after* her drowning, staring out from beyond death with clear, still eyes, in a faraway gaze, algae on her face. I was passionate about that painting: it was not just a work of a certain quality, it was also very apt. I couldn't see this at the time as it was the very portrait of my soul. My attachment to it was fierce and I had outbid a well-known local playwright to acquire it. It looked good, if a little gloomy, in my bedsitter, one of my very few possessions apart from an antique mirror mother had given me and a large piece of dark green fabric that covered a wooden board sitting on top of my two suitcases. I also exhibited art reproductions above my bed, pinned on the wall with drawing-pins. With a brass candlestick, my radio, and a bunch of flowers, it all looked good and individual, certainly not the typical student room. My mother's interior decoration magazines had obviously left their mark.

I joined the university drama group which took a lot of my time: I found it easy to be someone else, even weeping on demand. We toured villages around Bordeaux, and at the Air Force base performance I was thrilled to be brought flowers on stage at the end of the play. My work, of course, suffered, as I was needier of attention than capable to concentrate on my studies, and I failed a number of courses, sometimes going blank and weeping during the exam.

Men hovered. I was pretty. Accident of time or place, as well as a little perseverance on their part, got one or two what they wanted, but not always: this one was red-haired, not very attractive but strong willed-looking, and sought me out at the university canteen where we had bumped into each other a few times.

"I want to see you naked," he declared broodily one day, and I was shaken by his desire. My head filled with romantic and literary notions – the Surrealists and the mysterious intellectual and emotional moodscapes they wrote about – I eventually agreed to go to his room. I did not question it, even though I was supposed to be smart; something else must have been at play to which I was blind, something I had learnt a long time ago. He told me how beautiful I was, how much he wanted to see my body, he could think of nothing else. Flattered, puzzled, I undressed. I was seen. I stood there, my clothes on the floor, as he gazed at me. Then he started to undress, and I moaned:

"No! I don't want to!" as I attempted to grab my skirt.

"You're not going anywhere!" he assured me, throwing my blouse on top of his cupboard. So, I started to become a little intelligent: I had to make myself undesirable, repulsive even. I started to cry when he pushed me onto the bed, then sobbed, and howled, and whimpered, and let my tears drag mascara with them onto my cheeks, and snot drip onto my mouth; I retched and dribbled. He must have been disgusted to see the effect he was having on me, his own humiliation. He got up, threw my clothes at me and told me to leave. I finally made my way home, shaken, mortified, and very puzzled about myself. But not for the last time, as one day my friend the bookshop owner is lying on my bed, pressing me to join him. He undoes his flies and produces a very large member. Too large. I am a little girl and I start to cry. He gets dressed again and leaves.

Chapter Seven

I had always wanted to be a writer. To me as to most of my compatriots, there was nothing more noble, admirable and prestigious. I wrote poetry that no-one saw but it enlivened me at a deep level, made me feel real in a way nothing else did.

My high-school teachers had in the past commented on my essays; one had teased me during a sixth-form break:

"So, when are you going to write your first novel?"

"In a month's or a year's time?" I replied jokingly, quoting the title of the latest book by Françoise Sagan, a precocious and successful writer.

Well, it would take a little longer than that.

Writing was a yearning more than a desire for me, unable as I was to follow it with decision and even less action. It was a role I dreamt of but could not reach out to, living as I was in despair and imbalance, only coming out to perform the ordinary. The roles that came to me in the first year of my university days – I was very far from choosing – were those of a dependent and needy heroine in a sick comedy of errors. I was lucky to meet Gérard then, a mature student taking Physics, as the strength of his character and his decency towards me gave me at the right moment a much needed measure of stability. We liked each other, were good friends, and enjoyed each other's bodies except that, as usual, I was incapable of feeling any sexual pleasure. I never had, with anyone. I didn't see the contradiction: I liked him and what we were doing, but I didn't think to 'ask' for my pleasure, asking wasn't done and it wasn't on the menu – maybe I was frigid? I wasn't conscious of having any right to this: I just needed his need, so I stayed 'in neutral'.

Since there was no contraception to speak of – the Pill was talked about, but not accessible – we were always taking some risks and I got pregnant twice which forced me to resort to abortions performed by an understanding doctor, one of them causing a haemorrhage that very nearly killed me. Gérard was supportive throughout. We parted after two and a half years after finishing our studies as had always been understood. Saying goodbye one afternoon in my room, he took me in his arms to hug me and stop me crying, saying: "Promise me to try and stop being so passive, it's unhealthy, it's very bad for you, please try and turn towards action." I kissed his face, his hair. I knew he had been good for me, but also that he wasn't for me.

So, I was passive –was I? – but not like Odile, surely? Not like my sister?

★

I didn't want to go into teaching. In France, teachers are civil servants and sent to work wherever there is a vacancy, it could be in any town or village, and far away from your family and friends. Another *carcan*. I visited a psychologist who gave me several tests and concluded that I could make a very good teacher, doctor or nurse, as I was gentle and cared for people, particularly children. Then she produced a sheet of paper and asked me to draw my close family. I drew the heads of my mother and my sister which took up all the space. I asked for another sheet since there was no room for my father, and his dull and solemn face this time filled the whole page.

"Your dad seems very important, I see…"

"Not at all, actually."

She then asked me to draw a tree and I did, a large tree with lots of branches stretching upwards:

"Look," she pointed, "your tree has no roots at all."

Luckily, a new university course was created at that time, a Diploma of Journalism. I imagined autonomy, creativity, freedom and engagement with the world, so made a sideways move, abandoning my Literature degree. I felt more focused, to the point of deciding to stop my involvement in acting after our production of: *Tiger at the Gates* by Jean Giraudoux, a play he wrote under and about the German occupation of France, disguising it as the War of Troy. The role of Hélène had already been given to an insipid brunette with a blonde wig who played it like a Barbie doll and I played the modest part of a servant which was a great deal of fun; I felt the role of Hélène to be important not because she was Paris's pretty catch and the cause of the war, but because Giraudoux described her as the one person without political or philosophical dogma or commitment; she understood war, she understood men, she watched their passions with honesty and detachment; to her, conflicts were but seasonal crises in the history of mankind, to be observed and understood at a calm distance: her character was attractive since it mirrored my need to understand more while being less affected. So that year, I would change my name to Hélène.

Changing my name didn't just give me permission to be myself, it also separated me from a past that had always felt heavy. My mother understood it straight away, becoming angry and resentful and refusing to call me Hélène. Prone as she was herself to feeling rejected, she necessarily saw it as a repudiation of our family. Of course, for the orphan she had been – and still was – repudiation of one's roots must have seemed a double sin. Any explanation on my part would have seemed like criticism, so I didn't attempt to justify myself: I couldn't say that it signified a separation from them, that it was a rupture, and I would no longer be their creature as they had chosen my name. She also remarked that 'Hélène' was no prettier a name than the previous one. It wasn't about 'pretty', I argued, I felt more 'at ease' as Hélène. I also see now that it freed me to give myself what I needed instead of expecting it from others, a tentative step away from passivity. I was also coming to terms with my perception that if God had proved unreliable as a father figure, the idea of God-as-God was ever more precarious and possibly spurious. I felt orphaned of God in the same manner as I had felt in my family. Maybe, quite possibly, it was the same thing. The price to pay of course was to try and survive the emptiness that ensued and tied itself to my rootlessness.

However, it was now sometimes possible to experience other, lighter bonds since no longer living with them distanced me from my parents' life and the atmosphere they generated. When I went home, afternoon tours of the countryside with my mother in her new 2CV looking in antique or bric-a-brac shops for bargains for the country house, stopping for drinks in village cafés was very pleasant. Exhausted after my separation from Gérard, I told her one afternoon in the car that she was my only successful love. And I remember feeling, if not clearly thinking at the time, that it wasn't quite right that she should look so fulfilled, leaning her head back against her seat: the destiny she had assigned me was to make her the centre of my life regardless of my own needs and that wish was being granted.

I later asked her for René-Jacques's letters which I had given her for safe-keeping before I left for university.

"I'm not sure where they are," she said, frowning. "I've put them away somewhere, may be in the attic…"

"I'd like them back before I go, Mum, I want to take them with me."

"Don't bother me with all this now, I have so much to do," she protested, "I don't have time to go in the attic and rummage everywhere…"

She sounded angry, displeased at my request. I sensed danger, a no-go area, and did not insist. I would ask again another time, since I loved her and it bothered her so much that day.

My father, who for most of his life had found security in work and routine, seemed happy to see me when I came for these holidays. The old toxic brew of family life was diluted by the fresh air and good food. Lying in the sun with a book was bliss, as both time and weather were clement. Odile must have been around at the same time, I do not recall any salient contact or conversation and she didn't seek my company, but I met Arnaud Niklaus again at a drinks party and told him jovially that I had followed his advice, slept with a lot of young men and found they were all better lovers than him, wasn't it extraordinary?

★

I am not strong, my mind wanders, wavers, crashes. I weep. The discarding, if not the death, of God had left me orphaned, but the Truth had to be somewhere? Without God, there is no ground, no North. I spin, spin, unravel. I am a box but don't know what's inside. Men have sometimes looked in without noticing me. I try to shut them in, fail, remain empty. No-one knows what it's like not to be. Even so I speak the right words, do the right things. Some people think I am nice, intelligent; I make friends. It is important to look normal.

The loss of God has left other doors open, it seems. I have a series of premonitory dreams which fill me with wonder and fascinate me as they are all verified in fact, and this makes me feel special, interesting: others listen. Two of those dreams I remember vividly and I wrote them down at the time. My mother, who was visiting me in my Bordeaux bedsitter at the time woke up in my bed one morning (I slept on a camp bed when she stayed) to hear the story:

– It takes place in the South-East of France. A thick river of mud crashes into a valley, swamping a village; houses collapse and are carried away, cars, trees... A lot of people die in the mud. It will happen in about a week's time.

These dreams are special, differing from ordinary bad dreams or nightmares, which I occasionally have like everyone else, by what I can only describe a certain 'weight' to them, so that I have learned to recognise them. A week later, in the South-East of France, a dam collapsed and millions of gallons of water destroyed the entire village of Malpasset where several hundred people were killed, the country's greatest catastrophe since the war.

When I have the other dream, I wake up alone with a rhyme in my head, many times repeated, which accompanies a scene of panic-stricken people in long robes and veils running away from the street where they are being shot at: "Téhéran, ville en sang, Téhéran, ville en sang..." (Tehran, town in blood). A few days later, a demonstration in the Iranian capital sees a few people shot dead: the Shah's police disperse a crowd of religious zealots protesting against the new freedoms recently granted to women which allow them to discard the veil. This was the first protest of many, announcing the end of the Shah's regime.

These dreams continued for a few months. In a way I was

gripped, feeling strangely privileged. I was tempted to probe further but did not feel I had the strength to go down that road; besides, all those dreams announced disasters. So one evening, in my bedroom, I declared to myself aloud: 'This has to stop.' And 'it' stopped.

Part of my Diploma of Journalism involved hands-on training at 'Sud-Ouest', the dominant paper for the South-West region of France, where Henri Amouroux, a well-known historian of war-time France was editor-in-chief and our main tutor. We became friendly, and my training the following summer in all sections of the paper – local, regional, national – I found fascinating and entertaining, allowing me to nurture more fantasies about being, later, a journalist in Paris. Shy of that more demanding reality, however, I thought to spend a year in London first to perfect my English. I explained to my parents this would be an asset in my future career, but it had the advantage of allowing me to prevaricate further as well as stay away from them. Having spent a month in London on three consecutive summers in the past had made me aware of a measure of safety when away, and feeling a stranger abroad was after all easier to accept than feeling lost on my home ground.

I therefore found myself in London teaching at the Berlitz School for Languages. They would employ any native speaker – even former waiters – paying me one pound a week more than my colleagues since I had a degree. I stayed in a number of bedsits in Holland Park and Notting Hill Gate that very cold winter of '63-64, when I soon met the young man who would become my husband.

Men had been problematic: I had no clear vision yet of a pattern in my relationships, haphazard and unrewarding as they were. It seems that the occasional predator would predate and leave me diminished, wary, uncomprehending and no less needy. There seemed to be a gaping hole in my heart that needed filling almost at all costs. In my childhood dreams, a Jack London figure stood against the light in the doorway in his brightly coloured lumberjack shirt. I looked at him and greeted him from the fireside where I was dutifully cooking. What bonded us was indestructible.

In my dream of Elsewhere, England, or rather London, seemed to fit in a tame and reassuring way: all these rows of identical houses in identical streets could make one a little dizzy by their stubborn sameness but the people were gentle and unassuming: mostly they left you alone, speaking kindly when addressed and seemed amused by my Frenchness. I had kept good memories of my educational stays in London. Having been lucky to board with families who did not see it as part of their role to exercise any pressure on me, this left me free to wander around the town with my friends and make more friends: Hand-Dieter from Germany on the steps of the Eros statue in Piccadilly; Prabhu, an Anglo-Indian student. We corresponded for years. We walked along the banks of the river, sought refuge from the rain in the cheap cartoon cinemas in Piccadilly Circus, eating vast quantities of Smarties, and felt trendy in a dark basement bar in Soho called Le Macabre that displayed plastic candle-lit skeleton heads on each table.

I was almost twenty-four at the time and my job teaching French at the Berlitz School was exhausting, consisting of endless private lessons at a very basic level. Good humour was essential and kept alive by the knowledge that it was temporary. I had struck a friendship in the past with Pandora Huggett, my last hostess in England and a divorced mother of five noisy boys. (I remember showing a photograph of her to my mother who decreed she looked ridiculous.) When I contacted her, she invited me to spend the following weekend with her in Aldermaston, near Reading. Her older son, John, who had become a teenager since I had seen him a few years previously, came to fetch me at the station and declared that we would attend an end-of-term party given by his Art teacher before driving back to his house.

The lights were down, the music was pop, and pleasant and shabby young people smoked, drank wine and seemed content with modest bread and cheese and carrot sticks. I relaxed, sitting down with a glass of wine.

A pair of hands came to my attention: strong, beautiful, they were rolling a cigarette in Rizla paper with the help of one of those small gadgets I remembered my father using after the war: I was fascinated by the nimble fingers handling the paper, the loose tobacco that had to be tamed and the final seal with the lips. I hadn't seen one since childhood so went towards him and initiated a conversation. The face matched the hands: strong, handsome with an air of calm gentleness. With short brown hair, a short beard and a smile, Johan was a young man of average height and strong build, an artist, a painter. Our contact was easy, friendly, and we chatted pleasantly till I left with John to spend the night at his mother's.

It was very quiet when I woke up the next day in Pandora's house, the younger children spending the week-end with their father. I had a quick breakfast in my own time and hung around Pandora for a while in the kitchen, chatting, recalling the days when my English was still tentative and her house a lot noisier. As she was getting busy preparing a good Sunday lunch, she suggested after a while that I might like to look around the area, as the countryside was very pretty at this time of year, and lunch might be almost ready when I returned.

So I started on my way along a country path, only to catch sight of John soon after, who seemed to be waiting, or watching. He asked if he could come along.

He was a tall youth, over sixteen I imagined since he

was able to drive, and quite hairy, with a bushy beard which wasn't unusual in the sixties. Not being in a position to say otherwise as his mother's guest and not minding either way, I said 'sure, of course', and we ambled together, no doubt talking about his school and studies, until after a while I found myself pushed against a fence with the boy all over me, and being assaulted so quickly I could hardly believe it, although I was wearing a skirt which would have made it easier. There was a confusion of words and sounds, and wild gestures on my part, fearing I was losing balance and falling, but I was firmly held in place until he had finished.

I was stunned. I hardly knew him, lunch would be ready soon, we would have to face his mother at the table, make conversation, and his sperm had begun to run along my thighs, which was embarrassing as well as unpleasant and I felt sore and confused. I don't remember him saying anything in particular as we proceeded to walk back towards the house. When I caught my breath back and some of my senses, I asked why he had done that, and he replied that, well, I had agreed he could come along, and so he figured… I was dumbfounded, speechless. Later, on the train back to London, all I could think was: what a nerve, what a bloody nerve!

I was barely agitated, just astonished and annoyed. I didn't realise for decades that this had been a rape and I should have been more shocked, maybe traumatized, and certainly not treating it as something that can happen when you go for a walk with a boy in the countryside. Because why on earth would anyone believe it was just one of those things?

Two weeks later a letter arrived for me at work addressed to: Hélène, Berlitz School, London. It was a thick package of a letter in an unknown handwriting: inside, the bold and moving outpourings of love of my party acquaintance Johan. I was filled with wonder at this letter, which could by all accounts have been deemed premature, where long-held yearnings were displayed disarmingly. He had fallen completely in love with me on the evening we met and innocently wanted us to make a life together. I was stirred, touched, amazed. And at least these yearnings matched mine.

We had our first meeting in a cafe near the school, in Oxford Street. Almost speechless with emotion, we could do little but stare at each other, elated and awed by our feelings. This was our very first date and I found I liked him. Looking back, I glimpse that I was sucked into that situation; his feelings, not mine, had decided that we should meet again, but precisely because his feelings were so strong and I was weak, I responded with my needs and romantic notions all at once, a sucker for 'a situation' which would steal me away from my loneliness.

Johan would 'do' just fine, and he was saving my life.

Chapter Eight

The time of meeting Johan represented an exciting move, an adventure of sorts. I was thrilled to have met an artist and the occasion fulfilled my desires for 'dropping out' of the bourgeoisie, linking it cleverly to my love of art.

Johan lived in the country with a couple I instantly loved, Eric and Helen. Eric was a sculptor and had been one of Johan's tutors at Reading School of Art; his wife was also an artist, specialising in woodcuts. They lived in near poverty in a wooden chalet nestled in a clearing in the middle of soft silver birch woods not far from Henley-on-Thames, which they called The Burrow. Not being able to have children of their own, they had started fostering, hoping one day to be able to adopt the three little mixed-race boys who filled their lives. Johan occupied a chalet on the grounds – no better insulated than a garden shed – which served as his studio, with a sleeping bag on a mattress on one side.

When he showed me his paintings, I felt they were for the most part stunning: well-balanced abstract compositions, sometimes abstracted landscapes, they shone in my view among the best in contemporary art, showing a vibrant and mature sense of colour. His mother, Kathleen, lived in London with the last of her three husbands, a retired army major; his real father, an Afrikaner, worked in Swaziland as an irrigation engineer. Kathleen had been married and divorced in her early twenties, already with a child. Her chance meeting with Johan's father (also called Johan) at a cinema, became a passionate love affair and their little boy was born in London, but due to return to Swaziland he asked Kathleen to come along with the baby. She refused, appalled at the prospect of a simple life in the African bush, so Johan did not meet his father again until the age of thirteen when the man appeared one day without warning at his boarding school: 'I am your father.'

Kathleen, a pretty and lively woman of great charm, chose to marry instead a rich industrialist who had made a fortune in car accessories. He subsequently adopted Johan and they had a little girl called Noeline. Johan was sent away early to boarding school, an experience that he talked about casually, without great feeling, as he did about most things.

Johan was intelligent, kind, knowledgeable, and his easy-going manner allied with charm was very attractive. His great talent also put him in a category apart from many men: he was purposeful and driven by his art, and we often talked about it on our walks together. He was full of dreams and mine easily merged with his. We were in love and best friends – except that apart from occasional embraces and warm kisses, our sex life was non-existent. It wasn't just that after a short time of intense emotions, Johan, feeling all this to be exhausting if not alien to his nature, had relaxed into a more casual mode of loving, but intercourse was seemingly impossible. He was upset with himself – 'I'm not too good at this sort of thing!' – but never to the point of facing up to his condition. I was tolerant and accepting, my desires 'on hold', telling myself 'it' was bound to get better with time. There were more important things: we loved each other and lived for his art; my present was lit up by this new happiness. The little girl in me was quite satisfied with our relationship. I knew he loved me, I could see it in his eyes. And I felt safe.

When the news came that his earlier application to spend a year abroad with the Voluntary Services Overseas was accepted, I was distraught; he would be leaving the following September for the West Indian island of Dominica to teach newly qualified graduates the skills of art teaching, not to return until the following June. He was rightly looking forward to the experience. I remember my excitement at receiving his well-written letters full of anecdotes about his daily life, work, friendships and particularly his painting which he described in great detail and passionately: he was developing his skills in new directions, immersed as he was in the easy atmosphere and rich colours of West Indian life.

For my part I spent that year of 1964 in Paris, cutting my teeth as a journalist at a weekly rag with pretentions, *Candide*, thankfully now long defunct. When the time finally came, Johan and I were overjoyed at seeing each other again. He seemed – slightly – more interested in a sex life thanks to a wild island carnival where he allowed himself to drink and dance all night, a revolution for him, later falling asleep drunk on the beach under the palm trees. His many paintings, which I was longing to see, were sailing slowly back to England on a banana boat so we had the summer ahead of us, and it was the right time to meet each other's parents since we would get married in the autumn. While his mother Kathleen and her husband were warm and welcoming, my own parents had been fretting at the idea of their daughter marrying an artist. The idea – I had mentioned he had a beard – of someone hirsute and of course unkempt, terrified them: what would their friends and the town people say?

Their relief was palpable as they greeted us at the railway station: the beard was short, the face amiable, and the manner friendly. My mother, knowing just enough English to allow herself a Freudian slip, shook his hand with a smile, saying:

– Goodbye, Johan.

Our hilarity set the general mood on 'fair'. Mother soon decided we should have an engagement party to introduce Johan to family and friends and formalise our situation. We tried to resist the offer: not having any money, we had dismissed the idea of an engagement ring and could not afford a honeymoon either; nor did we care for formalities. In vain. My father lent Johan a cream-coloured summer jacket for the occasion, gifting him the required gentility. Odile was there, quiet and pleasant if withdrawn. The whole family was won over by Johan's gentle disposition, but Mother, monitoring the situation, warned me not to be too affectionate in public, 'as people could see you are intimate'.

While Johan, happy and well fed, was painting contentedly and selling a few canvases to my parents' friends, Mother pleaded with me to get married in church, 'what would my father think, he would be so upset, and he would blame her for being too lax with me when I was growing up, she wouldn't be able to bear another argument,' etc. Newly stronger because of my recent status, I retorted that it was out of the question.

"At least," she implored, "tell our friends you will be getting married in church, albeit in London, your father wouldn't know what to say to all the relatives and friends whose children had done the right thing and had beautiful church weddings." I countered I wouldn't dream of it. It had become easier to resist her pressure as I was no longer alone and so susceptible to her tyranny: she knew that her power was much diminished since I had in her eyes moved under the 'authority' of my future husband. I resolved to speak to my father.

I arranged to go for a drive with him and when after a

while we stopped in a country lane, I put my case to him calmly. I believe he felt flattered and relieved that I should choose him for an adult talk, since he had long been bypassed by Mother as far as decisions were concerned, big or trivial. I saw as well that he could not let the opportunity pass to acquire a little of the closeness that he would have wished for all these years and had been denied, often through his own doing. I didn't see at the time that it provided me with the chance to make a genuine contact with a father who had been absent from my life and couldn't give himself the role I needed him to play. Now that he no longer relied on an authoritarian persona, I could see, more and more, the little boy underneath. Predictably, he assured me that a Registry Office wedding was fine by him.

Our wedding, on a cool Friday in October, was fun, with many friends and few relatives on my new territory, London. We had given Johan's aunt's address as ours so we could get married at Chelsea Town Hall, while the reception would take place at the Army Barracks along the King's Road, courtesy of Johan's cousin who was an officer there. Having met his mother just before the ceremony, Mother took me aside:

– Why hadn't you told me Johan's family were the right sort of people? Her relief was obvious, she would be able to share the wedding photos with their friends back in France.

For a year Johan and I were very privileged as his parents lent us their flat in Putney while they went away, allowing us to save for a deposit to buy our own place. Johan got a job teaching Art in a secondary school, painting in our small spare bedroom in the evenings. Prior to getting a teaching job myself, I worked for several months as a sales assistant in Liberty's, doing some baby-sitting in the evenings. We were safe and secure, but life seemed so narrow: what do you do with such vast feelings as love and artistic endeavour when you have to imprison them between four walls and subject them to such mundane routines? I burst into tears one evening, despairing:

– We have Life, this life, and Love, and we have to live like this, and it is such a small life!

Johan, painting beautiful things, was the happier of us two. Although we both went back to work on the Monday that followed our wedding, he was also preparing for an exhibition at the Richard Demarco gallery in Edinburgh the following month which would be very well reviewed in 'The Scotsman'. His career seemed to be able to take off, which thrilled me. The Dominica paintings were vibrant with soul and emotion, shaken as he had been by such a raw and luscious world. At night though, we still slept like babies, his rare attempts at intercourse being disastrous. I was dying for affection, but Johan found displays of love awkward even when they came to his mind. He called me, at times of closeness, 'my little love'. Starved, I asked for cuddles one day:

– But darling, he replied innocently, you give enough affection for the two of us...

I was baffled, but had slowly grown to understand that great trauma in childhood – only ever mentioned casually – had left serious wounds: Kathleen's husband had been a violent drunk who beat her up every evening. Johan was often beaten himself as a little child, and a padded door had to be installed between his bedroom and his mother's so he wouldn't hear her screams. She escaped one day, taking the two children and fled. When her husband hired private detectives who tried to kidnap the children on a beach, a determined Kathleen fought them and she and the children managed to run away.

Is any emotion a safe feeling for a little child when he sees such violence around him? He will withdraw from it, freeze, repress, denying any pain and damage: he is, after all, still in one piece and outwardly functioning. I was very young in my understanding of such things, psychological causes and consequences were not commonly talked or written about yet in the sixties, and I only later came to realise that our marriage wasn't really a viable marriage at all.

Johan found a flat for us the following year, at 238a Sydney Road, in Muswell Hill, opposite a council estate, a long way off the bottom of Colney Hatch Lane. It was all we could afford but we were happy there. Johan bought a garden shed to paint in, the spare bedroom being too small for his now large works on hardboard. I myself took extra work which led to my meeting Antonis, a handsome Greek architect who filled my Wednesday visits to his flat in Westbourne Grove with lust and excitement. To be able to live an adventure in a completely separate compartment from my marriage gave me an outlet for some of my needs without endangering my marriage to Johan who never knew, and it lasted a few months. I remember my simple joy at meeting my lover every week, eating strawberries on his bed, privately marvelling at his enthusiasm for me – 'Helenaki, Helenakimou', he called me, my little Hélène. We made love breathlessly in the summer heat.

Johan painted. In fact, he gave up his teaching post without consulting me, which did not outrage me half as much as it should have done although I did feel let down: we were supposed to be a team, a partnership, and there I was now with the sole and heavier task of earning both our livings and pay the mortgage. We never argued, as he was easy-going and I was still on the wrong side of gentle: bearing up was second nature. We even used to laugh about it: "Could you say 'no' sometimes? Do you always have to agree?" On this occasion, his excuse was that I would have been very angry had I known of his plan. "What do you think I am now?" I retorted, but had to accept the fait accompli. Brought up to be ever compliant, I found it easy to surrender my needs to others' when the relationship or the situation required it. Mother had written it early as a law: "One must put other people first." I had come to realise that at home, for Odile and me, other people meant: herself. In the cocoon of my relationship with Johan, where I was safe because I was needed and never criticised or ignored, it was natural for me to concur, to collude even, as long as I felt I belonged.

I resorted to giving private lessons on Sunday mornings, and found a new full-time job teaching French at an East End school. Johan, now painting happily full-time, became anxious to develop his career in a more welcoming environment than our dreary little suburb. He decided, convincing me against my better judgment, that we should sell our flat. He wanted to take a lease (with a rent that was twice our previous mortgage repayments) on business premises on Islington Green that he thought we could easily convert into a workable flat in spite of having no bathroom; the lonely sink in a small room we baptized 'kitchen'.

I enjoyed living in the area which was lively but money pressures quickly made themselves felt. All this taking place in the blessed sixties when the world was metamorphosing and everything was possible, I thought, discovering in me some creative enterprise, that I could make some extra money in a small fashion venture:

'Chokers', as they were called, were flattering black ribbons worn around the neck, adorned with a motif of some sort in the middle: they would team up nicely with the long flowing skirts of the time. Mine would be made of strips of soft suede which Johan would cut from the pelts I bought wholesale and I would embellish them with antique embroidery motifs or mother-of-pearl counters and sometimes fabulous old buttons found across the road in the stalls of Camden Market. This was fun and it took me out of the drudgery of teaching full-time and the terrible difficulties I was having in the classroom.

Few of my students, from deprived backgrounds for the most part, were in the least interested in learning French, making me pay a high price both for my assumptions and my inexperience. It was often havoc during lessons and I was torn between my duty to teach and my reluctance to impose a discipline: if it was at all strict, I would merely add more misery to many of their already harsh lives, of this I was more and more conscious. So at the end of that year I changed jobs, finding a post at Starcross School in Islington, closer to home but a great deal worse.

Johan was finding opportunities to exhibit here and there. This was in the main more a cause for excitement than a source of income, as a gallery would have to be rented for a period and would take a hefty percentage of each sale. Then there was the cost of framing, which Johan would do himself but for which tools and materials needed to be bought. There was sometimes a small profit, but it was just as well I was earning fairly good money with the chokers I managed to sell in Hampstead boutiques and West End stores – our life was precarious.

Johan, when he felt stirred, could paint extraordinary things, like his vast pictures, in great part figurative through his inventive use of collage, inspired by the sufferings of the people of Biafra during the famine. But then, seeing little commercial benefit in them, he would often paint over them, much to my despair and that of our more knowledgeable friends. It seemed that once he had expressed a deep emotion, he was unable to sustain and maybe integrate it, and so would have to dismiss it. I couldn't see at the time that our marriage was suffering the same fate.

When he painted for an exhibition, he would at times resort to commercial styles which did no justice to his talent and the results would be disappointing. We were lucky once though: a couple rang our bell, having seen the sign for our 'gallery' in the entrance hall of our building, and they bought several pieces for their business of Art for rent to television and film studios. This stroke of luck postponed the moment when we would both have to face the consequences of living so much on hope.

Chapter Nine

Not for a single day did I suffer from depression in the five years Johan and I were together. I felt empowered by our companionship where I had been able to find an active role, and by Johan's apparent if relative commitment. I had at last found a visible and legitimate place. This was confirmed one rainy Sunday when we decided to go to the Planetarium, a first for both of us. I had the devious ploys of the French thinker – and mathematician – Pascal in my mind, presenting man (woman too, presumably) with the infinitely vast space beyond our world, the stars, the galaxies, comparing it to our insignificance and aloneness: wouldn't we be convinced of the greatness of God's creation, awed by his power, and fall to our knees? Besides, we had everything to gain in entering the fold, he claimed, and nothing to lose: who wouldn't bet on salvation when the alternative was damnation? I was full of anticipation: was I about to have a religious experience? Would I become again the Catholic I had shunned?

I was far from being entirely earnest about those concerns, since I never could take Pascal's arguments seriously: his wager was indeed stupid, and he the theological equivalent of a cad, full of intellectual contempt for his would-be converts: didn't he understand a real truth-seeker would despise any such bribe and that he had himself fallen for his own argument? For me, the search for truth, free from any enticement, might have been put on hold for a while, engaged as I was in earning a living, but I had never renounced it. Faith was a different matter altogether: I hadn't become a cynic, but growing up surrounded by so many fallacies both at home and convent school had not prepared me to fall at the presented hurdle: whether to put my trust in the biggest parental figure of them all, the god of our Western religious galaxy. I would take any opportunity to doubt and argue, but also heartily welcome debate and new arguments. It was all very interesting. With my friend Johan next to me, reassured of my place in the world by my place at his side, engaged in our common endeavour: his success, I was far from the vulnerable youth seemingly spinning in space, who mourned God, wandered aimlessly without compass, begging to be told: life is this way, this is where you go, what you do.

So on that day, sitting in an uncomfortable seat and my neck crooked, I was unequivocally seduced by the entrancing display of the world beyond: stars glittered and winked joyfully, constellations glided, galaxies floated in elegant parades. It is easy to feel part of the exceptional when the exceptional becomes visible: so we were all part of this, in fact we were all, each of us, as stars in a sky which now turned to heavenly by the simple magic of its order and beauty: we all belonged. I felt very happy and told Johan who laughed contentedly. Pascal had lost.

At the beginning of our marriage, encouraged by the ambient atmosphere of creativity I was living in, I tried to pursue my interest in drawing and painting in which I had dabbled in over the years without much success, having lacked any proper tuition. Certainly Johan, if he ever had the inclination, never found the time to tutor me. He had looked at one of my drawings once and said:

– Not bad, but quite flat. Why don't you take up sculpture or pottery to get a sense of the third dimension?

Intimidated at the thought of sculpture, I plumped for pottery, in my eyes less demanding of hard ambition. And so I attended weekly pottery classes in an Adult Education Institute at Putney School of Art, which was to be for several years a source of discovery and enjoyment. I was quite good at it but stubbornly declined to go on the wheel, far preferring to build my vases out of coils and slabs. I found the slow hand-to-clay relationship profoundly rewarding, and when, at the end of one term, I brought home my dozen or so pots and put them on the table for Johan to look at, I was amazed: bold, balanced, they exuded single-minded ease and firmness of purpose, they were what I did not know about myself and had to admit to: 'God', I thought, 'I am so strong…'

It was just as well.

The student riots of May '68 had come to an abortive and depressing conclusion but the feelings of frustration and hope that had been shouted in the streets left little doubt that all our yearnings, be they for a better economic, political or cultural order, had a spiritual lining: *'panem et circenses'*, bread and circus games, were not enough for people throughout the Western world who demanded life should be about more than 'Métro, Boulot, Dodo': commuting, slogging and sleeping. Expressing these yearnings was for many cathartic, but for others depressing if it led them back to the status quo. I felt proud to be French then, and would have loved to have taken part in demonstrations but I was the sole earner and the borders had been closed. I followed it all eagerly, at first hopeful then sad, on the radio and television.

I didn't know that Johan cared much for all that, engrossed

as he was in his work which varied: if he allowed himself an emotional content, the painting was not just skilful or attractive, but it spoke to me, shared its feelings, it had a life of its own. As so often, when Johan refrained from emotional engagement he took refuge in experimentation, thinking development lay there, and his work still had some appeal but a lot less soul; similarly, there was less content in our relationship. I didn't feel he treated me at all differently from any of our friends. I dared to suggest we both go and see a doctor together, to no avail. I left *Forum* magazine lying around the flat for a while, open at the sexual problems pages, but he had a calculated blindness to it. A close friend warned him:

– If you don't do something, you will lose her, she will leave you.

It was probably too hard to contemplate.

At the same time, like every hibernating animal, he needed eventually to emerge from his slumber and allow feelings to soar: an acquaintance of ours, a photographer called Sophie, with a gentle presence and beautiful eyes of turquoise, was an occasional member of our group. Johan wrote to her declaring his feelings, inviting her to a party at our flat. He stood that evening by the window, waited and waited, yearning. Then he turned towards me:

"I love you too, you know."

I knew. I watched him wait. I understood. I myself had started a relationship with an artist friend. I loved Johan, but with resignation now, and that night Sophie did not appear.

At least I had found a new and far easier job this time, at St Godric's Secretarial College in Hampstead, teaching nice middle-class girls how to become bilingual secretaries, a convenient baggage to possess until they found a suitable husband. The pay was poor but compensated by classrooms in beautiful houses overlooking well-tended green lawns.

Free to leave the College between classes, I took walks around Hampstead, learning the new geography and the magic of beautiful trees, stopping dead one day at the sight of a bright pink hawthorn in full bloom: it stood in front of a grand white Victorian house with a porch. The scent, heady, seductive, was of countryside in the middle of town. I marvelled at its beauty and shape, transfixed: how wonderful it must be to live in a house with such a tree in the front garden, what privilege! And I walked on, enjoying my freedom in the peace of a London spring.

One day, we heard through a friend about a Housing Association flat in Hampstead and declared an interest. The small sum we needed as deposit had just been given to Johan by his half-sister Noeline on her father's death. Having inherited the bulk of his estate she kindly felt she should give her brother a small share. Serendipitously, the flat was in the very house where I had stopped to admire the hawthorn in bloom, one of these coincidences that seem to give meaning to new choices and departures. We had to wait however: the conversion of that grand house into flats had yet to be completed and would take a few months. We had chosen the garden flat, down a few stairs at the front but level with the garden at the back, with a private patio that would lend us relative privacy from the communal garden. With two bedrooms, it was more than we had dreamt of and as much as we needed. We could make a home for ourselves there.

A while later, Johan claimed to have a wonderful idea: he had been visiting a warehouse near us in Islington, an ideal space to convert into studios, and he intended to partition it for sub-letting to other artists and craftsmen. I was encouraged to see him act decisively. A friend of ours who was separating from his wife financed the venture so that she could receive a regular income out of the good profit Johan would make. However, I later learned what Johan had omitted to tell: the lease forbade him to sub-let and just as soon as a couple of artists realised that he wasn't entitled to charge rent, they stopped paying him and it snowballed. Our friend's wife had to wait a very long time for her money, Johan having bought himself a new car with her husband's investment. I felt angry, discouraged, and tired of carrying an irresponsible, weak and dishonest man.

I have no memories whatsoever of our discussing my decision to leave. The conversation would have been kept short. *"No post-mortems, dear"* was one of Johan's favourite phrases. I do not recall looking for a room. It was all done amicably, I am sure, and he would have helped me move my few belongings out, driving me to my new address, saying:

"See you soon, dear," as we parted.

My temporary new home was a bedsitter in Belsize Park, a small room in a busy house full of lodgers where I felt quite lost. Johan and I saw each other occasionally. I even lent him some money which he couldn't repay but I settled happily for a painting in return. And the day I came to collect it, I stopped dead in front of a sculpture he had just completed: a larger than life young man with the exaggerated torso of an athlete but in a wheelchair, both his legs missing, who carried his future with him as we all do, only more visibly so. It was the end of the Vietnam war, and shocking images were shown on television of young wounded American soldiers being brought back on airplanes, some on stretchers, others rolling down planks in their wheelchairs, their eyes empty – beautiful, strong young men recently at the peak of their powers, now ever powerless, limbs amputated, carrying on their bodies the defeat and scars of their country.

And I understood what Johan felt. Whether he was aware of it himself, I didn't know, but he had put his heart and soul into this, all anguish and despair. Only the sculpture was heartbreakingly potent.

Chapter Ten

Where was Odile? What was she doing when all this was happening? As I retrace my steps on my own map, I am aware of being a very poor cartographer of her life, estranged as we were. She so often seemed, towards me, animated by the anger of the spurned lover, at the same time as using summary text-book definitions – she was taking Political Sciences in Bordeaux – to impress me with. Then she would close up, inaccessible. We occasionally shared confidences during the summer holidays we spend at my parents' country house but she seemed set in a groove, with disdain the weapon closest at hand. One day, I suggested that she applied her lipstick too thickly. Immediately, she started applying more and more layers all the while staring at me defiantly. Did I call her silly? Quite possibly.

Madame Niklaus came round again with "a wonderful book written by Father So-and-So, very profound," she added, "a great story by a very holy man…"

I thanked her and declined, but Odile again took it eagerly, looking at her with reverence and gratitude.

Another time, on a rare walk together, Odile confided she had an abortion:

"Oh, no!" I exclaimed, appalled. I knew it from my own history to be a very painful experience, ambiguous at best. She reacted with fury:

"If you had one, so can I!"

Did she mean that my actions gave her permission to behave like me, or was she seeking to protect herself against criticism by implicating me? I now sense that, having at that time rejected both our parents, she had turned her focus even more desperately on me. But she was conflicted: there was jealousy there. I had felt jealous towards her myself as a child whenever she had seemed closer to Mother and I felt excluded. I got my own back when I could: if she would grumble at being woken up for Sunday breakfast in the bedroom we shared as children, I would coo in my mother's arms all the more, winning her praise and preference at that moment at least. Our rivalry was such that we seldom used our common enemy, our father, to make peace with each other, when an alliance could have brought us some comfort.

I remembered Mother telling me much later that Odile had also been in love with René-Jacques, which always seemed to me such an oddity: how could she sustain that love when he paid her not the slightest attention in our teens? She must of course have been very upset when he died in the Vespa accident and unable to weep openly. I can only understand her state of mind if I acknowledge it had a lot more to do with me than with René-Jacques, that she had made me her only focus, her model for existing, feeling, behaving, and that it got out of hand, that she needed to merge more than she wanted to be herself, almost a religious way of being: she was being 'me-in-love-with-René-Jacques'. It was also likely to have been the hopeless love of the needy child, never to be assuaged.

Seemingly caught in an emotional Gordian knot, she was setting up, time after time, the conditions that would lead to her rejection and isolation, I am sure a familiar feeling. Having her turn at Bordeaux University when I left, I suspected that she had a hard time, mostly with herself if my own experience was anything to go by. Having failed to complete her degree in Politics and mortified (her tutors had decided she 'lacked the required maturity'), she took refuge from the family by fleeing to Madrid, officially to work on her Spanish. I understood she must have been desperate at her failure and lack of direction, confiding in a cousin later that she had felt so lost she prayed for *'someone to come and kill her'*, priming herself for the shocking tragedy which was set to take place.

Mother telephoned me one evening, fretting with anxiety: Odile had met a man in Madrid, an Australian quite a few years her senior. Bill lived above her in the same boarding house and had apparently taken wonderful care of her when she got very ill with flu. Odile and he, now a couple, were due to visit our parents for a few days on their way to Paris where they planned to live. Mother wanted me to be there at the same time: she was concerned about my sister's choice of partner, Odile having been very vague on the telephone about Bill's profession and the arrangements they were planning; she needed a buffer and an ally; besides, neither she nor Father spoke any English.

Bill was tall and thin with very deep-set eyes and a small nose that gave him a look that worried us, and he didn't speak French. He seemed to be well in his thirties, Odile being about twenty-three at the time. His dress sense was as incongruous as it was outrageous: a black velvet suit as everyday wear in our backward town would have been out of place in itself but its impact was aggravated by a white silk shirt complete with lace trimmings on his frilly jabot and cuffs. He didn't, however, have the winning presence of a Hollywood musketeer... I was too green and naive myself to think of examining him too closely and conversation was sketchy. Odile, on the contrary, seemed very happy. She proudly – if bizarrely – announced in a short visit in my room one morning: "We have done everything," boasting about the breadth of her new sexual experience. That odd piece of information, coming out as it did without preamble, left me at the time unconcerned and I merely thought her silly.

Work was calling me back to London, and as usual I was relieved to go. However, soon after I got home, several concerned telephone calls from Mother informed me that the day after my departure Odile demanded a substantial sum of money before leaving with Bill: she claimed to need it for six months' rent on a flat in Paris and to buy the lease on a bar that Bill wanted to run. Although my parents were horrified and tried to resist, Odile was adamant: she had not just made up her mind, she was determined, Mother said; and fearing they would otherwise never see her again, they relented.

From Paris, Odile gave news to Mother on occasion. She and Bill had found a flat but life was expensive and she had to wash their sheets by hand in the bath 'to save money'. When Mother rang one morning, Odile sounded evasive, her tone of voice flat if not sad. "How are things with Bill?" Mother finally queried. "Oh, a bit difficult at times," she replied wearily that day.

My parents' anxiety at a pitch, they confided in the Niklaus; their son Armand, it was rumoured, was in the secret services and they would ask for his help. This gave my first sexual partner another role to fulfil in my family. He found Odile in a room with Bill and a few other men. She was crouching on the floor in a corner, head down, seemingly terrified. Acting fast and firmly – he must have produced his Homeland Security card – Armand ordered her to come with him right away, the men letting her go without argument. He then put her on a train straight back to our parents' town in the South.

Mother was full of sadness and solicitude, Odile looking broken as well as withdrawn. One morning she surprised her in the bathroom and saw my sister's poor body covered in bruises. Mother cried, Odile cried and confided. They would go to the nearest large town to consult a gynaecologist who confirmed that my sister was in a bad way: a serious infection had ensured she would remain childless, and she was not even twenty-four. Bill knew how to break a woman into prostitution.

Remembering how passively I had seen her behave in the past, I feared it would only have been too easy... I was later given to understand there was worse but Mother had been sworn to secrecy. She had always in my eyes been closer to Odile and was distraught for her little girl.

After a while, Odile decided to take a year off and find work in Canada. She had a good friend in Ottawa who would help her find a job. Of course she remained there, as Mother had feared. She worked first as a teacher and attended courses, I do not remember which. I wrote to her sometimes, albeit rarely. She confided in me once on the telephone that she hadn't gone away far enough: "Communist China might have been safer," she joked, deluged by a flood of letters from Mother who, as ever and more so now, demanded, pleaded, counselled, complained and admonished. "Her letters make me ill," she added, "I often have them on my table for weeks without being able to open them."

It was only years later, when I started remembering what had happened to me, that I began to realise the magnitude and horror of what she had been through, and why.

I wasn't my sister's keeper – seldom was, but we communicated for a while. She didn't volunteer much, mostly complaining of 'Mother's 'tentacles' reaching across the Atlantic. I felt relieved to be living in London since

I was less the butt of her criticisms now that I had been 'legitimised' by a man. Until the day, of course, when I decided to leave Johan. Mother, who was fond of him and had come to visit, was shocked at the news:

"But I thought you got on so well!" she exclaimed, wide-eyed in astonishment.

"We did, but..." and I explained why we were never a real couple, why I had to leave, prudently deciding to omit Johan's unique ways of making money.

She looked astounded as well as concerned:

"Oh, my God, don't tell this to your father!"

"Why not?"

"Because, – it was the same with us, your father had terrible problems, he couldn't either, or else at times only in the middle of the night, and he would wake me up suddenly, and we had to do it, quick, quick ... I couldn't bear it in the end..."

I do not recall what I told my father, who showed mild surprise, may be that Johan and I had merely grown apart; this ensured there would be no real questions and therefore, as our divorce papers eventually allowed a few years later, no blame attached. This I thought right and proper in our case, as Johan and I were keen to remain friendly and I had no wish to humiliate him.

That conversation with Mother lingered in my mind for a long time: I was shaken by the similarities, the obvious symmetry: it went a long way to illustrate, albeit retrospectively, so many scenes in my childhood, my mother's pleading behind closed doors ("You can ask me for anything but not that!"), her shrinking at my father's touch, the kiss on her mouth the day we celebrated her birthday, when he pinned her against the dining-room wall and she turned her head, pushing him away:

"No, please! Not this! Not in front of the children!"

She had been on the verge of tears.

I remember being torn at the time between the wish not to see and the desire to know, as when 'the word' came into use much later, she exclaimed with passion:

"I hate that word: sex!"

It was clear this was a no-go area and that 'it' should all be kept out of the way by not asking any questions.

Chapter Eleven

Meanwhile, alone in my bedsitter that winter of 1972, I was losing my footing: cooking on the tiny stove one evening I set fire to the pan as well as the lampshade above it and the kitchen curtain, desperately lonely, out of balance and lost: who cares for me?

I telephoned Mother to ask her to send me René-Jacques's letters, it would be a comfort to be able to read them again now, but I got a rebuff in the style:

"Oh, please, don't act like a child! I'm not sure where they are, I'll look for them next time you come. You can wait a while longer."

Since I didn't know what to think, I avoided thinking. Not that Mother was not present in my mind, on the contrary she now lived in my head more than ever, chattering away non-stop and we always ended up in arguments: she advised, recommended, admonished, preached, reproached and dismissed endlessly as in a fast-forwarded film of my childhood. I felt exhausted, overdosed by this endless tyranny. I did not seem to be able to get rid of her, she forever stood in front of me, an eyebrow raised ("You are hurting me a lot, my little girl."). There seemed to be no room for me in my brain, she has conquered it like a disease, meddling in all the conversations I had with myself. My father stood in the background, neutered.

At times of creative anger, I entertained myself with a huge picture in my head of my own 'Holy Family' where Mother sits, larger than life, in majestic plumpness, on some kind of ceremonial stool – rich velvet and golden curves. Eyebrows up, eyelids down, in resigned suffering and eternal wisdom, she rests one hand on a young boy, my father – child Jesus like – standing in front of her; he has a finger raised in warning of the next platitude he is about to deliver with solemnity. Mother's hand on his shoulder, he is unaware he is her child forever: powerless and malleable. Unsurprisingly, Mother is herself oblivious she is sitting on top of me lying on my front on her seat, my arms and legs gesticulating on either side of her. I screamed in protest and pleaded to be freed, to no avail. She was deaf to my cries, I was ignored.

In retrospect, where was Odile in this family portrait, as she didn't appear in the image I have created? Was she even there? Or was she invisible? Maybe, just maybe, Mother had swallowed her, which is why she sat there so much fatter, even more powerful. It could be, though, that I have cancelled Odile from my life, there was barely room for me as it was, I might not want any competition. In my mind, caught in the pincers of Mother's needs and demands, I acted in scenes where I was endlessly the butt of her criticisms, yet she wished me to be totally hers, as in a state of osmosis. She had frequently told her friends in the past:

– She tells me everything.

It was not, of course, entirely the case, and when I was thirteen or fourteen, I once retorted:

– No, I don't.

It was easier that day, daringly, to say it in front of a witness whose presence acted as a buffer. Mother could not systematically ignore it that way, but it meant intending to hurt her, a mortal sin, and the guilt it gave me fed into my anger.

I dreamt a lot, dreams similar to those of my childhood when I used to find myself lying on the ground, paralysed but conscious, as an enormous black spider swung threateningly above me, all the time getting closer. I was already conscious that the spider was Mother, just as Odile was later when she dreamt that she had a huge boil on her left breast near her heart, and an endless leaking of pus was seeping out of it, to her unbearable shame. These things we had been able to share on rare evenings alone as we grew more aware of our family life.

Attempting to define myself had always been a painful and tentative enterprise, full of clumsiness and anguish, not least when Mother rounded me up in one of her definitive assessments, if she saw me trying to paint or draw or attempt anything new: my results had always been classified as 'not bad' at best, damning me in my own eyes as I loathed mediocrity. She got quite close to the bone when she declared one day:

"You're a bit like a duck: you can walk a bit, swim a bit, fly a bit, quack a bit, but you do nothing particularly well."

She had complimented me once though, for a present I had given her on her birthday, a rather nice pen and ink drawing of thistles and reeds which she chose to hang in the country house... but between a wall and a door that hid it when open.... She much later returned it to me – there was, she said, ' no room' for it in her now smaller flat – so I chose in turn to hang it in my London house cloakroom like the unloved child it was.

In the same way I used to look for my reflection in shop windows for reassurance, I now incessantly checked on myself, questioning, pondering, weighing, watching myself feel and systematically asking 'why?', taking notes: how to be? I was filled with emotions that were inaccessible, but overwhelming as in a Rothko painting, as in a Johan sculpture... I functioned well enough on the outside, except when I collapsed in tears between lessons in the middle of a teaching day, distraught with anguish and despair. And I knew it was not about the absence of Johan but the absence of me in me.

When I finally moved into my new Hampstead flat, a little burrow down some steps on the street side, I was delighted to see that it had plenty of light as well as being surrounded by trees. The patio off the living room, level with the communal garden, was half enclosed by a low wall for my privacy, with a flower-bed-to-be on the side. Johan hadn't wanted to take any of our few possessions (merely a bed, a table and four chairs, our 'wardrobe' in Islington having consisted of a few stacked wooden crates from the greengrocer's). Since he planned to go and stay with his mother in Spain for a while, I started my new life with a modicum of furniture.

However, alone in the flat that autumn, I was frightened at night: I sat up in bed, rigid, stiffening at the smallest noise, eventually daring to get up to check the French doors to the garden: dried leaves brushed to and fro by the wind were the only visible cause of the disturbance. I could easily sweep that danger away in the morning but could not stop the rustling of branches. Night after night I sat up in bed listening, eventually resigning myself to sleep. In the end I resorted to reason: I might well be burgled one night, but not every night. I should therefore not be scared every night, once would suffice. And I slept well thereafter.

Except that one evening a snake came to my door. It should in theory have been a short visit, merely to return a book I had left behind at his girlfriend's. I had never met him before. As he stood in the doorway, grinning, I saw a flash of light in his eyes. He could give me news of her since she now lived outside town. I should be friendly, invite him in for a cup of coffee. But after a while he didn't want to leave: I was so attractive, he said, and sadly lonely, very unfair. He should like to stay the night, he felt I would like him to. I protested weakly, and he darted at the weakness, he knew his game. At the same time, I was aware of my dislike: bad skin, sly eyes, smug demeanour, he was repellent to me, yet I was spellbound. He coiled around me as, limp as a wounded mouse, I whimpered in resigned complaint. And he took his time, as I realized he was waiting for me to come, which didn't happen and lengthened my trial. Waking up in disgust in the middle of the night, I took refuge in the other bedroom where he found me in the morning and dragged me back to my bed where he complained again that I wasn't 'tactile'.

I was totally unable to do 'angry', 'confrontational', 'decisive'; it would require clarity as well as courage. Far easier, less painful and complicated, to collaborate, to be quiet and good, obedient. Could I pretend he is my boyfriend and there was love? Isn't it what one does? The fantasy didn't fit, though, better forget it.

After he left, I knew I would not see him again. I rushed to the bathroom and washed, and washed, and washed...

Other people had moved into the house and it was now full. There was a lively, friendly couple with one child above me, occupying a similar space to mine, whose life seemed inspiringly normal. Above them, a seemingly dashing divorced man in his late thirties, Trevor, who made a bee-line for me, and I suddenly found myself going with him on outings to the country, out to dinner, to the theatre, receiving flowers. He was so suitable that I surrendered with enthusiasm. Mother would love everything about him: his looks, manners, position (he is a doctor), polished fingernails… I made every effort to please, tried to anticipate every one of his desires or whims, dressing for approval, conversing for effect. My life could be taking a turn for the better, the safer.

Of course it didn't: an ex-girlfriend of his had reappeared and I became 'such a wonderful woman, the right one at the wrong time, who will understand, he knew, I have such wisdom'… As I watched myself suffering almost unbearable pain, I also at the same time undertook to dissect that relationship as ruthlessly as I could, as minutely as I was able, because I sensed it held secrets about me I had yet to discover and needed to find out if I was ever to grow up. The pain seemed to go well beyond the bounds of the conventional and systematic emotions I had invested in that relationship. I had to admit to myself I did not like Trevor very much at all: he was too smooth, suave, charming, standard, a bourgeois with slithery good manners. Strangely, he had no body smell whatsoever, a confirmation of his blandness; that lack of smell of his had been an odd relief in a way I couldn't explain at first, but at the same time, confusingly, a dis-attraction. He reminded me in his demeanour of those smart acquaintances of my parents whom Odile and I as children had been directed by Mother to greet with a curtsy when they came to dinner, and who smiled condescendingly at us, tapping our cheeks. I remember feeling the red-hot pain of humiliation of those moments when Mother beamed, fulfilled in her own need to impress.

I also had to concede, in my now ruthless examination, that I had never felt any physical desire for Trevor, for he was bland in body as in soul. It took me several months of agonising self-analysis to conclude that this particular role of mine in that particular play with that particular man was merely telling a story about me without even being real.

And as I stood brushing my teeth one morning in front of the bathroom mirror, I had the lightning realisation that all the angles and facets of that story were about getting Mother's approval, being her thing again, and I experienced an exhausted feeling of achievement, having reached the top of that tall mountain on my knees.

I thought I had better talk to my GP, a kind and mature woman who offered me three short appointments a week in surgery time. She had a strong interest in psychoanalysis, and we both felt she had better check my conclusions. She confirmed what I thought after two months, gave me a lot of praise and encouragement, but warned me that self-analysis is incredibly difficult, dangerous and rare, and that if I wanted to pursue my quest I had better see a psychotherapist one day.

My teaching work was not enough to keep me sane or satisfied. There were all these hours after I got home when I found myself alone not knowing what to do with myself. I wrote some thoughts about politics (Sheik Mujibur Rahman of Pakistan was inspirational but got assassinated), freedom, self-realisation, doubt, loss, often mere paragraphs, never as long as essays but nevertheless attempts at definition.

Johan wrote to me from Spain: he had felt very lost and aimless for a few months but was thinking of returning to England and settling in the West Country. Our friendship was still there, casual and undemanding as our love had been. After two years of separation, I occasionally toyed with the idea of divorce but kept putting it off, since there did not seem to be any hurry or even necessity.

It was around that time that the government passed a new law allowing no-fault divorces after a two-year separation, which didn't just promise to be painless, it was also very cheap, so maybe the time had come for me to sever the knot. I wrote to Johan to ask him if he minded, I could initiate the paperwork myself and we could go halves on the fees? It would only cost eighteen pounds, probably the cost of the stationery, and going halves meant we did it together, not one against the other, which seemed the friendlier way out. This new divorce being 'Made in England' in the early '70s meant it was easy to the point of casualness: I found myself at the Law Courts swearing my affidavit to a clerk who sat at a counter alongside others, no more intimidating than if I was buying stamps at a Post Office. On the forms, I was the petitioner, Johan the respondent, but there was no guilty party; a neutral phrase described us as having grown apart and we were divorced after a few months, apparently unscathed.

After a while, weighed down by loneliness and a feeling of the absurdity and pointlessness of my existence, I emerged from a heavy sleep each morning wishing the old death wishes: can one die by merely wishing it? I often thought of suicide, the only way to stop such pain, but the expression of imagined suffering on Mother's face forbade it and I struggled on.

When I reappeared at my parents' country house for the summer holiday – I had no-one to go with anywhere else, another source of grief and frustration – I sought and found some nurture in Mother's marvellous cooking. Since she made a lot of the dishes I liked, I found myself at mealtimes a fulfilled child. I sunbathed, read a lot. Friends of theirs came and visited, good food was plentiful, wine flowed and the weather was warm.

Odile was also there this time, the first summer after her terrible ordeal, half-cancelling her presence by having brought a friend from Canada as a buffer, and opportunities for intimate talks were almost nonexistent as they were always together. As I asked her one day if she had read *Siddharta* by Herman Hesse, one of my favourite books of wisdom which I thought might help her, she replied contemptuously:

"Oh, *Siddharta*, I've been through it and out the other side!"

There seemed little point in seeking any closeness as I would be rebuffed. I had partly forgotten her trauma, liked to think she was recovered since it would appear she had escaped prostitution. No-one talked about it of course, and I had had more than my own share of difficulties.

At mealtimes, I tried to entertain my parents about my do-it-yourself divorce, astounding Father who as a lawyer earned a large part of his income from the acrimonious ones he knew how to fuel and prolong. I have made photocopies of the forms I had to fill and translate them for him. He studied them, bemused. Mother was cross, didn't even look at them, in fact she was cross with me for appearing to treat lightly a life event which should be painful by definition. Also, if life isn't so bad, you stay married, what does sex matter, it's disgusting anyway so why should I care?

That there had been some pain in my marriage she evidently didn't see and never asked about. I had been careful to play things down because my unhappiness would be, to her, punishment for my failure and inadequacy; in her eyes I already failed on several counts: I did not seek to live a magazine-format life nor did I seem to care about the code she and my father lived by. It all caused her worry 'she didn't need, adding to a life of sacrifices'. I now made things equally bad in many ways by air-brushing every aspect of my life as being 'fine, absolutely fine', which gave her no grip, but she was fond of Johan and sad of his exit without goodbye, depriving her both of role and recognition: did she not matter to him? I could see she found him safe because he was gentle, and manageable since he never objected. She had no idea his frequent smiling was hiding indifference and silent sarcasm, as he was aware, beyond their genuine kindness and generosity, of their own childish need for approval and unquestioning observance of social conventions.

As I faced my mother's silent condemnation I guessed there was also, implicit, the feeling that, since she had stayed with Father for Odile's and my sakes, I should equally have remained with my husband for hers, her peace of mind, her view of the world according to her need, I owed it to her and was breaking the rules. This was unsaid but somewhat audible in resentful comments about how self-indulgent I was, and visible in shakings of her head. For once, she was faced with the reality of our difference.

Whenever, as little girls, Odile and I saw Mother cry and begged her in tears to leave our father, she always replied she had to stay because of us. We didn't realize this wasn't totally true: she couldn't do it because Father had stolen her money, but she was also terrified of losing her social standing, and it wasn't done at the time. There was moreover the fear of the unknown: like a Black Hole, it could swallow you... . By insisting throughout the years that she had put Odile and me first at all times, she was pointing to her sacrifice (admirable) rather than her naivety (infuriating) and lack of luck, the better to lock us in eternal devotion, guilt and debt. If and when I had a child, I swore to myself, I would never imprison him or her in my needs. There would be no blackmail. I started mentally to make a long list of 'Don'ts'.

With Father, I had seemed to agree a sort of cease-fire that was easily liveable in a large place like the country house and in the summer, when verbal exchanges were kept to the minimum and with the right tone of voice, pleasant and harmless. Physical closeness was almost totally avoidable except at the duty times of the 'good morning' and 'goodnight' kisses my mother had always insisted on. At those times, I held my breath as usual, neutralising my feelings. Father knew I didn't like to be close to him. He had remarked once in the past, when I had recoiled at his touch, his voice a mixture of surprise and hurt:

"You don't like me to touch you, do you?" I had remained silent.

In the country, we didn't have to negotiate our corners, there was plenty of space. From my London safety, I had emptied myself of feelings for him to the point where I may at times feel benevolent: I had moved 'elsewhere' and no longer saw or wondered what took place between him and Mother. On the surface, they seemed pacified, smiled, even joked. Of course, they were happy I was here during our holidays and we were in a beautiful place. The view over the Pyrénées was vast and serene, we were surrounded by gentle hills, the summer lay a shimmering haze of heat over the landscape and we all mellowed. I would have liked to ask Mother again to give me René-Jacques's letters, but knew in my bones that I would at a stroke cause the collapse of our particular House of Cards. Forbidding myself to think about it gave me a pang of burning anger. Shhh...

On a good day, I could laugh at the way Father still tried to endear himself to acquaintances by prolonging forever a simple handshake, assuring people he agreed with them, he was just like them – so much did he want to merge. This was the same father who asked me as a little girl: "Who do you prefer, your mum or your dad?" and gave illicit extra pocket money asking me not to tell Mum. I saw his game, his need, winced. This was too much like childhood, I wanted to go home.

Odile would also go back home, to Canada. She often made it easy for me to dislike her, though with added pity if I could see her pain. Her frequent animosity towards me allowed me to appear the more balanced, pleasant daughter.

It gave me the place I must have required in the family. Somehow she had remained the young girl who stopped playing Ray Charles's records when she learnt he was taking drugs and had to be sanctioned. May be somewhere along the way I too, for some reason, had fallen from grace.

Chapter Twelve

Early in my marriage to Johan, we had gone one evening to see the Louis Malle film: *Les Amants,* (The Lovers), which told the story of a couple who, meeting by accident, quickly come to understand the overwhelming nature of their attraction. We watched their tender and passionate love-making, their grateful smiles as they discovered each other, their hands stroking each other's faces in amazement. I could have wept to see such closeness: this was something I would obviously never know; Johan and I seldom held each other; his kisses, child-like, were equally rare, our love-making non-existent, caresses absent. Yet I loved him then, as loving seemed to be one of my functions: my heart was married to him.

Looking back, particularly since the disastrous episode with Trevor, I saw that I attached my sentimental needs around the man's neck like a placard: 'LOVE!' it said in large letters, 'THIS IS LOVE!' – what the doctor ordered, what I-the-child craved; it gave me a place, reassured and defined me, but mostly settled me like a lullaby. If someone had asked me why I had chosen Johan, I would have replied it was because we got on well, we loved each other, I enjoyed being with an artist, and I didn't mind the shortcomings too much...

'Why didn't you?' could have been the next question but I wasn't ready for it yet. Mother always advised to be patient, accommodate, compromise, minimize. I didn't know yet that every single thing is meaningful, and that the discovery of meaning can be elusive for a long time. Although some markers were already there for me to read, I was still unable to do so.

The French say that 'happy people have no history' – no stories to tell, since nothing disturbs the peace that inner contentment brings with it: it is self-perpetuating, good feelings give birth to more good feelings in a joyous momentum of their own. Some people even took it for granted, claimed it as their birth right, went as far as enshrining its pursuit in their Constitution! I was astounded by the simple and to me naive American optimism: didn't they know what life was like? I thought we had little more than duties, but then the French poet Jacques Prévert said once that: *'We have a duty to be happy, if only to give a good example.'* Now, that's a different kind of duty, I mused.

My upstairs neighbours seemed very satisfied with their marriage, their children, their life, in spite of occasional material problems. Their parents, who came to visit, also exuded contentment and pleasure, chatting with them, playing and laughing with their grandchildren. I watched them and marvelled. Seeing fathers and young children together filled me with intense emotion, part pleasure and part grieving at my own lack of it all, and I almost stopped to stare, my heart melting, my eyes watering: how wonderful, they made better fathers nowadays, thank God, they knew how to love and how to show it... . It was at that time that the husband of a mere acquaintance committed suicide on the very spot at the roadside where his beloved daughter was killed in a car accident. I attended the funeral and wept my heart out, in fact I was just about conscious that I was the person there who cried the most.

I ached with loneliness, starting the day in tears, feeling better only when working or in the company of others, but always disconnected, watching myself and others through a sheet of glass, never able to reach: how do you do it? I could understand dying of solitude and misery: why didn't it kill me? And if the remedy was no other than love, where was it hiding? Was it so little natural, even if it didn't last, that even spring came without it, leaving me in such pain at the close of day?

I wondered about returning to France. My country still breathed and whispered in my veins, I was not from here. I quit my job, attended two interviews in Paris where friends had lent me their minute flat overlooking a courtyard, and I realised how lucky I was to be living in Hampstead so close to the lush beauty of the Heath, hearing and seeing birds at all times, surrounded by trees and with my own outdoor space. Then deciding to remain in London gave some urgency to the task of finding work. I rang all the schools I knew of and a job luckily appeared in extremis at an American school whose language teacher had just let them down. The place looked like a nuclear shelter, all brick and hardly any glass, a ghetto in every detail of its design and intent, and I would be teaching there for the next twenty years... . Although I was given tenure after a year and was very well paid, the isolation I found myself in, a rare foreigner among practically all-American staff, was not a new feeling to me, in fact it hardly shocked me, so much was that school a home from home. It seemed I played with mirrors which sent back images, ever so familiar and urgent, demanding inclusion. And one fine day, sharing jokes with friends and looking back at my poor starved childlike marriage, I declared incautiously that I was now ready for a big passion...

I therefore soon met Jeremy, at a party. The Gods must have been present at that meeting, and it is not that they do not care, but although some might weep, some will shrug, and others, I now know, will laugh: they were the Gods, so belonged to other spheres, and were themselves powerless before the Forces: our needs, our blind compulsion to re-live our childhood patterns that decide how we live our lives and at whose mercy we usually remain.

Very tall, strong-looking in his late forties, he towered over most of us, laughing under the praise lavished upon him for a television programme on wildlife he had presented the night before. His laughter was loud, released, child-like, endearing, and he was wearing a red-checked lumberjack shirt which immediately struck a chord: the Jack London hero of my young days had materialised. I stood there in the middle of the crowd as he made his way towards me with a drink, flirted about my Frenchness and having been a Catholic, the secrets of the confessional, standard adolescent jokes wrapped up in charm. As he jested and quivered, I melted.

At our first meeting alone, a lunch at my flat during which I burned nearly everything, the sofa led promptly to the bed. We both trembled with excitement and emerging passion, couldn't stop making love, again and again. I had never known such enthusiasm and energy. He was astonished at his own prowess. To me this was all very welcome, abundance after famine: surely, it meant something, this hunger, this joy? We repeated our first meeting on a regular basis.

Jeremy's story, showing unresolved feelings as well as divided loyalties, was revealed to me over the next few weeks and months: separated from his wife, Diana, a journalist with whom he had three children, he had only recently moved in with Jane, a scientist, and her brood. So the 'friend' he had mentioned initially seemed to be more of a life partner, in an adult arrangement decided upon before I appeared on the scene. I was an accident, evidently, as well as another betrayal, since it turned out – he admitted to it all – that Jane had been his mistress throughout his marriage to Diana. The birth of their son at the time tipped the balance in Diana's favour, and two baby girls were adopted after a few years. When he finally left – or was pushed – Jane was the obvious choice, and being the same age seemed the mature and definitive option. 'Pipe and slippers' is how he described it to me, hinting at resignation. I was, of course, younger than both by thirteen years, incidentally – and tellingly –the same age difference as between my parents. Then aged thirty-six and looking much younger, I evaluated my advantage, understanding the odds, determined to seize the opportunity: this bright and adolescent man, having seemingly toyed with life and lacking direction, opened up to me, showing his disarray. I would guide him towards the right choices in spite of his frequent jokes arguing for lots of eggs in different baskets:

"With a little here and a little there, you can make up a life, no?"

"It's not a life, it is patchwork."

"Lower your standards!"

"That's not what they are for."

I was articulate and convincing, and in his needier moments he found me wise, sought counsel, seeing I had deciphered his needs. I was as needy as ever, but with an opportunity now to fulfil my hopes. I also saw my hold over him, which empowered me in a way I had never known: he sometimes visited me, having apparently decided to resist making love to me, feeling some guilt, but I watched him struggle and then give way to his impulses, every defeat strengthening his desire. I laughed at it with the comfort of reassurance, being just as mesmerised by him: I felt safe with this powerfully sexual man since my desire matched his.

Brought up with two brothers in the Home Counties in a middle-class family that worked closely with local aristocracy, Jeremy had inherited, without having means other than his own eclectic talents, a view of relationships where money, wherever it came from, was very much boy's own. He had greatly suffered from being sent away to board at the age of eight – 'an exile', he often told me, fighting tears – but he had more fun at Oxford where he acquired, as well as a degree in Zoology, more of the self-assurance and ease that would serve him well in his later career as a journalist and writer. I soon noticed the former often depended on competition based on assumed rivalry: "If you met Diana, you wouldn't win!" he assured me once. Exploring 'girls' had been a matter of making in-roads in alien territory, conquering what could be conquered, measuring degrees of victory as so many points scored. He had found Prep school easier: "I always knew what to do with boys, but with girls..." he admitted so innocently once that I was left speechless, ignorant as I was of the warped and tolerated predilections of the British system of education, which horrified me later when I understood the harm it had done –was continuing to do – to its children, the future builders of the State. I could only see he was wary of women and therefore anxious to have the upper hand, but he didn't always boast about his achievements:

"I am a successful lay-about," he joked, alluding to the many arrows – radio, television, books, ballooning, travel – in his bow, which kept him entertained and free to use his time as he wished. Although he seemed to enjoy belittling me and what I aimed to offer ('bo-o-oring', he would yawn behind a playful hand), his quips and sarcastic jokes, shocking as they could be at the time, appeared as so many challenges to my stubborn feelings.

"He will become good when I have made him happy," I told myself, and I didn't flinch.

Provocatively, innocently, he wore his lack of self-love on his sleeve – his sweaters, full of holes, advertising his emotional orphan status; I fell in the trap, rushing to buy him new ones which he scorned. He also preferred to take my love for mere desire, and, knowing no better, I mistook his desire for love. I was filled with an urgent need to show him the way and that he had found what he needed, I was his solution.

"You wouldn't like me so much if I wasn't so tall," he jibed once, "you need to look up to me" – and I laughed, recognising the accuracy: his six foot three was entrancing to my five foot one. Standing on tiptoes against him to be embraced, I felt a fulfilled woman as well as child: I knew nothing as heady as being embraced by him.

More than anything, Jeremy was fun: being lighter than air quite naturally extended to ballooning, in which he was expert and frequently involved. A glamorous pursuit, it delighted me. It mattered little at the time that he kept most of my fee when he used me in a film for which he had been hired – he would boast of it later; I was having fun too. Being taken out of my teaching routine and more conventional pastimes was outlandish, I was addicted. I also felt a vicarious enchantment listening to his stories of travel, for this man enjoyed the world as his playmate and he relished skipping from place to place like a child in a large playground.

However, a pattern soon developed between us which was wearing me down: he showed intense, joyful and reassuring interest in me when he had been away for a few days, or after I had asked him to leave me alone after one of his many sneers or put-downs, only to show cruelty and flippancy again after love-making. This left me emotionally exhausted;

insecure, I then got clingy and was scorned as 'pure lead'. When Jeremy eventually boasted of hurting me and assured me he hated sharing, I understood our relationship had become so painful and hopeless that I finally had to admit defeat. He had warned me, his wife had long ago judged his shallowness: "You do not like what you have," she had said. So I decided to go away for a while, only to see him arrive minutes before I left for the airport, wild and dishevelled, having walked the streets all night and finally, believably, promising me the Earth...

My body as much as my heart knew its demands by then and with Jeremy it had slowly come to life and given itself permission to experience full sexual pleasure. Indeed 'that place' between my legs, even if it had expressed its right to life in the past with spontaneous sensations and yearnings, had been deemed of scant regard when not disgust in childhood. Was I around seven – a late age – when Mother declared I should from then on wash myself at the bidet? It seems now, oddly, that she had so far performed that function. I remember protesting: "But it's dirty!" – another fact of life I had learned from her.

Now awakened, my body was slowly making other demands. Two years into our often frustrating if compulsive liaison, I told Jeremy I wanted us to have a child. I was thirty-seven, and did not just want this man as my life partner, I wanted a family, my family, a family life, so I warned him that I would stop taking the contraceptive pill, and he should have to decide whether to continue to be with me or not. I knew this man adored children. Seeing him with his young boy and two little girls on outings with them outside London, I was moved to tears when one of them would hold my hand during our long walks in the countryside, delighted by his attentive and playful affection towards them, his sense of fun, his lightness of touch and ability to enter into their conversations and games. He loved taking them out at weekends and paid them lots of visits at home – the highlight was to give the girls their evening bath – and cooking pasta for them when Diana was going to be late back from work. This man was the ideal father for the child I now so desperately wanted: I wept at the mere sight of a small baby on television, even advertisements depicting a cat with her litter had me sobbing helplessly.

"Let me be a mother," I prayed to the Gods, I would be such a good mother...

Well, Jeremy didn't stop coming to see me, nor promising to leave Jane's house and live with me while endlessly putting off his move, and after a while I found I was pregnant, while the future had been postponed and I remained on my own. Being pregnant, though, seemed to me a state of delight and fulfilment that I was born for: I grew and sheltered inside me new life, a little child, a little being, what marvel! And when I felt its first movements inside me, my joy soared to Heaven. I was well, too, and having 'a textbook pregnancy', I was assured. My body stretched wonderfully to prove it and I was proud of myself, even though Jeremy, strangely, kept refusing to touch my glorious belly.

"I don't love you," he spelt out bluntly one day and watched my face intently as tears rolled uncontrollably down my cheeks. I believed him that time, he was looking quite satisfied with the effect he was having, had an air of pride... All I could do was to withdraw into the intimacy of my flat, my cat, the baby growing inside me, wishing to be pregnant forever. Even so, I was passionately envious of the young parents I noticed everywhere around me enjoying their child together, being a family. My existence, so often questioned, needed just one thing to be complete, what I had always lacked myself: a father, and the feeling was this time amplified. I walked the streets alone at weekends, watching couples strolling hand in hand, and I mourned as Jeremy had never held my hand... I was so familiar with deprivation that I didn't think this foreign or even strange. At work, I continued to perform my duties with care and the satisfaction of being useful to young children. Taking a chance on the sex of the baby, Mother knitted dozens of beautifully made garments for a boy, and receiving them almost every week cheered and amused me.

Except that one weekend, a few days before I was due to give birth, I realised that I hadn't felt the baby move for two days... I told some friends who came to visit that October Sunday afternoon and they hurriedly drove me to the hospital.

The poor young nurse who saw me first tried in vain to get any sounds of heartbeats from my womb. I was shocked, but not surprised: what was happening had been inevitable, the doomed conclusion of a doomed relationship and the result of many injuries to my feelings and hopes. Mumbling that she was not expert at using that machine, she rushed to get a consultant, but I knew I wouldn't hear those sounds again. It had always been such a joy, each time I came for an ante-natal check, to hear my baby's heart sounding loud and powerful as a galloping horse.

The consultant held my hands and brought tears with kind words but I couldn't afford to break down yet, I had a job to do. He would examine me internally and try to get the contractions started that night, and we agreed I should return to the hospital when they did. A friend was waiting for me at home now, having left a message on Jeremy's answerphone. I remember it was eight o'clock when the contractions started and I braced myself to ring my parents and tell them the news. My mother cried. My father, for the first time, was moved to give me recognition:

– You are so strong, you are so brave! At that moment, briefly, I felt I had a father.

I was driven to the hospital, feeling brave only to a point. I had a lot to do and there would be no end result. Hard with despair, I told the midwife:

"Knock me out when the time comes, I don't want to be there."

At eleven o'clock, Jeremy arrived. We cried a little, talked a little, waited. The night was long. I seemed to be stuck with contractions every three minutes. At six-thirty in the morning, I barely protested when he told me he was tired and going home to sleep. The second he left, the contractions got much stronger. Hardly conscious because of so much pethidine, I was tossed in the storm, and I was also that storm. At the end, the midwife said gently:

"Would you like to see your baby boy?"

"Oh, yes," I replied longingly. I could only feel overwhelming tenderness as I took him in my arms and stroked his cheek with my finger. He looked so much like Jeremy. He was asleep… . Then the midwife took him back and I was sedated, as the placenta was not coming down and had to be removed surgically.

I woke up with strange and eerie cries of kittens mewing everywhere outside my room. I emerged slowly: they were babies. I had no baby and wept back to sleep. When I came to, Jeremy was sitting on my left, the consultant on my right and I was in the middle of their conversation. Jeremy was asking when I would I be ready to conceive another child. The answer was: very soon. It all felt so unreal.

I was kept in hospital only two or three days. Walking through a ward full of mothers and babies in order to go to the bathroom was near unbearable and I tried not to look. I remember being told there would have to be a post-mortem, the results would be given to me at my post-natal examination. I was given mild tranquillisers and was exhausted. I must have been asked if I wanted the hospital to 'take care of the baby', or else they asked Jeremy and I must have agreed, I don't remember any of it. When I got home, the cot and the baby clothes had been removed by my well-meaning neighbours. My flat was like a desert to come back to alone; Mother had knitted so many lovely things, all boy's clothes too. I did not know or dared to know that I wanted to hold them and mourn. My body was a mother's body, my breasts were full of life-giving milk and my heart full of living love for my child. A health visitor, kind and curt, talked matter-of-factly of "very bad luck, dear" and gave me tablets to stop my milk. Friends came and were kind, a few cried with me… . My dentist visited, held my hand and quoted the French philosopher Alain: "*We haven't been promised anything.*" These words, appealing to realism and courage, were immeasurably helpful at the time.

The time came for my post-natal check, when the appointment was made tactfully at the gynaecological clinic so I wasn't confronted with living babies everywhere. The consultant gently explained the causes of death which were multiple: the cord was tightly wound around the baby's neck; the placenta had detached from the wall of the uterus; areas of infarction, like black holes, had blocked the way to the cord. It all felt like a murder plot. What came to me, bursting into tears after hearing these facts, was my own pressing need for an even more crucial fact: "WHERE IS HE?"

The answer, meant to be soothing, was spoken softly:

"Well, he is everywhere, he is in the atmosphere…"

I screamed out, sobbing:

"I have nowhere to go!!"

I was too distressed to ask for more and nothing more was volunteered. A nurse was called to fetch me a cup of tea. I was given time to recover. Besides, I was in very good health.

Chapter Thirteen

Well, pain has to be a teacher or else it is nothing. You fight it with knowledge, but only if knowledge is what you seek – and if you are aware that knowledge is out there to be sought. So you can't know without this previous knowledge: 'To those that have…'? This quote from the Bible had for so long shocked me: 'To those that have it shall be given, and from those that have not it shall be taken away…' It was outrageous, unjust, and ruthless; I had for years been in revolt against that notion but it had hovered in my consciousness like a wicked confirmation that, to pain already there would be added more pain. This didn't entirely make sense though it squatted in my mind, insistent. Could it possibly mean that we may only profit from the knowledge we seek? That we have to have the desire if not the will, perseverance and skill to seek in order to find – to be 'given' – and that without these prerequisites we could discover nothing of worth? Besides which, a desire to be could often be sidelined by a desire to have, only to confuse the issue…

My father was ill: cancer of the bladder, which had to be removed and a bag fitted to his poor amputated body. I rushed to his hospital bedside and, astonished, watched Mother care for him in the most dedicated, loving way.

"You are so nice to me," he told her gratefully, and she replied, full of compassion: "But, my darling, why shouldn't I be nice to you?" I was astonished: Do we love because we must, is it one of our functions? It seems we need to express it, rightly or wrongly has nothing to do with it... but, of course he had become harmless now, he was in her hands – and so because she was safe she could be good, as she wished to be, and finally could enjoy some harmony without obstacles.

Just as I had made a conscious effort to overcome my old loathing of his touch and spontaneously placed his hand on my pregnant belly only a few months before ("The baby's moving, feel!"), such was my joy and need to share it, I could now take him for short, slow walks around the neighbourhood streets, holding his arm. He had become childlike, to be protected. One morning, as I was getting ready in the upstairs bedroom, I was struck by the strange anguished barks of a nearby dog – only to realise that it was my father barking downstairs with horrendous pain, the cancer having now spread to his bones.

When he was near the end, my mother called me and I arrived from London late in the night, too late, at the family house. My father's body was lying on his bed, ready for the undertakers who would come in the morning. Mother, steeled against so much to feel by so many things to do, was adamant I must not see him before going to sleep and against my heart I obeyed. "Tomorrow," she insisted, "tomorrow." The next morning, I got up and made my way to his room, and there he lay in the middle of his bed. The soft day light filtered through the net curtains. I looked at him, a very small body in his larger clothes, his breath extinguished.

"I am so happy that you are no longer in pain," I whispered. I was calm, tearless.

In the kitchen, Mother was already dressed, busy with

the preparations for the day. I put the kettle on and helped myself to some bread and butter.

"In a moment," she declared solemnly, "I want you to go and see your father."

"I just have," I replied.

"YOU HAVE??"

Her shock and astonishment was total but she also looked outraged, angry even: I had taken the liberty to go and see my father without her mediation, without her previous knowledge and sanction, and it came to me later that it was probably the first time this had ever happened.

The funeral took place on a dull spring day in the old parish church that Odile and I used to attend on our own on Sunday mornings as children, in our little white socks and gloves. I still remembered the heavy, haunting smell of incense which used to make me feel faint during mass. My mother wept endlessly and I kept my arm around her shoulders during the service so she might feel less alone. Odile, far away in Canada, would not have made it in time but would pray for him, she assured Mother on the telephone. Outside the church I noticed, among a small crowd, my old philosophy teacher, monsieur Coutant. We nodded and smiled in understanding. A long slow day stretched ahead.

I didn't feel my father's loss, as he had always been missing and I was well used to his absence, but 'things' seemed to be falling into place somehow, like the last piece having found its place in a large puzzle, after which you know you can get up from the table and give yourself to another occupation. There was a sense of duty accomplished through the family reunion and the later lowering of the coffin into a patch of soft ground near the cemetery wall; I had also participated in his leaving ceremony, but there had been no need of goodbyes on my part, just a need for completion.

★

In January, about two months after baby Thomas died, Jeremy suggested we could take my mother, who was coming to stay for a few days, to some nice places in the country that she might like to visit and would lighten her stay. I knew she would be touched by the thought and that her presence would signal that a new life was beginning for Jeremy and me, an affirmation of his desire to start a new family. Mother was in awe of him: working freelance for the BBC, that beacon of friendship and courage in Britain's alliance with France during the war years, he was endowed in her eyes with a kind of halo; I too could just about remember my parents listening to its broadcasts as a little child. It was with some hurt and frustration, though, that I seemed to be following Mother and Jeremy around during our visits to this town or that museum, until I eventually burst into tears when stepping into a church and immediately rushed out. The church seemed to be speaking to me of unfinished mourning, but I also found myself isolated among company that was meant to support me: Mother was looking at Jeremy with favour, and indulgence for his hesitant French at which he himself laughed charmingly. She approved, her long eyelids conveying both understanding and liking, feelings his own mother had been cruelly incapable of manifesting. I thought to myself later: he laps it up, he quivers like a young child who is going to get a treat, and *she* is under his spell. This entente made for a peaceful couple of days but somehow left me out of it.

Pacified after Mother's visit, Jeremy had eventually declared he loved me and even moved in, in his own peculiar way, that is to say bodily but without warning or any of his belongings: his clothes and books would remain in his large study in Jane's house as he seemed to keep there the very little he owned. When I protested, some clothes appeared for which I made room in a cupboard. He was often absent however, travelling worldwide to research his next book, which did not make our aim of trying for another child very straightforward, and I fretted.

He had also reverted to his old, cruel ways, occasionally bringing back token presents only to describe them as 'dirt cheap', and scornfully refusing to utter the words 'we' or 'us'. However, he maintained his role as a lover. I still felt at times disarmed by his wit and a joyful week in New York, the only time he was kind to me for a few days at a stretch. But he also had moments when he saw himself with pitiless clarity ("My brain is full of facts but without a single truth…") when he moved me and I thought I could reach him, make true contact, we had a chance… But *As it was, so it will be*: did anyone say this? Am I inventing it or rather discovering it? My head was full of questions again, divided as I was between my need for another child and the belief, slowly more pressing, that I should protect myself against Jeremy.

He had, that summer, brought back rather proudly a recording that had been produced of his latest good idea: an audio documentary of all our human breathings, swallowing, heartbeats and gurgles. He had given it to me with the warning that one side contained the cries of a new-born baby and that I should avoid listening to it, which I appreciated: we were nine months into our first year of living together, I was still not pregnant and the first anniversary of our baby's death was looming.

I felt very ill that day, had taken time off work and lay on the living-room couch weeping most of the afternoon. Jeremy came back for dinner in the evening, noticed the state I was in and advised me blankly to go to bed, which I did, feeling oddly chastised. I fell asleep quickly.

What woke me up, screaming and sobbing later that evening, were the piercing cries of my dead baby. I rushed out of bed to take him in my arms and soothe him, and found myself in the hall before I realised that Jeremy was still in the living room, the door having been opened, 'that' side of his record on at full volume, and my own baby was dead and forever silent.

I howled at him:

"HOW CAN YOU!! HOW CAN YOU!!"

He seemed unconcerned, and I went back to bed crying. For three months I slept away from him on my side of the bed, avoiding his touch, rigid with apprehension and in total despair: I had to decide to let go of everything, all my hopes for a relationship, a child, a family. I felt numb and powerless. Jeremy seemed aloof and kept himself busy, watching a lot of television in the evenings. We communicated rarely if quietly.

Finally, he felt sufficiently confident to turn the charm on again. I knew what he wanted. For my part, I wanted a family. When I relented after a few days, he looked at me afterwards and sniggered:

"There! It didn't hurt, did it?"

We had intercourse once more the next day and I remember my tears when he had finished, as I knew, exhausted, that he was now ready again for the slow and subtle violence of cruelty. I was right.

Heartbroken but knowing I had to save myself, I determined in the end to tell him to go. The following evening, I asked him to join me at the table where I was sitting. I said simply:

"Jeremy, I shall be going away for the weekend. When I get back, I want you to have left this flat."

He blushed, stammered, lowered his glance:

"We could – would you like – try again for another week?"

"A week?" I replied, "I have not known you *once* to be kind for a whole week…"

"Oh," he protested, "you are so rude!"

This would have been funny, I thought, if it wasn't so pathetic. I stood up and left the room.

The Gods, usually too busy, had for once looked in my direction and flicked a little gold dust towards me:

– There, let's do something for Hélène! and I was pregnant. Indeed it felt like a miracle, and in the state of deprivation in which I found myself it shone like the brightest star, assuring me of some benevolence, even possibly some happiness. I even started to see myself taking my baby to the Heath to show him the ponds and the ducks in the bright summer light. I would watch him gurgle and smile, I would kiss his lovely cheeks and smell his wonderful milky smell... We would play... and I realised at that instant that not once during my previous pregnancy had I thought beyond the birth, I had never visualised my baby as an independent little person with whom I would share a long continuum of moments of leisure and play. He hadn't existed in my thoughts except as this amazing little being that moved and stretched inside me and whose feet and fists I would stroke with my fingers, laughing, through my ingeniously elastic skin. Had I created him so mortal through my limited vision? Or had the repeated blows of Jeremy's cruelty mortally wounded him? Had I just known then, unconsciously, that his life would be finite, starting and ending in my body? Yet that pregnancy in itself had been such bliss: for all my grief, I would have to be grateful for it. To be able now to think of this brand new baby in moving and living images assured me, I felt, of a happy outcome: 'it' wouldn't happen again, surely.

Mother, who was staying with me when I got the results, insisted that I tell Jeremy immediately. I wasn't ready for it, could not bear to see him, and when I described to her, in tears, his many cruelties, it was with him she sided, with me she found fault ("You should have been more understanding, more patient, you must have done something to make him cross with you…") Though I balked at her words, appalled, I eventually gave way through exhaustion:

"All right, you tell him if you like, but I can't see him." And so she stood in for me yet again, her sense of being enhanced by this added power: she knew how to live my life, while I lay on my bed with a pillow over my head. I knew they had an alliance, I had seen them together: ('a real man', she told me once, eyes down as if over a secret understanding.) I didn't know what to make of this alliance, which I sensed more than I saw it, my mind blurred by loneliness, failure, abandonment and fear, but I understood later that she was profoundly attracted to him herself: why, she was only ten years his senior… . At the time I loathed her interference, her assumption that she knew best what I should do, and most of all I felt bitter at her desertion in Jeremy's favour; yet I lived this more as an injustice than as a betrayal since she had so often found fault with me that I was quite used to it. I knew that the stomach aches I suffered from at each one of her visits – it used to be nausea when I lived at home – every time I felt obliged to ring her because I knew she expected it, or had to confront her, would not leave me until long after she was gone. I was caught in the eternal dilemma of fighting for myself at the same time as feeling I owed her because of the many sacrifices she had made for Odile and me, her daughters.

In spite of it all, I had waited and yearned to be pregnant for so long that it was now bliss: the wriggling of the baby inside me was again a tangible sign of Nature's happy designs.

I felt the need one day for a special kind of music and went to a record shop, asking for some 'happy flute' and came out with Mozart's complete Quartets for flute and violin.

When I played them that day – "Listen, my baby!" I said – I was in no doubt that she could hear it, as I felt her – for it was a little girl – 'dancing' even more strongly inside me. In the same way, I felt she could hear my voice and I also sang to her: it was essential that I should be as happy as possible.

One fine day in August, my little girl Sophie was born. I didn't care about all the wires on and around me, the monitors, the bright lights. I didn't object to being induced since it assured safety, I could finally hold her perfect little body on top of mine, heartbeat against heartbeat, and close my eyes. She didn't cry but cooed, purred.

– Be careful, they said when passing, or you will drop her if you fall asleep! I smiled, I couldn't stop smiling:

– I wouldn't dream of falling asleep, I shan't drop her...

Later, I would take her to Hampstead Heath, show her the trees, the sky, the world. I would watch her grow, eat, sleep and laugh, did people know how wonderful it is to have a little child?

★

I had braced myself and postponed Mother's visit until I got back home from hospital a week later, much against her will: "I wouldn't understand it," she had warned threateningly a few months before, "if I wasn't there for the birth!" But I had found her presence too much to contemplate, knowing that she would be a grandmother before I was myself a mother. "She is mine too!" she had exclaimed angrily. Once with us, happy and helpful though she proved to be, she forever interfered with the baby when I breastfed, lifting my arm, turning Sophie's head: "No, no, this way, there!" After two days, needing some peace away from her, I decided to go to my bedroom to breastfeed and she protested: "It is also MY pleasure!"

Baby Sophie smiled and I responded with delight. She

paid me back with more smiles, and a wheel of contentment was set in motion. Feeding on demand, although she had regular needs, required waking up twice in the night after a late-night feed but in spite of the fatigue, those feeds were incredibly precious: nothing, no-one disturbed them. There was the silence of the night, the privacy of the bedroom and the softness of the light by my bed. The intimacy was total. Smiles were exchanged again after the feed, then we both dozed off again. When my milk dried up after three months I reluctantly made bottles, missing the softness of her lovely cheeks against my swollen breasts.

★

The realisation came to me abruptly one day that I would never be free of Jeremy and it filled me with dread. He would ring the bell unannounced on odd days, when he was not away travelling, announcing cheerfully: "Just popping in to see how things are!" and it tore me apart that my life had now become one where my baby's father could simply pop in, pop out – never enquiring about me or offering any help, practical or financial; that all the love I had had for him was reduced to his coming to play, to reassure himself that he was still allowed in my home and had access to his child. I knew with certainty now that he was only ever concerned with his own needs and that I would have to protect myself and make sure to remain strong. He visited one evening after work carrying a bag full of food which, surprisingly, he offered to cook for me as I had just started breastfeeding the baby. Uncertain, I accepted, only to see him later fall asleep in front of the television as I was finally ready to go to bed. Upset, confused, I sensed this was his way of coming back. I felt angry that he seemed to override my feelings and my anger saved me. In two minds, I threw a blanket over him while at the same time exclaiming, half-crying:

"Jeremy! This isn't fair on me!"

Startled, he got up and promptly left.

When Mother next came at Easter, Odile was also due to visit us from Canada, and Mother, who had not seen her for several years, was overjoyed. I had booked a room for Odile at a nearby hotel since Mother would be sleeping on the living-room couch and I didn't have a bed for her. I also knew Odile would also use the opportunity to feel excluded, justifying both her lack of self-love and anger.

Apprehensive at her visit, imagining also she would be pleased to see her baby niece, I decided finally that in fact Sophie would either bring us all together or else be the ideal buffer, it should work. Mother, having recently sold the country house after Father's death, had bought beautiful presents for us which we opened at the end of our first meal together: for me a pair of good pearl earring studs; for Odile a smart, chunky silver bracelet that my sister held at arm's length with contempt, exclaiming:

"What on earth am I supposed to do with it? I wouldn't dream of wearing a thing like that! Still, I can always give it to a charity shop."

Mother was crushed, on the verge of tears, and I was horrified. Odile, her face frozen over her own turmoil, then declared she needed a long walk every day to fight her chronic constipation and left us, to go and explore Hampstead Heath. I had hoped that Odile would leave me free to go for real walks myself; instead, I would have to spend all my time with Mother as my sister systematically avoided her company... . Conversations at meal times, either strained or artificially cheerful, tended to concentrate on baby Sophie who, for her part, smiled contentedly, unperturbed.

Finally saying goodbye to them both was the greatest relief; it was wonderful to have my home back, my shelter and peace. I could again feel in harmony with my child, my cat and the garden birds, and live my life as I wished. In spite of the loneliness that clung to me like my own shadow, I had a most precious thing, I had my little child.

★

Then, one day, IT hit me, what became the start of a long nightmare, like someone in a crowd bumping into me from the side then revealing themselves, unashamed: a large and powerful image of a dishevelled Jeremy standing, holding a naked baby and rubbing her against him, panting, absorbed, insistent. I wanted to scream but there was nothing to scream at. I shook, struggled to push it away, silently shouted: NO! NO! NO! in horror: NOT HIM! – and was filled with hatred for myself, disgusting woman! – What is this? Why? GO AWAY! GO AWAY!!

1 Above: The author in the garden.

2 Right: René-Jacques Baumer in 1953, age fourteen (photograph taken by author).

3 Right: The author's parents in Bordeaux in the late 1960s.

4 Below: The author with her baby sister on the balcony, 1943. (She still has the small armchair.).

Chapter Fourteen

On the last day of my maternity leave, the Sunday papers came as usual through the letter box. I picked them up and stared, stared, and stared at the front page as I could not believe my eyes which were only able to read the headlines; everything else was a blur, as if a fine rain had evenly dissolved the print. Panicked, I rushed to my upstairs neighbours. They comforted me and took me for lunch at his father's, who was an optometrist and might be able to help; so, later on that day, I was luckily fitted with a temporary pair of glasses that would allow me to face my first week's teaching after so many months and put on a brave front.

Over the next two weeks though, it got much worse: my hands and feet, then my arms and legs, had become like paper or dead wood. I had no sensations and was losing strength. Sophie was only five months old and felt so heavy I could barely hold her. Fortunately, another friendly neighbour offered to take and collect her from the nursery. I spent my days crying, defeated. Of course I was off work again and felt terrible about it; I feared 'they' would all think I was faking it. I had now lost all sensation at the top and bottom of my spine, and the papery feeling reached my face: my nose, mouth and cheeks had gone dead; I was hardly able to walk. Like me, my doctor feared multiple sclerosis and sent me to hospital for tests. Those eventually came back negative but I was still in a bad way: a rare virus named Guillain-Barré had attacked my nervous system. Only complete rest would bring me back to health and the doctors wanted to hospitalise me. I was horrified at the prospect, fiercely refused to be an in-patient: if I surrendered to this, I told myself, I was finished, I would become again a thing in someone else's hands, please God make it a psychological problem instead and I will get my teeth into it and see it through, I have done it before. For I guessed there was at work much more than a virus. Indeed it all resembled a huge panic attack and my doctor, questioned, seemed to think along the same lines.

"So, what are you going to do with this depressed hysteric?" I joked.

After an assessment at the Tavistock Clinic where I was watched interacting with Sophie ("It's nothing to do with her," I offered, "it's me…") I was referred for group therapy, where the psychotherapist was a kindly old man with a red face and a white beard, Patrick de Mare – a benevolent Father Christmas figure, also a remarkable group leader – and I threw myself into the experience since I had no time to waste and must work on my goal, my survival.

Mummy – Daddy – Mummy-Daddy – Mummy – Daddy, – who said parents did not make children? I was familiar with 'the ropes' already, both reading and regular probing had more than acquainted me with family dynamics. However, I felt very weak, quite frightened, and being confronted with Jeremy on the occasions when he merrily popped in and equally cheerfully popped out not only revived my pain but raised acutely angry feelings. I could no longer bear to see him at once so carefree and distant from my life while all my hopes for a family had been destroyed. I finally wrote to him one day telling him to stay away: this time I must put myself first, I had to allow myself to recover.

145

I did not tell him I was ill, but he knew I went to group therapy and had on occasion disdainfully alluded to my 'mental health problems'; nor did I tell Mother, she would be too worried and make me responsible for an extra burden on *her* shoulders; I would be at the receiving end of her cloying solicitude, the butt of endless queries, recommendations and sermons. So I would pretend all was fine, I knew the tone of voice, the glib phrases, all learnt in childhood, they now had a use again. I was split between increasing anger at her tyranny and sorrow at the sadness of her life: her courage, endurance, her obvious sacrifices, were a capital that was banked early and was now threatened with diminished returns. Her more recent lack of loyalty anguished and wounded me more than anything, as her criticisms had never been so frequent. I began to see that The Big Mother had been toppled by the new mother, myself, and she must feel displaced if not made redundant. The role she had constructed for herself and clung to all the more while her marriage disintegrated, was threatened, her dominance lost and she was angry; as motherhood endowed me with a power she never wished me to have, it deprived her of hers. And I was angry too, watching her take the bottle of water from Sophie's hands when *she* decreed Sophie has had enough: ("Now, now, that's enough now.") and I exclaimed:

"No, let her drink, she is the one who knows how thirsty she is!" I was catching a surreptitious glance at the infant I was at Sophie's age, the time when Mother was the measure of all things – well, no wonder.

This was all very disconcerting, as I still needed my mother, my mum, and even now at times found solace in her smiles, our occasional connivance, and dreamt of her support and approval. I knew I had upset her by turning down her presence at Sophie's birth. My keeping of Johan's surname after our divorce had deeply offended her – "Why, Mum, it's an ordinary English name here, everyone knows how to spell it, that name is fine, it is who I am now." Of course I knew that according to French – and most – customs, a divorced woman was supposed to take back her maiden name, but I had decided to take advantage of England's more casual ways; I did not dare tell her I wouldn't dream of using my maiden name again, one Madame Dufresne was enough, thank you very much; besides, it would represent a huge step backwards at a time when I was striving to move on and at long last become my own person. I had also added to my sins by giving Sophie that very name: why, that little child of mine would bear her pathetic father's surname when he had done nothing to give her a family and I, the only parent to care for her would be called differently? Never. Mother and child will bear the same name, on that I was adamant, we were each other's family now.

Jeremy had no problem recognising Sophie as his and didn't dare object, if he even thought about it, to her bearing my borrowed name. Of course there was no baptism: Mother knew I had long since turned away from religion but would have loved me to put my beliefs aside to conform to her views. My anger at the growing realisation that who I was never mattered was fuelled by her spontaneous exclamation one morning when I played and laughed with little Sophie who giggled and screamed with delight:

"You make her too happy!" she frowned, as if witnessing a tasteless oddity.

– What was I like as a little child, Mum? I asked her later, and she barely cast her eyes back at that already distant past before replying casually:

"Oh, you were quiet."

Was that it, then? All you had to say, all I was? I marvelled bitterly at her lack of awareness of her detachment, her indifference.

At the same time, she could be kind and sweet, and still so beautiful she must be good, which added to the confusion. She frequently talked of love ("Everything I have done, I have done out of love for Odile and you.") but I was slowly becoming aware that you just cannot call everything – or anything – ' love', and that '*love*' may be a blunt instrument. As I refused to go on playing the old games, both Mother and I, for different but complementary reasons, were very resentful women.

I wrote her a letter begging her to listen to me so we could get on better, have a closer relationship. She replied with a long letter of recriminations describing her role as a long-suffering mother and grandmother whose life of endless sacrifices had gone unnoticed and unrewarded. She demanded recognition, gratitude, and pay-back: I owed her, and she listed all my debts in relentless detail.

I had recently learnt, though, through therapy, that not only was it not wrong to feel anger, I had a right to it, it was mine and in part defined me, so, notwithstanding my own contradictions, I was empowered to reply :

'*Dear Mum,*

I nearly rang you after receiving your latest letter which made me extremely angry by the amount of emotional blackmail it contains, but I prefer to write, more calmly, because after all, at my age and thanks to my newly-found strength, my survival no longer depends on tranquillisers.

You always imagine that we have a fixed, one-way relationship: I am a bad daughter and I cause you pain. This suits you because I am therefore obliged to feel guilty and responsible and you can more easily put pressure upon me.

But I need to tell you that THE ANGER you cause me by your manipulative behaviour has been going on since childhood and that the ban —for it would hurt Mummy — on ever expressing it has been the cause of a deep depression that has affected me for decades because it meant, in essence, that I was forbidden to exist: YOUR feelings, YOUR wishes, YOUR pain, were all that mattered. If there was the slightest conflict with my ideas, my feelings, my desires, you acted exactly as if mine didn't exist.

Sorry, Mum, but I exist now and if we are to have at least a dialogue, it will have to be between equals, between adults. You completely ignore, as usual, the feelings I expressed gently in my last letter. I am therefore obliged to speak more sternly today: all is not credit on your side and debit on mine, you may talk of love but you always present the bill. You have the nerve to accuse me of depriving Sophie of her grandmother, when we came to you for Christmas (and I would have loved to spend it in my new flat) but it doesn't count; you came when Sophie had chickenpox, but because she was ill it probably doesn't count; I was suggesting that you come for her birthday, but for some reason it doesn't seem to count.

I understand your solitude and your anxiety concerning your health and I think about it with sadness and affection, but you are not the only one to suffer, I was myself extremely ill a while after Sophie's birth and I thought I was going to die. I am not saying you are well but health is in part a question of attitude, and I fear yours is becoming an ideal means of pressure to get what you want.

I sincerely hope this is the last time I have to get this angry but you are going to have to choose: either you continue to play the martyr, or you finally accept to read my letters, listen to my words and hear my feelings. And please, stop your blackmailing letters because they may no longer affect me and I don't think this is what you want. For my part, I feel a more balanced and adult relationship between us could lead to more affection.

To finish, if you decide to come, could you reserve me the week of August 7th? If the weather is nice we can go on easy and pleasant excursions around London.

Hélène'

With the benefit of distance or separation at least, I now had a better view of Jeremy and was appalled at my poor choice for a partner, a fact that my colleagues in group therapy had pointed to by their comments and impatient exclamations, ("Wake up, woman!" a man interjected, therapeutically enough.) and I cursed the day I so foolhardily called for a big passion. I felt responsible: a more mature person than me, and a less needy one, would have seen how immature he was, and a more guarded one, how harmful. Were we all, Johan, Jeremy, myself, like little children just managing to live both the little we have learnt combined with what we wish for or need? I feared so: after Johan, another but similar story had written itself. I had chosen for myself an older man, a possible father substitute, a reassuring thing only in appearance: an Oxford graduate, Jeremy was well educated without being well brought up at all. Bright without managing to be properly intelligent since he was no more aware of other people's feelings than of his own, he was dangerous for that very reason.

I cast my eyes back at his marriage to Diana such as he had described her to me in small touches in the course of our affair: very beautiful, very intelligent, very successful – this used to make me wonder why he was with me at all, and value him all the more but he blamed her for alleged drinking, and begrudged her the care of the children: "if she fell under a bus" he would be such a fulfilled dad. He missed the children: Alan, the elder and his only son, was the apple of his eye. He was obviously fond of the girls, but they were mere girls, the gender close to a birth defect in his eyes, who had moreover been adopted. They amused him though. Holly in particular was bright and sweet, expressed herself unusually well at the age of eight for she read a lot. Paula was also gentle and affectionate but had suffered in her babyhood from breathing accidents which had deprived her brain of oxygen, condemning her to limited development. Jeremy had described to me the devoted care his wife had showed her over many years, trying a dozen techniques to stimulate the child and improve her brain function, sadly to no avail. He had not participated in those, feeling they should have 'returned' Paula like the faulty acquisition she had been; this shocked me greatly. I could see he resented her, as on the occasion when he put a strong detergent in her bath (they 'had run out of 'bubbles') while knowing Paula suffered from eczema; inevitably, the child had a severe reaction. He had related the story possibly as a confession, to get rid of it in some way: if you could talk about it, wasn't it more acceptable? Forgivable? As when he would throw too many little pebbles at her on the beach and she cried because they hurt her back...

So what kind of a father did that make him? He had told me about being away from them for months on end while travelling, never sending his wife any money for their care; I would soon learn myself that his commitment to my Sophie did not go as far as participating financially either. I only had to remember his protest when he moved in with me and I suggested he pay a fifth of the outgoings on the flat, only for him to reply weakly that he did not like to spend his money on such things – and felt exploited... this at a time when I had offered to put his name on the deeds of my flat. Now, with Sophie, he had finally agreed to make monthly payments "but I want you to ask for them each month..."

Added to this was his belittling of me at almost every opportunity, which I took with little argument at first, thinking possibly I was not worthy. *Plus ça change...* His scorn at my tears at the loss of the baby had been plain to see when he had visited me in hospital and I had started crying as he entered my room: "You always cry when you see me!" he had laughed. But not just at my own pain, I recalled, as the haunting television images of starving people in Cambodia in the Seventies were flooding back to me: "Pure propaganda!" he had declared. A psychotherapist acquaintance had even warned me at the time: "He is a psychopath! Get out fast!" Of course the big trap had been sex, my sudden addiction to that physical turmoil; the headiness of it had overcome all judgment at times, surrendering to the ecstasy was the compulsive goal...

Now deprived of Sophie who instantly became the most important thing in life, Jeremy seemed to have gone to pieces. He couldn't bear the exclusion. Some of my friends had put pressure on me for a while – "Your baby needs a father, it's wrong to exclude him..." – finally admitting that he had been paying them visits and shedding warm tears over his deprivation, how could I be so hard? (My turn to be wished under a bus?) I was getting a much more severe version of that treatment from my mother, his all-time ally, and felt appalled at their collective betrayal: did I not count? Couldn't I be given time to recover? Thank goodness for group therapy, since eventually, after some six months, I did feel stronger and told Jeremy he could resume his visits.

I must have been a fool, and no doubt still was. I knew as an adolescent that I must unlearn nearly everything I had been inculcated with if I wanted to become the person I really was, but the process was long, arduous, subtle, and slow, slow... I had been a late developer, indeed had only started to develop properly in my thirties.

And before that? Well, I was just late...time to catch up then, there was nothing I didn't want to know, and the intelligent and demanding work of therapy was as thrilling as it could be painful for enlightenment was at a price. Looking at baby Sophie, I was aware that children know, that they are closer to a true way of being when they haven't yet learnt all our modalities for it, and how we, the parents, society, wish them to be. I came to see there were also ways of knowing that we are not taught and I was attentive to those; they were the secret language, not merely of the unconscious, but of a different way of relating to the world which at times the world itself made manifest. And so one Christmas Day, when Sophie was four and a half, she unwrapped her presents on the living-room floor, squealing with glee in anticipation. And as I re-discovered them with her I was stunned to read the message I had written – for myself – clear as clear water among the garish paper and fancy ribbons: three little story books the pages of which folded into the shape of a house, a cardboard doll's house, and a puzzle in the shape of a... house. So perhaps it was time to move.

Chapter Fifteen

I do not know if time passes but we certainly do. Memory bridges the gap between being and having been in an often haphazard display of images. I had my first real garden in that new Belsize Park flat; not shared this time, but my own, and I slowly acquired the necessary skills through a quantity of books on gardens, gardening, visits to gardens with Sophie and friends and membership of the National Trust. I turned it into a magical garden and it saved my life as much as having my daughter did, and not in such a different way, as nurture pays back. Besides, getting your hands dirty is also therapy. You learn about being, you exist with the soil, the plant stems and leaves, and the glorious little orgasms of blooms. You pray for benevolent soil and rain even though you still feed and water, and you learn your place in the great scheme of things since you have to cooperate. You come to understand the value of time, maturation, and that there is order in life as in seasons. You belong.

We lived in Belsize Park for five years, the first half of ten years of considered and accepted celibacy for me: I had to change, stop being the person who would both choose and be the prey of damaged or malevolent men.

The strength I gained both through motherhood and gardening helped restore my health somewhat as my illness had for the first year wrecked my life and nearly my teaching career. I had very little sympathy from some jealous and petty colleagues – the ones who would never speak to me in French for fear of revealing their own imperfections of grammar and pronunciation, as I was the only native speaker. Besides, I had lost a lot of weight while being ill after Sophie's birth and looked good – neat and proper as ever, my well-cut hair washed and make-up dutifully applied. Still, my exhaustion and my stomach problems left me very little peace and I was forced to take the occasional day off work. None of this made me popular. Together with my two English colleagues, I was invisible to my American colleagues for whom life in London consisted in living in a tight little ghetto, and was aware of animosity between groups of teachers and some flare-ups. This invisibility, so reminiscent of my childhood, unduly and painfully prolonged my isolation from the world. People asked me why I stayed, but this was a well-paid job not far from home, I had tenure which I took for security, was a single woman with a child and a mortgage, and reasoned that I had no choice: I just had to put up with it. I knew how to, I had done it before.

Having made growth my goal, I wrote at night in my bed lists of things to not be: passive, confused, dependent on others, needy – the last one dictating that I should give myself what I needed, a tall order. My old Philosophy teacher, Monsieur Coutant, and the Circus people, had shown me I existed, but still so many said I didn't or counted for little. There were the false friends who claimed to befriend me but instead scorned me and put me down, like that writer of books on family violence and child abuse to whom I was close for a while until she let her bitterness and envy overflow one day; it was a treatment I was still too prone to accepting. I also remember the day I told her that I could read about any horrors except for the sexual abuse of children, and she had given me a funny look. I had to think about that.

I stopped group therapy after a year and a half, having made great strides while needing to go further and faster without being held back by others' fears and limitations. Beneath the woman still manacled to her mother's demands lurked a frustrated enthusiast: I was on a search for the meaningful, the numinous even, and attentive to it in almost every facet of life, since life itself had to be transformed. Among all the patterns that take shape from childhood, it was not merely, I felt, the women and the men that inhabit it that leave an imprint; it is also the atmosphere, the spirit of childhood, the form of its unhappiness, as well as the patterns of thinking and behaving sanctioned by encouragement or disapproval: we develop a 'way to be' in relation to life itself. I knew I would have to give birth to myself.

There was an elderly neighbour next door, old Mac, who was very sweet to Sophie and me. The day a teddy bear called Toto – the attached card said so – appeared over the garden wall in a cardboard box filled with ivy branches still one of her best childhood memories to this day. But he visited rather too often. I believed in being friendly and a good neighbour; besides, old Mac told wonderfully entertaining stories – why, he had once shared a mistress in Spain with Robert Graves! While I was making us some tea in the kitchen one afternoon, he came up behind me and placed his hands on my shoulders as I wriggled out of his reach. Nothing was said, but that very week, as if someone was trying to shake me out of a frozen stupor, those forgotten flashes rushed at me again as I wrestled with my disgust and denial, and this time it was old Mac rubbing a little naked child against him, panting.

Silently, I screamed, and screamed... GO AWAY! GO AWAY!

I couldn't make room for such hideous nonsense, there was obviously something wrong with me, but not with my Sophie who was growing up beautifully and was the apple of my eye: her sweetness, loving, curiosity and wit enchanted me and all who knew her. I delighted in her, invented motherhood and discovered childhood as the miracle of grace and opening to the world that it should be. I had to learn some nursery rhymes and she taught me the ones she learnt at nursery. She slept with Toto every night and he was in her arms already as I got ready to read her a bedtime story.

I recall her first proper sentence when, sitting in her buggy, she was teasing me by repeatedly taking her socks off and throwing them up in the air. She couldn't stop chuckling, and offered: 'I'm a nuisance, aren't I?' I was astonished that she had, so very young, managed to put herself in my place and could also handle the distance of humour.

But there was that other time I never want to forget, when the mood was very different. Being a lone mother and a full-time teacher – I rose at 6.30 every morning in order to be at work at 8 while Sophie had to be taken to the nearby nursery beforehand; being the sole material and emotional support of this household, without any moral assistance, was taking its toll. In spite of my joy at being with her, my latent illness and the stresses of all my obligations made me on occasion wish to put her to bed as early as possible at the end of the day so that I could collapse and rest. I must have been even more exhausted than usual that evening, and when bedtime came, she kept running away from me, laughing. After a while I lost it, and yelled at her:

"Come here, I tell you! Come here!"

I was a screaming fury but still she did not obey and kept on laughing and running away.

"Come here at once!" I screamed. "If you don't, I'm going to scream at you and hit you, I'm going to do something I don't want to do, please come here NOW!!!"

Before the yelling monster I had become, she didn't freeze and shake, she did not cry. Three years old – she came to me with her arms outstretched. Crouching, I was holding her pyjamas, shaking with anger, on the verge of tears. And with the sweetest, most loving look on her face, smiling gently, she embraced me protectively and said:

"You are my little darling," absolving me, knowing me.

Chapter Sixteen

My daughter didn't look like me and this was a very good thing. She took after Jeremy − his eyes − if she had my cheeks, jaw and mouth. 'She looks at me with his eyes', I used to think warily at the beginning. But this made it simpler for both of us to see each other as separate human beings; it was healthier for this very small family of two; it made respect easier, and here the word enlightened me: you can't respect another person if you think you own them.

In my previous incarnation as J, the name my parents gave me − I hated, and it hurt, to write the name − I was a part of my mother that she did not care for and used for her own needs. I saw that when I was not used, I had no purpose, no definition in the world outside and no role in it. I was shelved away from her consciousness, discouraged to have my own if it differentiated me from her.

As J I was alone in the flat and frightened because I had lost my role as a protector as Sophie was away with her father for the weekend. My defences were down, I wept: what is it, to BE? − To focus and see clearly, to act spontaneously? Watching others, at times copying what they did in order to understand what they felt, allowed me to explore ways I could be.

I watched a film, a documentary on television where

some of Sophie's school friends were dancing, where children were being shown that by allowing their emotions to inspire their movements, by touching and being touched, by working as part of that group, they were enabled to be themselves fully. They could feel acknowledged, respected, trusted and trusting, supported and needed. And they were safe. I imagined myself touching them in a dance, with my hands, arms, legs, body, and it was all fluid, fearless. Safe. Like being in a welcoming womb.

I wept and wept.

I used to hate and fear – be disgusted by – the reality of other people's bodies, their smell. I would stop breathing when they came too close, only allowing myself a sniff, like a shy dog, if curiosity was stronger and I felt sufficiently protected to attempt an exploratory excursion into someone else's being. What it was like to be J was to go through the motions, mimic and pretend until one day – a miracle – something might 'click' and feel real, giving me a vision of me, a measure of me. It might all add up to something eventually? I was a split atom, its parts connected only by threads of need…

Then all of a sudden, as clear as clear water, it came to me: I could only love a man in the possessive way my mother loved me – the fearful way I loved her – because, like her, I did not exist sufficiently to love him the way I should love myself. The shock of having a child had peeled away from me the hardened, self-righteous persona I had acquired. I was reeling from it, raw and close to despair. It put me right back in the middle of my childhood, and I had to achieve a clear understanding of it for fear of becoming the source of pain and harm myself. I knew I was in danger of looking once more for a symbiotic relationship and must at all costs understand my past or it would claim me again.

As is her wont, Mother loomed large. I was haunted by her imagined and real criticisms, comments and sermons. Her thumbprint on my brain, my head filled with our fights. To placate her and defuse possible conflicts I assured her again on the telephone that everything was fine, but she knew I was fighting Jeremy for a reasonable maintenance for Sophie – he preferred the bare minimum. I knew he didn't earn a regular income but he always seemed to have money for travel, and there was this rented house up North…

"Leave him alone," she said, "it doesn't matter since I give you an allowance for Sophie, he doesn't earn much, that's why I am helping you."

She might as well tell me she condoned the fact that he tried to pay as little as possible for his daughter's care, nothing could make me angrier.

"Listen, Mum, I don't need your help, I earn enough! If you wish to give me an allowance for Sophie, do it as a grandmother for her grandchild, but not to compensate for what Jeremy doesn't do! It's as if you are on his side!"

"No, of course not, but you have to be conciliatory, you don't know how to handle him…"

Because she knew, of course: the special relationship… to watch them together required a stronger sense of humour than I could summon. In front of her, this very tall man behaved like a coy little boy seeking approval while she smiled sweetly in acquiescence, lowering her long eyelids. I recalled one Mothering Sunday during one of her stays with us when the room was full of the flowers Sophie had just given me. That Sunday morning, Jeremy arrived with a big bunch of flowers which he handed …to my mother. After he left, I took the flowers from the vase, saying:

"If you don't mind, Mum, these will go in the bin…"

"Well, in the circumstances, I must say…" she conceded, twisting her lips in a grimace. The fact that we had witnesses this time, a friend of mine and our lovely Italian au-pair, might have helped her see how incongruous, as well as revealing, his gesture had been. But the fact is that my mother is very motherly-looking: nicely plump, still endowed of a beautiful face, smiling easily and with gentle manners, she struck a great contrast with Jeremy's own, a dried-up old stick of a woman who was fluent in the use of rejection. No wonder he seemed in awe of mine.

Odile wasn't writing frequently enough, Mother complained; she didn't visit often either, every five or six years seemed to have become the new pattern. When Father was still alive my parents had visited her in Canada and reported her well, working as a teacher and very involved in sports. She was in a relationship with a sports teacher, 'a very charming man' they declared, and she seemed happy, which reassured them she was recovered from her trials. However, the following year, she announced the sad news both of her refusal to marry her partner and her decision to end the relationship. Not knowing any details and not daring to enquire – she remained very prickly about her personal life – they were lost in conjecture. For my part, my contacts with her were sparse, as she would now only reply a couple of lines to my own rare attempts at communication. I could not say I ever missed her. Having so much on my plate, I forgot to care, but I wondered later: could it be that her partner wanted children and she couldn't bear to tell him the reason she couldn't have any?

It was nevertheless frustrating in the extreme to be the only one to have to see Mother at least twice a year as it cost me dear in heartache. My health suffered each time forcing me to resort to tranquillisers a few days before her visits and long after she had left in order to remain as detached as possible, but there were still frequent arguments. Odile had made sure there was such physical distance between them that it could only be bridged rarely, leaving it to me to be the only 'operational' daughter. I resented her for it with all my heart.

The day I learnt that my sister had taken up religious studies and attended religious conferences and retreats, I couldn't help thinking: 'Here we go!' It was bringing to mind Madame Niklaus of course, my seducer's mother who used to ply Odile with religious tomes: so Odile had caught the bait and entered another world. I had to share Mother's exasperation when, instead of replying to letters by giving at least some news, Odile merely sent back the odd religious quote as if discharging herself on God for her relationship with Mother and me. As was her habit, she merely hinted at what was going on. The mystery naturally increased Mother's anxiety and she wrote back pages of questions and speculations. I have often wondered these last few years if Odile didn't remain silent on purpose, to attract Mother's attention at the same time as perversely deprive her of what she wanted, as so much of her behaviour in later years appeared to be in that vein: punishment, vengeance.

Already with one divorced daughter, Mother was understandably upset that her younger one was shunning a more conventional life of marriage and children, for it soon appeared that Odile was intent on entering religion. Mother and I agreed that it didn't seem to give her the peace of heart she obviously craved any more than it improved her character and her attitude to both of us.

"But you know," said Mother when I complained, "she writes about you with great affection in her letters, so I do not understand…"

So it was love-hate, then? Not just hate-hate? I recalled a day as a child when I had bumped into Mother in the kitchen and got my arm badly burnt by a pan of boiling water she was carrying. Odile, upset at my screams, had rushed to the chemist to get some ointment for me. I couldn't remember any other moments of kindness on her part and still had in my mind the murderous words she threw at me once when we argued:

– I wish you were dead!

I wondered if she had felt jealous when I was sent to board at convent school. I think she knew I hated it there but my parents must have stressed that I would be given an excellent education so she may have felt deprived, and less valued. Could it be that she was now making up for the so-called religious 'experience' I had been granted at boarding school? My parents were not likely to have informed her that I was being sent away because I had worried them when asking what 'fucking' meant and had started 'looking at boys'. Mother may not have added that my arguments with Father were getting out of hand... . Nevertheless, Odile seemed to have chosen the opposite journey to mine: I was searching inward for enlightenment and serenity in order to have a life; she was relinquishing her earthly existence and even self to find peace in a God who – just like Mother – demanded that she give herself over to him completely. I was aghast.

I would have felt less superior, however, had I seen then that I was undergoing a parallel pattern of submission in my own job.

While loving children and enjoying teaching them, I had always disliked schools and wanted to NOT be a teacher. I hated the strict corseting of immovable timetables, the bells crudely separating work and play, the getting into line, the duties, the after-school meetings, the way each function was formalised, every instant accounted for, the days and weeks merging like clouds.

I hated it that there was no escape. It reminded me too much of my childhood and Mother's million demands from which there was no escape either. Did this look any different from the rules of religious life? Could Odile find enough acceptance and kindness in that world to achieve the inner peace she craved? When Mother flew back to France after a stay with us, I still had to contend with the many constraints of my work, the pettiness of some colleagues, and give in to my obligations. One day, a day I could not even begin to imagine, something might have to give, I might grow wings. But I still clung to the belief that my job gave me material security. I had tenure, a great asset I knew, but without ever experiencing safety — an old feeling, that.

Mother, of course, never accepted that I should dislike my place of work. "Such a good job," she endlessly countered, "you are so well paid"; "so close to your home"; "so convenient for Sophie". It was all true. But as ever she dismissed the fact that I was not well treated in spite of very good previous assessments; that I was terribly lonely there, ignored by my American colleagues and administrators alike. She judged that these were not essential things, sentencing me to an indeterminate period of imprisonment, "a duty to yourself and your daughter".

The poison between us rose, inflaming our words.

I recalled a leisurely walk on Hampstead Heath one sunny day. Sophie starting running ahead, to her astonishment was immediately restrained as Mother had grabbed her skirt and held her on the spot:

"Sophie! No! Don't run or you will fall down!" I couldn't but intervene, I was so angry:

"Let her run! She's allowed to run!"

"But she will fall down!"

"If she falls, she will pick herself up, and if she gets hurt, I will kiss her better! She is allowed to run and play!"

I was livid but also shocked. I have suddenly understood one of my own mysteries: my internal fury on the day when

Sophie, still a toddler, had pulled tightly at my own skirt and a wild current of violence had risen in me as compulsively as magma in a volcano; I had been astonished to feel capable of the insane rage my body had stored. I had felt violent to the point of wanting to actually hit my little girl... but why? It had always been fine when she clung to my hand, my leg, my arm. 'How odd,' I had thought then, 'how crazy, what's the matter with me?' So that was why: I cast my mind back at the little child I had been who could never play: "Don't jump, you'll get too hot!" "Don't go there, you'll get dirty!" And she would hold the hem of my skirt as I struggled to get free, held back as if with a chain and protested, crying at my lack of freedom, my enslaved body. And she wouldn't let go, tugged me back, eventually suggest I sat at her side like a proper little girl. That's what it was, the mystery had gone, my violent anger was finally justified.

No wonder I sat for years on the couch with a book on my lap.

"She will get all muddy!" Mother exclaimed reproachfully as Sophie was getting close to the water near the pond.

"It doesn't matter."

"Of course, it matters! She will bring all that mud indoors, on your carpet!"

"No, she won't, she'll remove her shoes at the door, she's allowed to go near the water..."

"You are spoiling her..."

"I don't think so."

She shrugged, scoffed, cast furious glances in my direction. Everything I did seemed contrary to her gospel – and it was: she stood accused; she could see that if I did things differently to her it had to be because I had judged that she had done these things wrongly and she hated me for my dissent as much as my autonomy.

But another incident came to my mind, an event at once

so trivial and monumental that it has survived in my mind because of its apparent irrationality: as the three of us were strolling one morning on a smart avenue in Bordeaux, Sophie, a toddler still, needed to do a pee. I naturally picked her up and, having lowered her pants, held her above the gutter. Mother fretted and protested:

"I don't agree with that, it is not a proper thing to do…"

"It's fine! What else am I supposed to do?"

"But that's how little girls are raped!" she exclaimed angrily, oddly disturbed.

This was so absurd I cannot think how I replied, except perhaps by asking her to keep a sense of proportion. It was a disagreement among several each day of her visits, they merged into one long feeling of frustration and desire in me to flee far, far away. But much worse than our clashes when our disagreements were at least in the open, were the times in between when she would act as if all was wonderful between us: her voice would go up a pitch, and you knew that her world order depended on it, that she would rather have the falsehood of that order than the honesty of dissent and anger, that she had to control reality and imprison you again in *her* need. It was as if the truth of a moment or a feeling revealed would cause her world to unravel and dissolve her insistent and frantic grip on things. So she wove you into her web. And while at times I went along with the pretence – for peace's sake, for Sophie's sake – I hated her for warping my world and dismissing my attempts at living a true life. At a time when it was more vital to me than ever, I came to feel that my efforts to claim what was mine were being stalled. That flimsy skin of peace had pus inside, an abscess made of lies, anger and sorrow.

Chapter Seventeen

That Belsize Park garden held me together tightly. For five years, it was my canvas, my planet-paradise where I was in turns the architect, the labourer, the lover and the supplicant. There was a huge sycamore in the far left corner and its long overhanging branches compelled me to be sensible and compromise: plant sturdy evergreen bushes beneath, sober ones like an eleagnus and a fatsia. Further on, I could allow myself a climbing rose of delicate pink, an 'Albertine', which would stretch along the back wall in search of brighter light. Then on the right and going down, wild crimson clematis, scented choysia, the deep blue of a ceanothus and yet more clematis that rested on the brick wall in arrangements of its own devising. According to the seasons, bright sturdy daisies, the luxury of lilies, the oddity of the candle-like kniphofias and the more secretive Japanese anemones and hellebores; masses of foxgloves... The garden, from its rigid rectangular beginning, had evolved as a wide alleyway of lawn winding boldly as I found my own boldness. I tended the curvy beds every weekend with new finds and Sophie got excited with me. As I dug the ground, I reached the depths, excavating more feelings and thoughts. I found there was no wisdom in tenacity, merely in perseverance, and that growth was the goal in life as in nature.

There had been, since a time so cloudy I cannot begin to fathom it, what I called 'the *jardin public* test': I was in a *jardin public* or a park with people – friends, family. We strolled among the greenery, stopped to look at the ducks, fed them maybe, made easy conversation, but nothing was easy as I was not truly there, or else I was there watching myself from a distance, disbelieving: do I exist? Why couldn't I be as real as grass, trees, ducks, children? As if I hadn't yet become flesh or else my mind hadn't synchronized with my body. Internally, I wept the tears of the ghost who yearns to be alive and whose fate leaves it in tormented limbo. However, this was happening less and less it seemed, perhaps getting my hands muddy was good therapy.

Of course I had a role now: I was a mother and a protector, which in itself made me strong. I did not doubt that, I did not doubt Sophie, her sweet face, the fun we had, the delight I took in her. I could take her to feed the ducks and feel real, and I knew I had a purpose since she had assured me one bedtime: "I am so happy you were born so you could be my mum." She liked to play pretend games, exploring possibilities, and her imagination thrilled me:

"Mum? If I wasn't your little girl, and you saw me in the street, what would you think?"

"I would think: 'Oh, that little girl, she looks such a treasure, I wish she was MY little girl!'" And we would kiss and cuddle and laugh, happy with our lot.

Nevertheless, as I watched her grow and wondered at how magical merely being the witness of childhood could be, I was aware how little I remembered of my own childhood, all the less so as Mother had hardly told me any stories about it – as if I hadn't been there with her but had done my growing behind some door... I was beginning to know that a past ignored will re-live itself throughout life, I must know it to own it, so where is it? And why so murky?

Sophie was always looking forward to seeing her dad, and Jeremy was often at his best when he visited or took her out. For my part, I had decided I could not possibly spoil things for her. I had suffered a great deal from having a father I despised and disliked and wanted her to have a good image of hers, so I spoke kindly to her about him even if it choked me at times…

I had learned that Jeremy had met his new woman, Lorna, while I was pregnant with Sophie as on one visit he had told me excitedly: "I have a new lady!" The choice of words was interesting: not a woman? An aristocrat? Was he still a child? I have no idea of his motives for doing so at the time, except to hurt me and naively to boast, but I remember marvelling at how quickly he was able to move on, and reasoning that if this put more distance between us it was salutary for me. A year or so later, they were married.

A widow twenty-two years his junior, Lorna had a child from her first marriage, a little girl called Zoe who had been a baby when her extremely rich father died. Leaving the totality of his fortune to the child, he knew his wife would live more than comfortably on the interest until the girl reached eighteen. Jeremy, I reflected, always made sure there would be someone to pay the bills: this had been true so far with all his women, including me.

A few years later, when Sophie was about three, he asked me if Lorna could come and visit as she wished to meet me. I agreed: since Sophie was going to their house it would only be civilised if we knew each other. Possibly he told me so himself, and so one day I opened my door to a fussily dressed thirty-four year old woman with little bits of jewellery seemingly everywhere. Her beautiful red hair was carefully tamed in a plait around her head. I was taken aback by her frilly appearance, so much had I expected someone sporty-looking, dressed casually and sure of herself, who would make me feel insecure.

Jeremy cannot have known the true reason for her visit, since after initial small talk she admitted that Sophie was a source of problems between them, so would I please consider stopping Jeremy from seeing his daughter?

I replied that this was out of the question: I didn't feel I owed Jeremy anything but wouldn't dream of depriving Sophie of her father, no matter how much it cost me; that's how it was. Lorna got upset, accused me of trapping Jeremy into having a child with me, which I denied. I felt dispassionate and unmoved facing this deceitful woman. Their problem, I thought.

Later, Jeremy hinted that there were difficulties with Lorna when he took Sophie to their house for the day. Indeed Lorna herself rang me one day, complaining that Sophie was the source of many arguments between them, why hadn't I had an abortion?

"I can't believe you are saying this when you know I had a still-born baby, are you completely heartless?" I was stunned.

"Well, at least," she countered blindly, "you could have told her, her father was dead!"

I had hung up, sickened. Jeremy had met his equal. All this meant that Sophie was not welcome at her father's house; Lorna would previously leave in a temper when he appeared with her or she would go out for the day, but very soon, changing tacks, she forbade Jeremy to bring Sophie into the house. Since it was *her* house, cravenly, he toed the line. Sophie was often distressed at her exclusion and I very angry at his spinelessness.

"You might be six foot three," I threw at him one day, "but as a father you are a dwarf!"

I was beginning to have teeth.

171

I lived in hope that Jeremy would finally tell his parents of Sophie's existence, time was passing and without daring to say no and prevaricating, it became clear that he had no intention to do so: his mother, he was adamant, wouldn't welcome her since we had not married; as it was, she had always shown less affection to his adopted daughters than to the more legitimate son and he feared she would be unpleasant to Sophie. Concerned that my own sense of abandonment and exclusion would be re-visited on her by Jeremy I cursed him for his cowardice: he still dreaded being blamed by his parents. I recalled the time when we had driven to Dorset for his father's eightieth birthday, when I would be officially introduced to them and he made me promise to keep the still-birth of our little boy a secret. I remembered how painful it had been to comply, that event was still very recent and raw. At the same time I was being made official as 'his lady', I was being required to also be anonymous in a vital respect: I felt like a mother, but a mother without a child. Sophie needed to know her family.

So, for lack of anything better and possibly because it was time, I would take my little girl to my long-discarded Pyrenean hometown to visit my father's grave. It would be easy to go there on the train for forty-eight hours during our next visit to her grandmother in Bordeaux, just Sophie and me, to show her where I grew up and for me to understand what I felt. I never missed my father, a measure of how little he had been present in my life, and the few moments I remembered I had always deemed either sad, bad, or disappointing. I knew there had to be more to it than that: I was missing a father, which is probably why I was overcome by floods of tears as I stood before his tomb holding Sophie's hand, saying to him without speaking the words : "I'm sorry, I am so sorry..." I couldn't have said what I was so sorry about. That it all had been a sad waste perhaps, a non-meeting, a missed opportunity? For he had been shy and restrained even in his moments of gentleness, uncertain as to whether his was the right kind of feeling, the right kind of action.

I could recall one time – and there must have been more, surely, surely – when I had adored being in his company: one summer evening, when I was in my early teens and in spite of Mother's arguments he and I had driven out in the night, after dinner, for fun, to catch in the headlights the occasional hare, the odd fox hurriedly crossing a country lane, or frighten an owl that would fly away in silence, displaying an unexpected wing span. We had both laughed like children, in shared pleasure…

I had long and often thought of writing about my childhood but, compassion apart, there was something in Mother's very existence which seemed to forbid it, I couldn't quite decipher what. Certainly, writing had always been about meeting myself on the page, which at serendipitous times produced in me an 'Ah!' of recognition. It was about being true. I wanted none of what I had inherited: remembering her more sophisticated public manners and judging them false, I could also see how costly it would have been for her to 'be herself' for it would have involved the disintegration of everything that held her together, every single defence built for her protection, every denial adopted for keeping up her courage.

Jeremy himself had some while ago written a memoir about his youth, but no publisher had wanted it; even his own father, he reported to me with surprise and mild shock, had returned the manuscript saying: "I believe my son has a dirty mind." Jeremy had seemed hurt and puzzled by this, but I remembered only too well his ambivalent attitude towards women, who were never called women, rather, jokingly, 'wimmin', but more often condescendingly labelled 'girls' and 'birds' or 'chicks', or else, coyly, 'ladies', as well as some of his coarser comments.

"May the light of the Virgin Mary shine upon your world…"
   This was the latest message Mother had received from Odile, she moaned on the telephone, just that one quote in place of answers to her anxious queries regarding her status, material security, her housing: was she going to join a particular convent? Which order had she entered? Would she be working in the outside world? Was she being 'looked after'? Mother was both desperate and exasperated at Odile's refusal to reassure her. "I am tired of worrying all the time," she complained, and suggested I wrote to Odile to try and find out more. I doubted I could but sent a short, friendly letter which remained without reply. Odile would have known that any news would get passed on to Mother. Wasn't she making things worse for herself, though, or was religion truly a calling rather than a refuge?
   I didn't spend too much time wondering. Without that glorious little girl of mine at the centre of my life, I would have drowned long before, but that centre was warm, joyous and it kept me sane. She always reassured me: "You are a wonderful mother and you deserve me!" I loved Sophie's littleness in those days when my body was still her playground, when climbing on me for play or having a book read was the most natural thing in the world. It made up for everything else, it seemed, the demands of my job, loneliness, and even Mother's relentless demands, as she was the grandmother, the only one at that, so had to be preserved. Naively, I would on occasion be tempted to confide in her when she was sweet and kind, relishing the moments when I felt I had a mother, but I could glimpse at other times that I was for her a rival, that she resented my independence and

the fact that I managed without a man as well as without her. Saved by a geographical distance I had been well advised to maintain, I was free to raise Sophie how I wished. Plainly being able to manage my life lay me open to blame in her eyes. She appeared much more respectful of Odile because she sensed the cold anger that my sister showed her held the threat that she would cut all links if she dared to cross the line. She also got a sense of her disarray through her more irrational decisions: Odile's anger ruled her as did her own terrible need to belong and she would do anything to try and assuage that pain. I had to admit that her exile to Canada had also suited me, since we had never got on: it had kept her out of the way with the advantage for me, absolving me, that it had been her own decision.

Odile never talked about herself in her 'letters' – out of choice? Or was it a punishing religious rule of self-abnegation? – so that all I had received for several years now were religious quotes from one Gospel or another, or well-wishing phrases talking of the grace of God. Highly irritating stuff, high-handed, holier-than-thou, well meaning in appearance only. I do not doubt that, consciously, she wished me well: didn't her religion order it? At the time she left for Canada, I recalled, I had been scathingly anti-clerical and an atheist for some years. So I suspected that her sub-conscious said other words than good wishes, continued a battle I no longer had any interest in fighting. But the letter she sent that Christmas was for me one pious message too many:

PAX!

Thank you to Sophie and Hélène for your good wishes! May the Divine Child and Our Lady of Peace grant us the gift of a New Year full of the grace and gentleness that men of goodwill, through the thorns of life's trials, are able to savour!

Affections to both of you! Marie-Odile

175

My own reply, I'm afraid, was incredibly violent:

You have a particular knack, with your pompous piety, of exasperating others to a very high degree. You totally fail to communicate because of your obsession to create a holy image of yourself. I am not impressed or touched in any way. If you want to reach people you need to treat them as equal human beings, not as inferior and needy beggars of your sanctimonious and patronising wisdom.

Maybe you will condescend, one of these days / months / years, to give some time and caring to your mother, I don't do what I do for her on your behalf.

Reading it again later, I was astonished at my own nastiness: surely it was more than her letter deserved?

The message was clear, of course: I am not the part of you that fulfils that duty. We are separate; we shared a childhood but not an identity, you are on your own.

No wonder she felt rejected, but she always acted in such a way as to provoke rejection, deliberately laying the foundations, setting up the modalities for the next incident that would confirm her badness and replay her exclusion: when was the first time she had learnt that? Who gave her the idea, made the imprint? Was it nature or nurture? She had always, like Mother, seemed a terrible masochist: had she sucked it from her breast, the first truth absorbed? – together with the silent misery, the angry resignation, the resentful self-justification.... If she had been born that way, if that is how one can be born and what being born means, no wonder she would have wanted to be born again, and gone headlong into religion to do so. To be saved. To find some grace. And there I was telling her it was all a sham...

Mother had been able, since Father's death, to find some solace in the Church and thus repair a relationship that she had never wished to sever. Having found herself excluded

176

by the very fact of her divorce many decades before was a high price to pay for straying from the rules of religion. Her return to the fold hadn't been the smoothest of developments, the priest in whom she had confided having explained naively:

"But, of course, Madame Dufresne, the death of your husband invalidates your marriage to him, so that now, in the eyes of God, it is your first and legitimate marriage only that counts. The Church can now allow you, if you confess and repent naturally, to come back to mass and receive the sacraments."

I had to admire my mother's indignant reply:

"You are telling me, Father, that my first marriage, which lasted barely a year, to a man who did not love but exploited me is the only one that counts, while a marriage of fifty years to the man who was the father of my children has no value? Do you realise what you are saying?"

If only Odile could find the same strength...

Chapter Eighteen

Then everything changed.

While I had managed the upkeep of a large flat, a car, and enjoyed the help and company of a devoted au-pair girl, I found myself after five years threatened with a very large bill for my share – two-fifths – of the work needed to re-paint and maintain the house. Managing agents were expensive and pressing. I took fright, thinking I would find it hard to cope, and decided to sell. It was not entirely a bad idea: property prices had gone through the roof in five years. Selling my Belsize Park flat would allow me to buy a house if I went a little further out of the area, Kentish Town for example: some of its Victorian streets seemed attractive, though the townscape had none of the prettiness and gentility that I was used to, as large council estates also bore witness to a great deal of poverty and hardship. I was reassured that there was also plenty of the less well-off liberal living there, particularly journalists, writers, artists, whose proximity appealed to my less conventional aspirations; besides, my political feelings had always been on the left. A good social mix, then. Besides, I told myself with bravado, we all breathe the same air!

Leaving was hard. Far more than the flat, it was my garden I would miss, so much of my soul was there. I had lived day after day engaged in a labour of love and the thrill of creation: my fingers knew every inch of that soil, had participated in all that flamboyance. It had generously repaid every visit and helped turn sadness and at times despair into a story of growth and reward.

Well, I thought, biting my lip, I'll just have to create another beautiful and fulfilling garden.

The new house was large, on three floors, but the garden quite tiny if not overlooked, the side of a tall house framing it at the end. All right then, I conceded, I could still plant some climbing roses, beauty is a requisite.

However, in the late eighties, Kentish Town didn't do despondency by halves: nothing subliminal about the desolation of rows of run-down houses, neglected front gardens where greasy newspapers and empty beer-cans often shared the ground with thistles and thorns. Behind dignified and attractive Victorian fronts, too many sad curtains betrayed loss of hope as much as they displayed slovenliness and poverty. Still, I could make my own home beautiful, so not all was bad. I always enjoyed a new project and home-making was my favourite: a home had to be harmonious, a good mix of comfort, warm colours and attractive objects as well as good paintings – many of them by Johan – and sculptures collected over the years. The first room to be redecorated would be Sophie's, while she was away up North on a week's holiday with Jeremy; her new school was just around the corner; we had a new au-pair, a Yugoslav; the neighbours were friendly; I could drive to work easily. But plenty was wrong.

I was exhausted inside: always being alone, the sole adult in charge, responsible and having to do everything wore me out and I felt as if my loneliness would never end. I had now been on my own for nearly eight years. In great part

I wanted it that way, concentrating on re-creating myself from the ashes of the past, sifting those ashes, throwing a lot away, mostly questing, growing. In many ways I felt quite adult, an achievement for me at forty-nine years of age! I might be a late developer but at least I developed. "Let go of your ego!" was one of the mantras of the time but this would have been out of the question, I was still working on mine…

I had quite an armour: I could appear full of enterprise, buoyant, and cheerful with that loving little girl of mine; I tried to make the most of what I had, gave the occasional dinner party, went on outings to the country with friends, conferences and seminars, alternative health and philosophies being of great interest to me at the time. Part of the armour was my old grey coat, worn over black trousers; it was so wide across the shoulders that I must have looked like a fat pigeon swollen against the cold, or preferably a strong and dangerous small person, defences out: living alone and mindful of my role as a protector I was very engaged in not being afraid. Except that I was afraid: the house next door, a council house that was empty when we had moved in, had just been invaded by five or six Irish squatters, and the wall between us felt horribly thin during the evenings when they drank themselves into a stupor. I spent hours listening to their appalling singing, arguments and shouts, terrified in case they should decide to pay me a visit by jumping over the garden wall. One winter night, eight of them, naked from the waist down, ran down screaming to the end of the street and back. Sophie was mercifully asleep as I watched behind my bedroom curtains, shaking. The police, when they came, were too late and unable to intervene.

I tried to laugh about it with some neighbours who had befriended me: a skeleton-thin Spanish woman, Rosa, had shouted a loud 'Welcome to the street!' at me the very day I moved in, and invited me into her house. We sometimes saw each other after work, when our little girls were back from school, and one day she told me her story: growing up in a Spanish village with a mother who beat and insulted her and a father who ignored her, she was repeatedly sexually abused by her brothers, a sister and her grandfather. She found it very hard to eat and refused everything I offered when she came to tea. Jenny, a friend of Rosa's, who confided in me the day she came for help with a French translation, had been brought up in a small boarding house by the seaside, where she was as a little child the 'sweetheart' of several male pensioners who gave her sweets and biscuits in exchange for letting them explore her vagina. "I was always so swollen down there," she would say wistfully, "huge.... . All I can say is, I must have been a very bad person in a previous life..."'

Involved as I was in making my home beautiful, my garden a small paradise and my life a meaningful whole, I fought it all as best I could, even buying packets of flower seeds that I sprinkled into the more unloved-looking front gardens, praying for miracles. But I could no longer watch the hospital drama *Casualty* on television on Monday nights with Sophie as I became prone to bursting into tears at the sadder moments. Sophie now warned me protectively:

"*Casualty* is starting now, Mum, why don't you go to your room?" Sensibly, she was sparing me inevitable upsets – I felt so close to all of them – and sparing herself at the same time. A sensible child, who was mothering me.

I was very ill again that January. It seemed a repeat performance of the illness of the previous November, and the February before. 'Gastric flu', as it was called, was striking me heavily for two weeks at a time, with its assortments of cramps, bruise-like aches, total exhaustion, inability to eat except at times the blandest, smallest amounts of food. Each time I thought I might die, leaving my little girl behind. I was shocked at my inability to cope and guilty about being unable to go to work.

I paid another anxious visit that week to a nearby therapist. She worked at the deepest level with emotions linked with physical symptoms. Together with the healing she gave me, things went very fast. This time I came with a riddle: I had caught myself talking about my stomach pains as 'contractions', adding: 'I am not going to give birth to much this time!' Now alert to signals of that kind, I was warned there was work to be done.

We tried visualisation and she prompted me gently:

"If your pain was a thing, what would it look like?"

I resisted a long while, going through objects in a haphazard way: an animal, a bird, an insect, an object, a stone... I didn't know. Then I screamed out:

"A BABY! It's a baby crying!"

"Why is it crying?"

Among delirious sobs, I cried out:

"He's crying because HE is in pain because HE can't breathe!"

The tears, the sorrow, were like a mountain bursting. My world was totally concentrated at that moment, nothing existed except that unrecognised child. After a long time, when I began to calm down, I could say his name for the first time: THOMAS.

There I was, ten years after his death, and I re-lived it all, clearly and consciously. The therapist suggested I might like to think about some ritual to allow me to mourn properly. Not having been to church for decades I found myself going with a friend to a service at the Unitarian Church in Hampstead and I felt quite overwhelmed during the service and the singing. I knew I would have one for my baby once I had all the facts: I rang the hospital to make an appointment with the registrar. I wanted to talk, ask questions, claim my story. I wanted to hear all the facts from a knowledgeable and caring human being, there had been too much silence and anonymity. His secretary rang me back the following day and suggested I make an appointment at the Neo-Natal Unit: they would give me all the facts it was possible to find out. If I was not completely satisfied with the answers, the registrar would be quite willing to see me.

That same week, I made contact with SANDS (Still Birth and Neo-Natal Society). I explained who I was, what I wanted. I felt embarrassed to tell them 'it' had all happened all these years ago. I felt a freak: who would be going through all this ten years later? I was reassured: plenty of people who, like me, were at a loss to know what to do at the time, were too overcome by grief to think properly, were not given much choice, and who were now able and desperately wanting, to hear the truth, face the pain, acknowledge the loss, give their dead child due recognition and restore it to its true place in the history of their lives.

They referred me to one of their team who befriended other mourning parents, or mothers, on a one-to-one basis in their own homes. I arrived at Rina's home one wet evening, and as we sat talking and her husband brought us tea, I was mesmerised by the photographs of her two children on the sideboard, the living one and the dead one: three years previously, their little girl had died, seven weeks old, and I listened to Rina with unrestrained envy as she told me of the photographs taken of her minute sick baby in the hospital ward, the funeral with the family and the friends, the open and shared grief. Then she heard me, and because she was caring I felt understood. It was as if it had all happened last week.

But I had questions to ask: what could have happened to my little boy? Would he have been buried? Where? Could he have been cremated? Is that what my consultant had meant when he had said: 'He is everywhere, he's in the atmosphere', or was he talking of my baby's soul? Could I hope to find out all the facts? Did she know what took place ten years ago? And, most important of all, would there be a *place* to go?

When she spoke, striving to be tactful, I knew it would be difficult to take: if they were buried, still-born babies were put in communal graves; there might not be a name; the part of the cemetery where they were laid was very neglected, the firm of undertakers insensitive. When complaints were made, the hospital chose a different firm. I might still not be quite satisfied with the state of the grave. It would be nicer if the baby had been cremated although there would be no ashes as they would have been scattered. However, she thought I would have been asked if I wanted a cremation, and I remembered no such thing. There was just a possibility, I thought, that I had been asked if I wanted the hospital to 'take care' of the baby, and I had consented. Or maybe Jeremy had done so?

On the 5th of April that spring, I went for an appointment with the counsellor and a senior nurse at the hospital. They had assured me on the telephone that they had all the information I had requested. The room was small and welcoming and I was treated in the most kind and caring way. The senior nurse had typed all the details I wanted, and she and the counsellor went through them with me, letting me ask, comment, cry, query, and they commented as we went along.

I learn that my baby weighed just over three kilos and was 50.2 centimetres long; a post-mortem was carried out and the findings were available. He would have been buried in a common grave, wearing a white shroud. He would have had a wooden coffin covered in white material with his name inscribed on a name plate on the top of the coffin. There would have been no burial service, but he would have been buried in a dignified manner as befits such an event. I could have a headstone placed on the grave if I wished...

It was a lot to take in. Although I was appalled, if prepared, at the idea of a communal grave, I was overwhelmed to hear his name spoken to me at last: so his existence was recognised, people at last were telling me they knew of him, his reality, his white shroud, his wooden coffin with his own name on. They heard my grief as if it was that day's grief and it was, it now could be, it was allowed to be, and I was so grateful for this.

The following day I went, accompanied by a friend, to the cemetery. I do not know if I could have done it on my own, but to have a witness was of overriding importance. We found the grave, the area it was in set apart from the main part of the cemetery. It was a large and shapeless mound of soil, weather beaten and overrun with thorns on which litter from overflowing bins got caught. You could not really distinguish one grave from another save for a few which had some kind of fencing, wood or wire, around them.

My baby's grave had two plaques, ten inches by seven, the only size allowed on public ground, with the names of two other babies who died at around the same time. The low, rusty fence was bent, which I straightened out. I cut the thorns off with my friend's knife. I was shattered, but too relieved to be angry: there was now a place to go. My baby would have his own ten by seven inches plaque with his name in as large letters as possible. I would plant a flowering bush. He would have a memorial service in the Unitarian church I visited and a few friends would attend. Music would be played. At long last I would be giving, and claiming, recognition.

Chapter Nineteen

There was, I now knew, a glorious logic to our lives: all beginnings had to have an outcome. There was nothing of consequence to us that did not have to be acknowledged and find its necessary conclusion. No matter how happy I might have been at Sophie's birth, I was certain that at some point I would have had to work through that devastating loss of the past to put order into my life, so that the past could be the past, the present be the present, to allow me to develop. As it was, the past was still very much in my present and it prodded me in unexpected ways, claiming attention. Moreover, I now felt more lucidly than ever that I had rights: to my life, my knowledge of it, because so much had felt, at times of puzzled reflection, unavailable to me.

Kentish Town brought me to my knees. The very day of the move, following the removal van in my car, Sophie and I had witnessed the almost cartoon-like chase of a thief by two policemen who brought him down on the High Street pavement and, passers-by barely ruffled, managed to handcuff him as he fought.

– Welcome to Kentish Town! we exclaimed cheerfully.

But not many days later, back from the local shop with bread and milk, I found myself walking behind a couple of down-and-outs staggering on the uneven pavement, drinking from cans of beer. The woman started to retch and vomit on her clothes as well as on the ground, slipped and fell in her mess. The man, himself barely able to stand, grabbed her somehow, helped her to her feet, brushed her soiled skirt then wiped his hands on his trousers. They hobbled on. This is what their life has come to, I thought with anguish, how had they come to this dereliction, they had been someone's children once ... . Nothing could reverse such wretchedness now.

And of course I felt disgust, revulsion, and a growing sense of gloom at living at such close quarters with that world. I could see that I felt threatened, compromised even. The best way to deal with it, I concluded, was compassion, love. If I won the lottery, I would create a Healing Centre here. Kentish Town needed healing. But I needed healing too.

Healing, indeed, came in many guises. I had a place to go and be with my baby now; I planted flowers which would soon wilt and add to the melancholy mess of the cemetery, but at least I could be there with him sometimes, and one day found me feeling particularly desperate and abandoned. I knelt there, trying to understand the link which maybe was merely in grief since I had been left behind, a common place wound.

As I sat weeping on the grass near the plot where he lay, I let my soul beg to him:

– I feel so lonely and I miss you so much... . Where are you now, when you are so much in my heart? My little one, my baby... talk to me... something, give me something: a gesture, a sign, some indication that I am making contact, I cannot go on being so alone...

I wept some more. It was a peaceful spot somehow in spite of the surrounding untidiness, and a robin was chirping nearby. I waited a while, calmer, before eventually leaving.

A mirror shop caught my eye as I drove back home along the main road, reminding me I needed to buy one for the new house. Stopping the car by the roadside, I walked across the road to look at the shop window, but seeing nothing suitable, walked straight back to the car.

As I fastened my safety belt and started the engine I became aware of a white lorry coming towards me from the opposite direction, bizarrely and illegally crossing the road from the other side. I did not immediately acknowledge its odd appearance as it all unfolded very quickly but it was a medium-size lorry, immaculately white with large shining chrome bumpers and lights in the extravagant style of American cars of the fifties. It was nose to nose with my car now, and as I had just switched on the ignition, I looked up in surprise: the driver, his hand raised, was signalling at me to wait. He was a huge, very black man who, defying his bulk, jumped lightly out of his cabin and his big face promptly appeared at my driver-side window. I think I expected him to ask me for the way somewhere, it all happened too fast for thinking. I lowered my window. He was crouching and his large friendly face was very close to mine now.

"Can I ask you a question?" he said with a broad smile.

"Well, yes, of course…" I replied, a little puzzled.

"But, really?" he insisted.

"Yes?"

I was becoming aware that, as he paused, his Adam's apple had started convulsing in his throat, until a chuckle transformed itself into a burst of irrepressible laughter, loud and released. This was oddly contagious, I was laughing too now, this was all eerily funny, and I was still waiting for his question.

"Are you happy?" he chortled, then roared again, and I could only join him, we were both inside a huge bubble of mirth, a world where we were best friends, mates, accomplices on an island unknown of others, sister and brother in understood magic. He leapt back onto the pavement as I pulled away, and there he stood waving at me cheerfully, and I waved back, grinning, elated, as I went on my way...

I looked for the truck for years, alert to any vehicle remotely similar that would confirm its probability, allowing me a glimpse of heavy chrome on a smooth white truck body but to no avail. Daringly at times, I concluded they didn't 'really' exist. In spite of superficially wondering who the man was and where he came from, I accepted that meeting profoundly and simply for a grace I had been given and there were no questions to ask. I did not stop smiling for five months, the joy that filled me swelled my heart. I was fulfilled, in harmony with the best of this world and incredibly thankful.

So I could be happy if circumstances permitted, but what permitted circumstances? You cannot search for the numinous, you can only live with your windows open and if you can, read the writing, acknowledge the serendipity.

My dealings with Mother were as difficult and rancourous as ever, so for a while now, survival having become a priority, I had shortened her visits to London as well as ours to Bordeaux, but I could still imagine her face, her grieved expressions, her suffering; the 'Mater Dolorosa', long imprinted on my brain, surfaced again, the better to imprison me, feeding on what was left of attachment and hope. She had suffered openly in front of our eyes when Odile and I were children, to the point when at times confidences would spill out, obscure to little girls: "I cannot bear him, I cannot bear to sleep with him"... Equally binding on us was the fact that she had stayed with him for us, so that we might have a father – even when, eventually seeing the kind of father he was, we would have been very relieved had we finally left, never to see him again. But as Mother had adored her own father, she could not imagine a life without one for us.

'Doing the right thing' had been prevalent for her, and at great cost.

From the moment Sophie was born, I knew the way I mothered her was bound to upset Mother, but this was an area where I would have died rather than surrender to her edicts; having long made a mental list of things to spare children as well as respectful and joyful ways to treat them, I never gave way. And if she saw me explaining to Sophie why we had to go somewhere or do a particular task:

– You're not going to ask for her permission, I hope! she would interject. The tone was contemptuous, hostile. I took note, took it in my stride, easier when I was on tranquillisers, but it made me feel quite desolate inside, like Kentish Town on a bad day.

"In the old days," she solemnly declared once, "families used to live together!"

"Yes," I retorted lightly, "but they used a lot of strychnine!"

"Oh! You are impossible! You obviously don't know what loneliness is."

"I know everything about loneliness…"

"How can you say that! You are young, you have no idea!"

"What a glib thing to say! In fact, there is nothing I know better…"

"In that case – " she looked furious and appalled but in her eyes I also sensed fear – "you should have sought psychiatric help!"

"Yes," I replied calmly, raising my eyes to her, "I should have."

And she fretted, threatened again now as I intended her to feel, in a rare moment of truth between us.

I never told Mother about finding my baby's grave and

the memorial service: it would have been an event for her to run according to her rules. I could not find it in me to tell her, she was no friend of mine. I was at the time becoming swamped by new, great fear and grief: I wanted to die, and couldn't do so because of my lovely Sophie.

For months now I had been collecting, cutting them out of newspapers and magazines on an almost daily basis, heartbreaking articles on the abuse of children. It had always been known and evident that many children were ill-treated and neglected, but the abuse now revealed was sexual abuse – an old secret kept well under wraps, and it filled me with acute horror and pain mixed with fascination. I had quite a pile of these articles on my bedroom writing table now, so many that one evening, looking at it, I had to face the obvious: "Come on, woman, what are you doing? This isn't just about those children, this is about you too!"

My soul was full of sick.

I was contemplating, horrified, the journey I had to make in order to find sense in it all: my childhood, my parents, my role as a victim, the nature of my relationships with men, those horrendous flashes and the incidents I remembered, unconvincing and puzzling in isolation but threatening if I brought them together. I didn't want to go 'there', but such was my need of my real self and my anger at having so often been preyed on by others that I had to see this quest as another urgent way of reaching the truth about my life.

God knows Kentish Town helped, although I have yet to feel thankful.

Women who had been sexually abused as children had made a bee-line for me as if finding me congenial and like-minded; houses conspired equally to tell me similar stories in the scenes they contained, particularly that house next door, a set for another battle-front. Why I didn't think, since it was a council house, of complaining to the Council, baffles me:

I was neither ignorant nor unsophisticated, and it doesn't need much sophistication to pick up the telephone. It just didn't cross my mind, finding me unknowing, powerless and paralysed. There was no solution, I would have to bear it, I knew how to bear things. Strangely passive, I just put up with it. I knew how to put up.

Those Irish squatters stayed on for at least another year fraught with menace and anguish. The next incident happened late one night and I witnessed it from my first-floor bedroom. If the walls were often too thick to reveal the exact sound of the words overheard, they were always too porous to disguise their nature. Several times a week the men had drunken binges full of their foul language, coarse laughter and arguments; however, that night revealed a different scene, as if one of them, or an added guest, had become a prisoner, to be beaten and abused: his screams, following his protests, became screams of pain, ominously rhythmical, mixed with crying and moaning. Crude laughter surrounded those screams. It was too late to put music on to drown it all, to pretend it wasn't happening. It left me frozen with terror, as I knew what the rhythm was. Calling the police wasn't even an option as I couldn't have found, let alone uttered, any words to describe it all. Another incident weeks later involved a woman, equally abused, and allowed to leave still screaming, her enraged yells filling the sleeping street in the early morning hours.

I had thought, when I came to London to marry Johan, that I was leaving, not just the constrictions of family life behind but also this un-ease of living and profound depression that inhabited me so deeply; that I would be shutting the door, wiping the slate clean. But I had to find out in many hard ways that you never leave childhood behind because it does not leave you, it inhabits your very cells, runs through your veins, it is the very texture of you; your body contains your whole history and it always tells the truth.

Opposite me lived Anita, a vital and loud West Indian woman, mother of seven-year-old Dwayne, the focus of many a noisy telling off for the whole street to witness. Dragging his feet, he follows her, who marches ahead like an angry soldier, berating him loudly after a talk with his teacher: little Dwayne hits other children. When they come for tea and biscuits, I can hold him on my lap and he lets me, shyly I sense, careful not to move, and I tell him he is a lovely boy while Anita rants and laughs about her work day, bracingly.

The evening she invites me in for a drink after the child's bedtime, she lets it all out: Dwayne is the spitting image of his father, and she hates the man who played around recklessly and abandoned her. She wasn't best equipped to cope in those early days, having been as a child put into care then raped at sixteen after she came out; she managed, however, to study to be a secretary and now has a good job and a one-bedroom council flat across the road from me.

She started hitting Dwayne when he was a baby, she confesses, "and when I saw what I was doing and that I could kill him, I went to the Council and I said to them: "You got to help me or I'm gonna kill that child and I don't want to do that!" and they sent me to this therapist: Jee-sus! They peel you raw! I couldn't stand it, but I said to her after a few sessions: "Okay, I get the idea, so I won't hit him again, goodbye!" And that was that! But he drives me mad, he is so clingy, he always wants to sleep in my bed…"

"You're not soft," young Dwayne said to her shyly on one afternoon visit.

" Well, Dwayne," she retorted, "you've got to learn, because you're a child."

"I don't like being a child," Dwayne replied sulkily.

"Never mind, Dwayne, you can get your own back when you grow up!"

She was telling him his future, shaping his destiny: no matter that he was suffering now, it was of no importance, he would be cruel himself when he grew up and it would give him the same satisfaction it gave her now...

It got worse over the weeks, the months, she lived her life under pressure, 'steamin', as she said. And I watched Dwayne reluctantly follow her home after school while she filled the street with her untamed fury.

I had made myself scarce of late, but I rang her bell one evening, to talk and try to calm her, only to be told that she was about to throw away all of Dwayne's toys. She was almost crying with rage as she spoke: "He keeps getting into trouble at school, he is always hitting other children, I'm sick of it, I've had it with him!"

Well, I too would be hitting other children if I was her child, I felt. And because she wouldn't hear me if I spoke to her, and because I did not have the authority of an official body, together with her next door neighbour who heard it all and was also concerned, I eventually wrote to the NSPCC. I also wrote to her, even though I knew it would cost me, but we had been friendly and I felt I owed it to her.

Dear Anita,

I thought I would let you know that I have done today what I have wanted to do for a long time, which is to contact the NSPCC, so that both Dwayne and you can get some help.

Nobody can be indifferent to the suffering of a little child, and I am not the only person in the neighbourhood to feel that Dwayne needs protection.

I know you will be very angry to start with. Do try and see that it is also a unique opportunity for you to get to the root of your anger and find the gentleness you yourself needed as a child and did not get.

I only want to help, Hélène

That very evening, Anita rang my bell furiously. I had been waiting for her. I opened the door and stood on the threshold as she poured abuse on me, all tearful screams and rage. I let her, waited for her to finish. She was a brave and strong woman, she might have done the same for me. She didn't allow me to utter a single word, so I let her rant.

Two weeks later, a letter from the NSPCC advised me that a child protection officer had investigated the matter and was satisfied that little Dwayne was 'not at risk of abuse in the home situation'.

Stunned, I immediately replied to express my surprise at her conclusion which flew in the face of everything I had known and seen in his family. I reiterated that I was supported by Anita's next door neighbour in my referral; that Anita herself had told me that Dwayne's headmistress had suggested counselling for her and the boy as he was constantly disruptive and beat up the other children; that Anita had refused, after her previous experience of counselling at the time when she used to hit him as a baby; that she frequently shouted at him in the street, and everyone was appalled at this woman 'who hated her child so much'. I stressed that I think she also very probably loved him as she sewed for him and bought him what he needed, but she had so much anger about her own life that she tried to control him completely just as she tried to control her own pain and couldn't.

I stressed that I had been a teacher for twenty-seven years; that I cared for children and for Dwayne, and I asked for someone to come and see me, this was worth another look.

My letter remained without a reply. Dwayne continued

to hit other children, it seemed, as Anita continued to scream abuse at him after school. I watched him drag his feet behind her as he followed her home and I wanted to weep. All I could do, the day he raised his eyes and saw me at my window, was to mouth: 'I love you', so he may know that love existed somewhere.

But love was elusive, I knew. Here was Dwayne suffering his lack of a father as well as his mother's fury. In spite of my own frustrations and anger towards Jeremy, I didn't want Sophie to think badly of him as I hated despising mine, and I saw that she wasn't always pleased to see her dad. So one day I stressed that he adored her, was so proud of her, but she replied sadly: "Yes, as a 'chick', Mummy."

I didn't like to see her upset and something inside of me forbade me to listen, so I offered to cook some pasta Bolognese for dinner, and this cheered her up immediately.

Chapter Twenty

Sophie was already ten years old when, on the well-meaning insistence of a friend, I went on my own on a holistic holiday in the mountains near Malaga. This went against the grain, so much had I always needed company to go anywhere and do anything, otherwise feeling lost to the point of bereavement and panic.

On arrival at the airport, I was aware of the footsteps of a stranger accelerating his pace to keep up with me. He was a member of my group: tall with a beard, and distinguished-looking, he spoke pleasantly without straining for effect. A young couple, both handsome and happy also made friendly conversation. This good start was confirmed later when, having been collected for a drive to 'the farm' – the '*cortijo*' – in the hills by a member of the staff, we stopped en route for a swim in the sea before enjoying a paella nearby.

The sea was marvellously blue, and I had not swum in years. This was bliss but I would be shy of going further than a few strokes into the water if the stranger, Paul, didn't reassure me that it would be all right, he would swim around me. Safety!

I had often blamed myself, sometimes jokingly, for having terrible taste in men, from the deeply inadequate to the plain nasty, but I knew bad luck wasn't just bad luck, that there was something in me that attracted those men: Johan, who feared emotion above all else, had known instinctively that I would make no demands but give what he needed: affection, companionship and devoted support; Jeremy would have known that he could use me as an emotional punch-ball and thus satisfy his deeper dislike of women with a cruelty born of his own pain.

As Paul eventually found a regular seat at my side during that week in Spain, I melted at his gentleness: I had given myself a few years to change myself, to go from passive victim to active player and I was proud of what I had achieved. I knew who I was, what I wanted. I was financially independent, the proud mother of a delightful child. I had vastly deepened my understanding of life and healed a lot of wounds. I was fifty-one years old, although I may have credit here because I was told I look years younger and had kept my looks, but time was passing, implacable: shouldn't I be sensible? Paul was so kind, so willing to please, so selfless…

Sophie, who screamed at first ("I don't want you to have a boyfriend! I don't want you to have a boyfriend!") was equally seduced, now even gave him some of her sweets, and I felt she was safe with him. We both were.

Twice divorced and the father of two pleasant grown-up daughters, Paul was, like me, on his maybe-third-time-lucky endeavour. He worked as a quantity surveyor, a good step ahead of his working-class background in staid Buckinghamshire. Under the influence of his second wife he had attended evening classes in Literature, and enjoyed art galleries, jazz, gardens. As I was a member of the National Trust we visited beautiful places at weekends. In fact he liked practically everything I liked which ensured peace in the home.

He was tall, yes. (Was it a need to look up to men that seemed to attract me to the tall ones, a too easy translation?

Jeremy had teased me.) I wondered what Paul would be like without the beard but without truly wanting to know, fearing blandness. The goatee, with its attendant moustache, was well-drawn on his face, brought his weak chin forward and gave him a distinction confirmed by his sense of dress. So there he was, a bourgeois convert in spite of a stubborn taste for cut glass and knick-knacks. His signature though, with dashing twists and volutes, seemed extravagant: who was he hiding? Tested further, he described himself curiously as 'horribly loyal' and I discovered later what he meant: to the point of torture in his self-denial.

It suited him well to have worked for the Liberal Party at election times, he was the epitome of the happy medium, pleasant and reassuring to all. My friends liked him, which was just as well as he merely had acquaintances. He blended easily everywhere, a chameleon, and if he applied himself it was seemingly without effort, he knew the nature of the flow.

This was not passion, thankfully, I could not bear the damage. We went for walks on the Heath and he held my hand, gazed at me and laughed with me. Those times were peaceful and good. I had such a feeling of achievement that I felt I should be content, I had reached my goal, it would be silly and reckless to be more difficult: I was not exploited, suffered no put-downs, Paul's love was sincere and his affection cheerful, undemanding. When he eventually moved into my house – we agreed he would rent his and participate in all expenses – it took place without foreboding, hitches or groans, and Sophie who was very fond of him accepted him easily. Contentment reigned, which was just lucky as the squatters had recently been evicted from next door and a Jamaican family had moved in.

The weeks and months slipped by in harmony, we even went on holidays to France which fulfilled in me so many cravings: my France, my land, my people, language and food, my sun! What was more, I was part of a couple at last. No more lamenting about loneliness, other people going places together, leaving me behind. We inhabited the planet like other families, were entitled to the same pleasures and freedoms. It made me feel promoted, freed from exclusion. As much as he tried to please me, I also wanted to please him: his devotion was precious to me and deserved more that appreciation: gratitude, for if this man treated me well, it meant I thought more highly of myself.

A year on, my application for a sabbatical was accepted by my school and my relief was profound. I had worked fifteen years for that American School without any rewards other than financial. Indeed it had been a very tough ride, as bullying was rife. Added to the jealousy and pettiness of some colleagues, one of whom seemed at times demented in her obsessive desire to harm me, I had suffered severe harassment from my principal who seemed to find cat-and-mouse games irresistible: vague expressions of 'people are talking', 'there have been some complaints', 'I need to talk to you, come and see me at the end of *next* week', 'some parents have expressed concerns', were destined to panic and destabilise me. None of it was confirmed by the classroom teachers, in fact they denied it, as they would have been the first ones to know. When, at the end of my tether, I went to cry and complain to the headmaster, I found support: my principal was spoken to, obviously sharply since he didn't talk or even look at me for the next two and a half years. I had become invisible to him, and this, added to the feeling of exclusion that living in a ghetto engendered, made me feel quite unreal at times. I knew that feeling well.

A year of freedom was more than welcome. I had chosen to do a Certificate of Psychology at London University (Birkbeck College), just about feasible in a year if I did not let up, and it was wonderful to feel intelligent again, I was getting my brain back. It had not completely disappeared: for some years now, trying to exorcise my demons, I had been writing poetry: outpourings of sadness and fears, where I revisited my childhood home, lack of love, tyranny and the stubborn loneliness that never left me.

Paul, who had seen some of my poems, was appalled:

– You write about horrible things!

Not that he would ever let himself feel his own childhood miseries. To hear him, his family was 'very nice', his mother 'lovely', his older brother 'okay' and his younger sister 'a darling'. He rarely mentioned his father, and it was true to say that Paul saw little of him as a young boy since his father went to war when he was seven, only to return long after the hostilities were over, having in the meantime been sent to South Africa – 'because he liked army life'.

Paul jumped into his father's shoes, becoming his mother's 'little husband', supplanting his older brother who may have had other concerns or needs at the time. He ran errands, fetched and carried, looked in on older neighbours, made himself useful and pleasant, won lots of praise and blossomed. Those were golden years.

He was thirteen when one day his father returned, welcomed with open arms by his beloved wife. As his parents had ears and eyes only for each other, his world was turned upside down. Paul found himself suddenly demoted, relegated to the role of a young child who was getting in the way and told to go out and play with his friends. He never said he was pleased to see his father again, they might have felt strangers to each other; whatever his feelings, he would have been on his best behaviour since it was not the time to lose the credit accumulated over all those years, but the wounding would have been profound, as his repression of it. When a baby sister was born a year later, he became the little father, he knew the ropes.

His sister was indeed very sweet and the bonds I witnessed between them were those of true affection but his father was seldom mentioned, it was obvious that there was a reluctance there, a reserve. Paul had learned the hard way how to be 'horribly loyal'.

We toyed with the idea of marriage, or at least I did, Paul declaring himself 'perfectly committed'. I felt him to be so, but I liked the idea, it flattered and gratified me. And we stood one day in a good modern jeweller's shop, as Paul had declared that he wanted to buy me a 'nice' ring. Not having had an engagement ring before – Johan was too poor and we did not, in those unconventional times, care about 'those things' – I was delighted: an opal simply mounted on burnished silver edged with gold looked unusual and stylish. As I tried it on, I recalled becoming vaguely aware, – as if the truth was being whispered in my ear and I was pretending not to hear – that I was being, not really devious, but certainly not truthful, when I asked him:

"Do you mind – do you mind if the ring is for my middle finger? I really like rings on my middle finger…" knowing it wouldn't look like an engagement ring this way.

As I dissembled, he reassured me with a smile that he didn't mind at all.

Kindness, in its odd way, ensured too many silences, surreptitiously built up its own walls, and the habit of it increasingly forbade it should be broken: we, each of us, were on our best behaviour, Paul because he had built himself such a strong and stubborn persona that he couldn't function any other way, and me because I was trying to preserve a dream. The dream of love was demanding, it had built-in criteria that needed to be fulfilled, and each unmet demand was a cause of anguish.

I had been alone, or at least the only grown-up, for too long – ten years – and I yearned for exchange if not debate, at least some adult conversation. But although Paul and I got on 'perfectly well' and life was 'nice and cheerful', I was drowning in platitudes, as nothing original or even personal ever passed his lips. As a teenager I had silently railed against my father's intellectual poverty and his readiness to agree with other people's views and arguments. With Paul, I again revisited the world of the bland, the dull, the commonplace, the cliché... I told myself the man was kind, decent, tried to reason with my impatient heart: Paul at least, unlike Jeremy, had chosen goodness, correctness, and lived comfortably in that persona. Surely, I should be grateful? I had been hoping that being fond would bridge the gap between needing and loving, but it brought other needs without giving the comfort of being at one with myself or with him. I had wished to fit in that mould where wisdom and resignation meet and survive, giving warmth and receiving care, protection and belonging, feeling the feelings that I should, but no manner of wishing would stem my old longings for being what I am, not what I should...

"You don't have to agree with me all the time!" I exclaimed, only half amused one day.

"I have no problem agreeing with you," he replied calmly.

"You know what you are, Paul?" I tried to joke. "You're a labrador."

He smiled:

"Yes," he agreed again, "I am."

I had a vision of a lovely black dog with his head on my lap, his eyes looking up at me, watching my every expression and movement, his whole being submissive, waiting for me to offer, at my pleasure: 'walkies?'

One winter evening, as we watched a moving television programme about a men's group who attempted to access and define their inner pain and share their feelings around a camp fire, I waited for something to stir in him, something real, raw and true, but it evoked nothing except another platitude. Exasperated, I stood up and left the room but he rushed after me, caught up with me at the bottom of the stairs and seized my arm forcefully:

"You can do what you like to me, you can hit me, insult me, abuse me, but do not ignore me!" He spoke passionately, in anguish, begging, other, true.

I shook him off and went upstairs, insisting I was dreadfully sleepy.

Living with Paul was like applying a poultice on a sore chest; what haunted me before he came on the scene was still there, but in his presence anxieties seemed attenuated or at least did not have the leisure to haunt me so. My studies occupied most of the day most days of each week, and there were always deadlines to for essays. I was stimulated by the variety of topics and encouraged by my results. Becoming confident, I could laugh at my mother's repeated anxieties on the telephone:

"But what if you fail? What will happen if you fail?" True to say that she may remember my many failures at university and wildly irregular school results, but these, to me, were far away in the past. I was in a different 'place' and failing was not an option, but still her image of me seemed to have changed little if at all. I replied, irritated:

"But I am NOT going to fail!"

The strong scientific slant of my course did not satisfy me fully, as it could be very arid: nothing relating to human feeling and experience seemed to have any validity, when it got a look in. Psychologists were badly anxious for their field to be seen as a science, the only way to obtain the government grants they needed for their survival. So Psychology had been trimmed, thinned, pruned, while the study of psychoanalysis, considered woolly, represented but a small section of the course. I wanted more of it. So I took an extra course: an attendance certificate will be the only recognition but it went to the core of my leanings and, I felt, aptitude:

'Counselling skills for individual and group work.' The tutor was excellent and I felt engaged, involved at last. It opened horizons. Having been in group therapy for two years after Sophie's birth, I valued the work and wondered if I might take this further.

Finally, in June, exams loomed and I passed with honours, feeling vindicated. This was new: action never used to coincide with passion: it was arrested by a familiar mental paralysis, an impotence which saw and hated itself; a discontent definitely not divine but instead terribly human, when merely being alive was insufficient, required its own proof and could produce none. This yearning was now set in motion, knew it had room to play. The word 'no" was no longer an absolute but a relative notion. The core of this desire was full of pain but its engine was alive with anger, violent in its need.

At the same time, it was tense with foreboding. There was an Alphonse Daudet tale that used to make me shiver when I was young: 'Monsieur Seguin's goat'. Monsieur Seguin had a she-goat that he was very fond of. She was, in fact, his favourite goat for she had great character. He kept her near his house in an enclosure that the animal frequently tried to destroy in her attempts to break free, for she was a young, lively and proud little goat, who looked at the green hills and darker mountains beyond and knew she wanted the liberty to live wild in those forests; she could not bear to be tethered to such a small existence. Monsieur Seguin had tried many times to reason with her: 'There are wolves in these mountains, they are evil when they are hungry and they are often hungry, can't you hear their howls at night?

You would not survive!' 'But these wolves are free,' thought the little goat, 'and I want to be free too…!' And day after day, while grazing, she contemplated the far-away landscape beyond where animals could roam free. One night, after many attempts, she was at last successful when the fence gave way at its weakest point. Surprised at the vastness of the space around and beyond her, she galloped towards the hills, elated, reaching the forest in the middle of the night. She stopped for a rest, lying for a while at the foot of a tree. The night was cool and the thick foliage of the forest seemed to offer shelter, until a siren-like howl soared among the trees not far away, and she trembled as she jumped to her feet. When the wolf came closer, she was ready to fight: and fight she did, till morning, with her horns and with her hooves. She knew the battle was uneven, the odds against her. The wolf was aware of it too and did not let up. And although she saw that she would be killed, she also knew that she was brave and that her fight would be the measure of her. At least she would die free. And when dawn came, finally she lay down.

The story made me shiver still. I knew I had embarked on a journey without a map, the signs being merely the feelings that took me there rather than here, guiding my steps. They had to coincide with what I could remember of the past, it would be a hesitant enterprise. Giving up on it was not an option but if I did not want to risk altering anything, neither did I want to accept an interpretation because it suited a theory or simply soothed my mind. The path I had followed since childhood had always been to separate falsehood from truth, fantasy from fact, in order that my life have some sanity. Now the time had come, because I felt such grief inside, to confront the past. I had no choice: articles about child sex abuse cases accumulated on my desk. I was reading, hypnotised, the details of the tortures inflicted on little children, knowing I knew what it felt like, and the mix of horror and pain devastated me. There was a huge fight ahead and I did not know if I would survive it.

Why couldn't life be the way it sometimes seemed in my house? Peaceful, pleasant, with a delightful, intelligent and lively child, a kind man, a cat, a garden...

One day, Paul decided to shave his beard and I couldn't stand it: his new face, the real one, bore no resemblance to what it was before, merely accentuated the very small eyes, the ruddy peasant complexion. I did not know this man: Paul had disappeared. With his beard he had drawn style and personality on his face, a kind of handsomeness, but also his need to be 'other'. Now there was nothing left but a blank canvas, a place almost devoid of character, a bland and anxious child so eager to please he had forgotten about himself. I could not bear to look at him, and when I urged him to grow his beard back, of course, he complied. Added to the fact that Paul had no body smell whatsoever, it had unsettled me. I had always found his odourlessness peculiar, as if he had left something behind as he grew up; or washed it off for fear that a genuine smell would betray and reveal him, a danger he couldn't contemplate since he made little room in him for the real and the true. It had made physical embraces of less consequence – incorporeal, they left me less involved.

Now even his kindness had become an irritant, so much did it smack of submissiveness, and I could not love a man who defined himself as a lesser being, an inferior.

"Really, Paul!" I exclaimed one day after yet another 'as you like, I don't mind'. "I wonder at times if it is blood you have in your veins or merely water!"

207

Chapter Twenty-one

Odile has announced she is returning to France after eighteen years in Canada. Mother confirms it is for good and frets in anxious expectation, for she imagines her visit to be immediate, full of joyful tears and loving reconciliation: the return of the prodigal child. Poor Mother lives so close to her hopes that she is endlessly devastated by their default: after her long absence Odile is now failing to materialise, writes from the North of France that she will see her later, she has priorities: finding work in a religious organisation where she may find lodgings as well.

Meeting her again would be momentous I knew, and was at once relieved, curious and concerned: at last I would no longer be the only one responsible for seeing Mother, and Odile might share with me details of her personal journey? But I was also anxious about our relationship: the letter I sent her last year warning her to face up to her duty and stop acting so holy, was possibly too brutal? What if her infuriatingly pious good wishes were well meant?

I had seen her entering religion nine years previously as a climax of glorified ill-ease and repression. She wanted to be good, accepted, recognised. She wanted to be healed and asked God for that gift. She might have felt unloved because she must be bad, had been bad, and so had to be punished.

She would have to: I knew *'they'*, the so-called religious, would make her atone for ever for her sins. Poor Odile, I knew she was not bad and I could imagine her pain, it ate her up, giving her a sense of existing which justified her in her own eyes and appalled me because she had become its prey.

What could she have done with all that pain? Buried it? I doubted it, it was too vast, too raw. 'Offered it up to God', I supposed, in the light of her religious commitment: this was what they told you about in stories of the saints and their martyrs, their self-imposed deprivations, inner conflicts and torments. This is also what the nuns had taught us at convent school. I hadn't been exempted, of course. I had at times in childhood immersed myself in holy surrender when God was the only solution offered to the search for meaning and solace, and my young heart had soared towards the great love that fulfils all. I recall the occasion when, ill with tonsillitis at the age of twelve or thereabouts, I was writing in bed about my sufferings, offering my sore throat up to God... . Mother, who had been sitting at the bottom of my bed to keep me company, had smacked her lips in irritation at being left out of my religious experience and let out:

"Oh! You annoy me so much when you do that!"

When Odile and I finally met in Mother's flat on that late winter morning I was shocked at her appearance. She was extremely thin, but the more remarkable feature of her body was its stiffness, her back seemingly obeying a rule of moral rectitude which had to find its physical equivalent. It never bent, never slouched, never relaxed. The same effort was visible on her face which used to be pleasant if diffident but was now still and expressionless as if any facial movement risked showing an indulgence of disallowed feelings. Her mouth, quite thin, at times made attempts at smiling, which her eyes denied. Her skin, exposed to too much sun in the past, was now thick and lined. I was astonished to sense so much fear in her. It touched me, hurt me, threatened me too, recalling many forgotten fears of mine.

I welcomed her with a kiss and a smile:

"Hello, Odile, I am so pleased to see you."

Not a word in reply, but she turned to Sophie who was a neutral if perplexed witness and greeted her kindly. Her coldness towards me soon prompted me to give up my attempts to reach her. She was supposed to have come four days previously but on postponing her arrival without explanation, had simply and bluntly commented:

"You'll manage fine without me."

Now she was here the family was complete, though a painful atmosphere of divorce prevailed.

Mother would sleep on the living-room couch, she said, offering Odile her own bedroom – Sophie and I shared the second bedroom – but to her chagrin my sister had already arranged to spend the night at a nearby convent. Crushed, mother fretted in the kitchen in preparation for lunch. After a while, wondering about Odile's silence, she went and knocked at her bedroom where she had been resting:

"Would you like some lunch, darling?"

"I want peace!" Odile shouted back angrily. Mother whispered to me sadly:

"Your sister is mad but we must help her."

I pointed out that, unfortunately, it was impossible to help people who did not want help; Odile would have to be aware that she needed it in the first place – she would have to break down first, I thought. We could only be there if she needed us: that was all we could do.

I wondered if both Mother's and my own fears had deprived us of what little imagination and courage was needed: we could have sat her down, held her hands – why did I balk at the thought? – and said: we can see your fears and your pain, there must be a way out of this, you need help and we are ready to give it. But how could she have accepted, even listened? We were ourselves sources of that pain. Still, if her past filled her with horror and anguish as it did me, wouldn't she have to do something about it – and save herself?

Having to be welcoming regardless of her conduct made me feel wise to a point but it was difficult to know what would have irritated her least and elicited the best response: mother depended on it, demanded it, and I couldn't after all have adopted a lukewarm, reserved, stance without being accused of hostility although it might have given my sister more room. I wanted peace too, and was hard put to know how to react as I asked if she had found a job:

"What makes you think I am looking for a job?" she replied sharply.

During lunch Odile adopted a tone of voice in the 'heavenly' mode, high-pitched and so soft you had to lean towards her to hear, and at that very moment she would jerk away from you as if you were trespassing on her space. The moment Mother asked her to repeat, saying: "pardon?" and wary of the aggression behind that softness, Odile shouted her reply at full volume as if the poor woman was deaf, forcing her to jump back in fright and humiliation.

We went to my cousin's later for an afternoon visit – we needed buffers – where Odile's voice was normal again: she spoke animatedly, in a friendly if not quite relaxed manner. The conversation was strange, balletic almost, a multiple exchange between my cousin, her husband, their daughter, mother, Odile and myself, except that my sister acted as if Mother and I were absent. I didn't infringe that edict in case 'things' became obvious and unpleasant. The other participants, unavoidably aware of the state of play between us, behaved impeccably and moved between and around us with great skill: complicated families become adept at these games, a surrealistic mixture of ping-pong and hide-and-seek.

At least we would be spared a repeat performance of the last time, many years previously, Odile and I had shared a bedroom when, getting ready to go to bed, she came out of the bathroom to comply with our old family training and kiss Mother and me goodnight, but that gesture had a sting in the tail: she had covered her lined face with some thick oily cream, compelling us to kiss her greasy cheeks – defiance and punishment all at once; Mother and I were being summoned to submit, the alternative being too frightful to contemplate.

I understood Mother's feelings and even found relief listening to her; we were for a brief moment allies, and it took her attention away from me. Her present concern was Odile's thinness which I agreed looked worrying: "I know she sometimes goes on fasts, you see, to mortify the flesh, but she may be taking it a bit far! And I was so concerned by her recent bronchitis: she told me she had been lying face down in prayer in the church's aisle, for three hours! I spoke about it to my parish priest, and he said: 'But you know, Madame Dufresne, some religious have a very strong calling, and it may seem a bit extreme, but it could be she is one of them…' I'm sure that's when she caught that bronchitis, church floors are so cold! I just don't know what to do about her, I feel really lost…" She mortifies her flesh, she hates her flesh: the thought appalled me. 'They' will have kept on shaming her for her past ordeal, made her feel dirty, soiled, for having been the tragic victim of a criminal, and locked her in an endless cycle of mortification and expiation with forgiveness an elusive goal: there would have been little compassion or support but harshness and endless reminders of her sin, as if they had attached it to her. Now her poor thin body merely evoked her privations and sufferings. I saw she had merely exchanged the family tyranny for religious incarceration, with no possibility of a rational Exit. If there was any fulfilment in it for her she would be at peace at least, and it would show.

Later on, in bed, I felt almost grateful to have been sent to board at convent school, it gave me the opportunity to rebel – in my quiet way – against something new: the nuns' hypocrisy, their petty rules and intense sexual obsessions. Giving us bad food had been the least of their sins in my view, but their lack of kindness was evident, I could see they didn't like young people at all, we were too alive to the world. Terrified of sin – having obliterated sex from their lives but incapable of excluding it from their thoughts if their sensations and dreams happened to remind them of it, those sad women lived in disgust of their own bodies: we knew the nun in her bedroom at the end of our dormitory switched the light off before washing herself at night in order not to succumb to any evil thoughts, and we had fits of giggles under our sheets when we heard her drop the soap, imagining her big naked soapy body crawling on the floor in attempts to grasp it.

I was having nightmares again: this new bolt out of the blue, this sick dream, where did it come from? I was used to missing life-saving trains or having to teach in front of an empty classroom before sharp-eyed colleagues, but this one, so realistic, so close to my past: Odile was assuring me that she and René-Jacques had loved each other and she could prove it: she had kept the sweet notes they sent each other; she could show them to me, he had never loved me, she assured me with glee. I was horrified, disbelieving, surely she was tricking me, taking away from me the dearest thing in my past. I would have to check, I should ask Mother, she had his letters, but then I remembered she didn't want to give them back to me...

Chapter Twenty-two

Reading my Counselling course diary a few months after I started it brought surprise and even astonishment, as if the person reading it could see beyond the words the truer language of the one who wrote it. This is as it should be, no doubt, all of us in the group had changed, even the ones who would not talk, would not share – and some of the people who talk had now stopped saying they had a happy childhood, so there was a reason they were here. For my part, a lot had happened. I had meant it to, and I was glad to be unable to control the change: it carried me, held me and finally revealed me. And although the process was painful, it was no more painful than before – only, usefully, the wounds were clearer.

Our family histories, the history of our development – or lack of it – held the front of the stage, and later, through the group work we performed, we mirrored the relationships, struggles, conflicts and anxieties born in the family, replaying them ad nauseam with each other until we could see ourselves not merely more objectively, but also with a measure of self-love or at least compassion. This could be a tall order.

However, we all had undertaken this course, this venture, because, acknowledged or not, there was a tall order, a high command of a kind. We might not have recognised it at first, but just as the child grows tall and learns to walk and play, it was willing itself in us, developing and demanding a voice.

Already the first day had given an inkling of what was to come. Although I felt quite calm and composed if curious, I saw myself fail in several ways: when my turn came to introduce my neighbour to the larger group, I 'missed' the death of her older son, probably because it reminded me of the death of my own baby which I hadn't disclosed. I had told her the least significant things about myself, which made me look as if I just wanted out of teaching because I was 'sick of it', so was introduced in a way that wasn't doing me justice and it was entirely my own doing.

How could I have said: 'The thoughts that fill me are all about the sufferings of children, I cry at anything these days, my heart is shaken by freak waves of horror, anger, and sorrow that are breaking me. There is too much pain in the world and I am afraid to succumb to it'? How could I? I had always felt groups to be potentially hostile, always critical, dismissive of me. Besides, these people were strangers.

We may all have felt threatened, for there was, in our first 'Personal Growth' group, a distinct feeling of frustration, impatience and aggression which directed itself at Mike, the group leader: the group needed him to introduce himself, reassure us, conduct pleasant conversation, make us feel cared for. We wanted to be led, shown a direction, and got none of it. Because I laughed, knowing the 'game', I received sharp, angry looks from J and knew she would attack me one day. Finally, under duress, Mike spoke of us as being in 'an open situation'. "Like a family reunion at Christmas!" I offered. And so we turned our frustrations on each other, and it was fairly unpleasant but interesting.

Over the next few sessions I imagined being in turns superior and inferior because I felt threatened by my isolation. I was objectively no more isolated than anyone else in the group, but felt extremely alone. There was protection there – the nature of the course was necessarily caring, benevolent – I would come to no harm, I would survive. Why was I feeling so alone? Why was I always feeling so alone? It was such an old feeling...

Of the many exercises we did, trying to be non-judgmental was the hardest. I could not think how it was possible at first, surely we all judged, all the time, spontaneously at that, and people who claimed not to were fooling themselves. I could see the value of the exercise in making us aware that we were always judgmental, in what manner, why we were, and how this could get in the way of first seeing and then accepting others as *they* were. I felt mostly benevolent towards others: wasn't that sufficient protection against discrimination? May be not: after all, some very hard people think themselves kind. There was something else going on in me, though, that I couldn't at first define, an anxiousness, then, surely, a panic at being asked to suspend judgement, to suspend thought, almost to not exist – the old commandment. It was going against everything that had kept me alive, if often silent: questioning, judging, because I had been forbidden to think, query, question, judge, too many unbearable challenges to my mother's existence and rule. I had nearly drowned, a silent ghost. No more.

Whether one believes in Freud or not, it would be difficult not to believe in the process of transference. I had long been aware of the phenomenon, which in turns amused and distressed me by its persistence – but then that is its role, to needle and nag the conscious mind until it takes notice. I took notice. Any group is a good playground for it to appear and disrupt. Sure enough, the younger French woman in my group, Sophie, is one of my mind's partners, unbeknown to her. A compatriot, she will do as a sister substitute: already, in my head, I have several times called her Odile. There are obvious things in common: motherland, upbringing, learnt social and moral values. But there is a double game at play there: I have, at times, unwillingly, secretly, been calling my daughter Sophie 'Odile' in my mind for years. This had started many years previously as a distant echo from the past, and forgetting had long secured safety. But these echoes had started to make themselves heard, first faintly, then with a louder and more consistent rhythm. The name 'Odile' had appeared, often superimposed on that of my daughter when I thought of her or addressed her. That my sister had lived in Canada for the last eighteen years and could therefore have been easily ignored seemed to matter little: what takes place in the mind ignores distances and boundaries, and it was drawing circles around me which made me slightly dizzy at first, as if I was caught in a spooky game of hide and seek.

Unsettled by that sly assault of the past, I soon decided to stop and listen. That slip-of-the-thought was warning me, pointing something to my attention. I felt that maybe the stresses of being a single parent and the necessity of putting a child's interests first must be reminiscent of those early childhood days when my baby sister burst upon my world and seemed to take up all the space, the attention, and there was none left for me. I could see the transference, understood it clearly, accepted the inevitable conflict, admired the psychological symmetry, took note, took care.

Does understanding put problems at rest? If it didn't, in this case, could it be that I was wrong or that there was possibly so much more than appeared, for the unrelenting pressure of 'hearing' her name in my head was amplified when, sometime last autumn, and a few weeks after my sister had returned to France, it seemed possible that we might meet at last.

When French Sophie took her turn and mentioned that she had chosen for her daughter a local convent school, I reacted with instant anger, pain, and disappointment. I reflected on this later and it took me back: I must have been shattered to be sent away from home to boarding school at fourteen. If I had been allowed to feel it, I would have felt it; I could feel it now. I shared my new thoughts with the group: although I was sent to convent school while Odile had remained at home, it is she who had become a nun, in a parallel exile. I explained that ten years previously, while still in Canada, she took the Holy Orders – so she may now justifiably, I joked, be holier-than-thou, as scoring points had often in childhood been the order of the day. Now, taking Holy Orders ordered order, certainty, a clear place in the world, a safe slot.

As I debated some of these questions in my group and admitted my fears I was met with a heavy silence, followed by platitudes: 'families can be tricky' and more loud silences. Talking of my previous therapy after the birth of my daughter, I became aware of enormous resistance in the group. Sophie hesitantly said she would undergo therapy if it was necessary but would rather not as it frightened her, she didn't want to change – she knew 'someone who changed', and would rather not question things. J added that when something bothered her, she tried to put it right out of her mind.

I was appalled, in a state of raging contempt. I wanted to leave the group, escape this dull prison: who were these shallow people who wanted to be counsellors? These very hurt people who couldn't see their own pain? My own survival had totally depended on change. I knew that if you didn't change, you died.

I dared to challenge them to let go of their fears and grow.

By the next session, having given my group up for dead

and with no time to waste, I had found myself a therapist. I always felt time to be short, I had work to do.

Fears were many and came out in the group, the opportunities were there! G was viciously beaten by her father as a child. She left home but her mother stayed, putting up with all kinds of bad treatments. C, a Portuguese, called the woman 'very brave' with what looked like respect. Even though J summarised her own feelings comically, exclaiming: "I think she's a wimp!" I saw red. I have cut out of the newspaper that very day an article which made me quite sick, about the Pope's exhortations to Croatian (Catholic) women raped by Serbs and forcibly made pregnant: he hailed women's special gift of acceptance and forgiveness as a healing force and inspiration in our world, and urged these defiled and brutalised women to forgive their rapists and bear these children, keeping and nourishing in them the seeds of hatred. That's how you subjugated women: physically and emotionally by raping them; psychologically, by confusing them in their desire to be good and redeemed, and giving them a goal that makes them more acceptable to the views of a religious hierarchy which thrived on their exclusion. Being brave would be to see this and take a stand, not take more beatings! I seethed.

I was feeling worse, feeling too much, plumbing the depths. I was the witness of many brutal happenings in my neighbourhood, and the confidante and sometimes helper of my own abused neighbours. Dealing with some of this myself in my own therapy made me feel quite raw, giving me a feeling of urgency to heal in others what was hurting me so much. I didn't feel I could tell my group so spoke too long and too often, of Anita, the single mother who was beaten as a child, later raped herself; how she used to beat her son as a little baby, and now, having given up blows, screamed at him, a seven-year-old, as if he was her worst enemy; of Rosa, who was, as a little child, rejected by her mother, sexually abused by her grandfather, brothers and sister, used as their dustbin; of Jenny with whom many men in her grandparents' lodging house interfered when she was four years old.

The horror of what I described disturbed, and the fact that I was talking about others – hiding behind them – irritated greatly. J attacked me with scorn and malice: "One more of your stories, you should write a Mills and Boons..." Two or three others joined in, contemptuous. T's eyes were flaring and that silly grin had left his face – now, *that* was more real! They obviously enjoyed bringing me down a peg or two. Why should I trust groups? Our tutor saw through it though, and as I raged at them at the beginning of the next session, accusing them of malice, cruelty and blindness, he intervened to declare that he had never come across anger such as mine without it being justified. They were stunned into silence.

Such isolation again, such exile. Here I was, a French woman in England working in an American school, twice removed from belonging anywhere and feeling an alien in the group also. Come to think of it, I had felt an alien in France too, when I lived there: French society had seemed to me too structured, attached to conventions – bound by conventions – too materialistic. The freedom to be myself I had found here in London and had explored ways of being that suited me, shedding old skins. I was a long way from the shy, self-conscious child who had dreams straight out of Jack London books in her head.

But of course I wasn't, I was still very close to her. I was very alone in my family too, either because I wasn't supposed to have an existence of my own, or because, having a brain in spite of everyone, I had felt the only one to have one – either exile or splendid isolation, both ways you lose – closeness, identity, hope – so that's where the loneliness came from...

While I had given God up as untrustworthy and improbable as part of my growing-up process, Camus and Sartre, with Existentialism, had found an open door in me. I belonged to the post-war generation of which they were gurus, leading intellectual beacons, but nevertheless offering deserts to the soul. Camus at least loved our physical world, but I could see how harmful Sartre in particular was; some young people gave up on life, even committed suicide after reading his work: what is responsibility in a vacuum? Not enough for some. I was very familiar with the feelings of Camus's *The Outsider*, endlessly wishing to be dead. But was it an intellectual condition, this alienation? Or, I questioned now, was I the product, more simply, of a generation who, having dared question, then refute the idea of God after a second exhausting war, was incapable of living purposefully because our upbringing had provided us with little nourishment, recognition and nurture? Was Existentialism conceivable, I wondered, in cultures where children's existence was given due acknowledgment and celebration?

When I thought of my sister's face, a frozen mask of self-loathing, hurt and fear, I shivered: so this is what they have done to you, what they have done to me... . It horrified and haunted me. She had chosen a path that aimed to heal and it had given her no peace. But when I thought of my own lovely Sophie, her ease at being, talking, joking, when I saw her confident and happy face, I could see I had at last begun to 'balance the books'.

Chapter Twenty-three

Among so many cloudy images of childhood haphazardly thrown back by memory, like unfinished phrases, a place name lingered: Couledoux. I knew I had been there. Years later, I asked Mother: she said it was for the country air: I had been ill, and needed it to recover.

I remembered vaguely a landscape defined by a mass of green, large grey stones in the green, a blanket of blue sky; the silence. I remembered the deepest bed ever, made of feathers and every morning the strangeness of large bowls and coarse bread. For a long time I thought I had been there on my own – the old feeling – but Mother assured me she had been there too, and my sister. I realised it must be true when I saw myself running to her after watching the farmer beat his screaming cat to death in the yard. The animal was sick, they said. It took a long time to die. She said they do these things in the countryside. Mostly, I remembered her silence, echoed by mine. I would try to play except that I never knew how to play. Did we make daisy chains? Find crickets? I saw nothing, felt nothing. Later, the name of the hamlet was never mentioned. I know it was a funny name:

Couledoux: 'Liveasy'. As if we could, ever. And since I knew that she hated the countryside, why would we go to the countryside since we already lived in the bloody countryside? After, my father would look at her slyly. She would return his gaze, resigned. I felt I knew that we had been running away.

As my therapy – my quest – developed, I told Ella, my American therapist, everything I remembered. It was a fact that practically everything I remembered was 'telling'. Even what I did not remember might be telling so there was little vacuum, really: who looked after Odile and me during the weeks Mother was away to spas in Thonon-les-Bains one year and Italy another year for her arthritis? She wrote, even telephoned occasionally, brought back presents and pretty sweets. Father would have been home in the evenings and at weekends. I don't know… I see no-one, no face, recall no event. There is a stubborn silence.

My close friends were 'telling', particularly Josy whose mother used to severely beat her and her sisters. The teachers and the relatives knew, saw the bruises, did nothing. She shaved Josy's head once to teach her not to be vain when the ten-year-old child was 'caught' admiring her own blond hair in the mirror. ("That was a good lesson," Josy says cheerfully now, "I never spent long in front of a mirror after that!") She once threw away all the girls' toys because their bedroom was untidy. The father never intervened.

But the more 'telling' people in my life now were those sexually abused women who gravitated around me and who showed no surprise or shock when I said I thought it might have happened to me too. They took it as a given, talked of karma, as if they had deserved their fate by being bad in a previous life: so this life is their hell. I refused this for myself, but could see they found it easier to bear if it was their own fault: they were not merely suffering, they were expiating, so there was justice after all… I was horrified. Should I have protected myself against such intrusions? How could I? I did not even see them as such, I was on a roll.

And these new nightmares, these men undressing in a room, getting ready for little children… and the children standing there, waiting, uncomprehending. If I was in the dream, I made sure to wake up in time, rigid with shock and anguish. How I hated men… I couldn't think of my father's body without disgust, his hot skin, his touch, his breath. Yet I remembered nothing, I say to Ella, nothing 'concrete', I was talking with the memory of a little child, it was different, impressionistic, fluid. But I still stopped breathing if I was too close to people, I couldn't have the intrusion of their smell, their breath, particularly men's – unless I felt desire, when it was *my* choice.

When still an adolescent, I had read in a rare magazine article a list of the characteristics of the typical male sexual abuser: a loner; a man incapable of showing affection; a repressed individual, closed in and sly; often professing strict principles, hiding under the guise of a respectable profession, etc. Strange, just like Dad, I thought, and promptly forgot about it. 'These things' were not talked or written about in those days. It would take the late eighties and the explosions of Cleveland, the Orkney Islands, the Children's Homes run by Frank Beck and others, not to forget nursery schools in Tyneside, or even churchyards… . Britain had ratified the United Nations Convention on the Rights of the Child and the Catholic Church – through the device of confession better informed than most (Helmut Karle, former Head of Psychiatry for Lewisham & North Southwark, notes that an eighteenth-century Vatican survey found that the most confessed sin was incest) – had yet to make abuse of children a cardinal sin, preferring instead to seek insurance cover to deal with future liabilities…

I wondered, I asked Ella, if I should write to Odile to see

if she remembered anything that could be helpful? "Why not?" she replied, maintaining professional distance.

The prospect of writing to Odile, for some reason, seemed easier now that she has returned home. I had increasingly yearned for France myself these last few years, cursed the obligations that directed my visits should only be to Bordeaux since Mother lived there, the rest of the country off limits. My friends worked and had themselves demanding family lives, there was no other choice. A past holiday in France with Paul and Sophie had confirmed the acuteness of my loss together with my revived bonds. I had given up a great deal in order to be free of family chains; unwanted exile was weighing heavily on me now and feeding into mounting resentment: was it the same for Odile? Hadn't she made a parallel journey and returned to reconnect with her roots?

It seemed there were movements of time where we both belonged. Consciousness had no part in it, nor will, and accident was something I regarded with suspicion. There we both were, I in need, she in deed, wanting to come back from abroad after decades of protective exile. We wished to make contact with what we knew and what was us, the nearly dried-up roots of our beginnings, before it was too late to say: this was me, and this is me still – and our yearning was great… Was it what she felt? Was it born of decision, a conquest? Or were we walking, hypnotised, along pre-ordained patterns of time like puppets on a web of strings acting a ritual, or mimes acting an old act in a circus ring?

Would there be peace now? Could I return to the vast womb of this landscape, its smells, its colours and its shapes in safety? And would we meet one day to see if we shared a language, not just a memory?

The news was that Odile was staying in Brittany in a

religious community where volunteers were trained by priests through religious teachings, exchanges, spiritual guidance, group recitation of the rosary, services, meals, etc. They were giving thanks that month to Father Thierry who, on his return from abroad, described his missionary works, inspiring the volunteers in their future endeavours to go and 'give love' to neglected and abandoned children. These volunteers, mostly young people, came to the Community for a compulsory training of at least two weeks before going to their place of mission.

As Odile seemed to have no money – she had returned from Canada penniless – and she was obliged to give Mother, in exchange for financial help, more details of the purpose of this training; Mother sent me a leaflet describing a typical day at the centre:

6:30 a.m. Start; 7:00 Prayers; 7:45 Breakfast; 8:30 Lectio Divina or teaching; 9:30 Worship of the Holy Sacrament; 10:30 Housework; 12:15 Lunch followed by the rosary, and one hour of free time; 14:45 Study of the languages and countries; 16:45 Teaching to the town's children; 18:15 Vespers and mass with the Brothers; 20:00 Dinner; 20:45 Community evening (witness accounts, guests, videos, relaxation, etc.) 22:00 Evening prayer.

When I next telephoned her one evening to enquire about Odile, Mother replied that my sister had finally admitted having broken her foot a few weeks previously and being in pain. She was very angry and talked fast:

"I have thought the question over thoroughly in my mind, and I am not sending them any money, only F200. You have seen the brochure? They want F2.300 to send these youngsters away to some foreign country. I won't give any more. I haven't got the money anyway but even if I had it, I wouldn't send it. Why should I give them money to have my daughter sent away abroad again? This is what they do, it is insane, a friend of your sister's, a youngster, she was sent to Romania and she came back on a stretcher, to be hospitalized! I have thought about things a great deal and have come to the conclusion that your father and I made serious mistakes in your education. These studies in Spain, studies in England that you wanted, that's done a lot of harm, we should never have given in to you, it's given you the idea of going abroad, that's been a very big mistake…"

I had woken up one afternoon not fully knowing I had slept. Sophie came home early and lay on my bed with the cat, bringing the dream back. Hard to believe it was a dream so much did I feel she had uttered those words: she had told me, in that dream, partly shyly out of a duty to make me aware, and bravely though wary of my reaction: "Paul loves you and cuddles you, but when you aren't in the room he always puts his arms around me, you know." I was aghast. She looked more and more lovely and attractive with her blond hair, her long legs and lovely body. If something happened to her, if Paul couldn't resist her, it would be my fault for telling him about child abuse, it must have aroused him. It would all be my fault. I don't understand… . It's all closing in on me.

But Paul left ages ago, and he loved me, this is just a bad dream.

The day after a session with Ella — a Saturday — Sophie went out with her father. I wanted the day to myself, I needed to go to the cemetery. I hadn't been there for nearly a year and felt ashamed of it. Thomas's tomb — a simple, small, slab with an inscription, propped up by a metal base set into the ground — would be in a poor state, I knew. I remembered the overall messiness, the look of abandonment in spite of the occasional fresh flowers, the weeds and brambles. I think I went because I was afraid that the grave would no longer be there, it could have been bulldozed and larger, fresher graves would have taken its place. I couldn't find it at first and panicked, but it was a few feet away nearly hidden by tall grasses. I pulled the grass off, the weeds, made room around the slab, placed a few daffodils in front of it, a few more on the little girl's tomb which my baby shares, and a few more on the slab of another baby close by. I wondered how many babies were there, all of them still-born, in that communal grave.

On my way out, I stopped by the guard's gate, called out. He came to the car, bent down at my window. I managed to ask: "Near the crematorium, where the still-borns are, it's not going to be destroyed, is it?"

"Where the still-borns are? Oh, no."

I burst into tears. – Don't take away my past, let it be a witness.

I was feeling much stronger after my sessions with Ella. It seemed that the possibility of action, approved, sanctioned, offered a way forward, I could legitimately contemplate it. I could find my power if I had the courage… I had fantasized about telling Mother on the phone: "I am having therapy because there are painful things in my childhood which I need to find out about. You know what people used to believe, that children would forget what had happened to them in their early years? Well, it's not true, they do remember," and see what her reaction would be. Or I would fly to Bordeaux for a couple of days after asking her to help me find the truth. She could lie, of course, she could always lie. But not so much if I said: "I am beginning to remember, and with hypnotherapy I will remember everything, and if you lie to me, I shall never see you again." The scenario made sense.

When, in the middle of a long weekend, Mother's phone

call arrived, I was watching myself for the strength to speak out and found none. Paralysis instead: terrible fear of finding myself caught in her net by the simple mechanism of responding to her emotions by my emotions and being swamped by hers. No wonder I would always pretend things were fine, I was well, Sophie was well, and very little took place that wasn't safe and ordinary. I was making a better job of it than Odile, but it was the same self-protection against the same menace.

I thought again of writing to Odile. Would she be kinder if I asked for her help instead of offering mine, giving her the easier role?

Dear Odile,

I was sorry to hear that you have broken your foot, it must be very painful and inconvenient. I hope you are well looked after and that you are finding the support you need in your community.

I am writing to you mainly to ask for your help, in case your memory is better than mine and could revive it. This is what is happening: for about three years now, I have been increasingly upset by the sufferings of children, the cruelty they suffer at the hands of their parents or those who owe them protection. They talk about it openly and frequently here now. I was affected by it to such an intolerable extent that I understood why it found such echo in me, and started psychotherapy a few months ago.

It seems to me that, of all the forms of violence inflicted upon little children, it is the sexual one which affects me the most, although I do not have any 'objective' memory, only images, sensations, disgusts.

Do you remember anything of your childhood and mine that might enlighten me? Do you know anything? Does 'Couledoux' mean anything to you? If you have the time, tell me what you think.

Love, Hélène.

I was in tears many times that night reading Ferenczi's *Confusion of Tongues between Adults and the Child*. Some unrecognised feelings were overcoming me. It had been quite a day. Apart from the fact that I could not – would not, almost – do my chosen essay: 'Coming Full Circle: from the Drive Theory to the False Memory Syndrome, a History of Denial', I either fell asleep repeatedly as I did the previous day, after reading only a few lines, or went shopping, or found urgent things to do like cleaning, washing (a lot of it was to do with order and cleanliness, I noted). But each time I escaped, I found myself later confronted with what I was running away from: a radio programme on adolescents who sexually abused small children; a television *Panorama* programme that very night, on priests and sexuality, with a big chunk on sexual abuse of children by priests. So I would have to do this essay after all...

I fell asleep later, having come across the word 'baby' in the last chapter I read and thinking of the most wonderful thing in the world to me, a happy baby's smile. In my dream, that smiling baby was holding its arms out to me, and I picked it up to hold and embrace it.

Chapter Twenty-four

Thank goodness for Sophie and the garden, a daily routine, for my job even, with its many trials which all enclosed me in an order that on occasion feels like safety. But I also felt lost and angry. I needed to *do* something, possibly break something, or fight something, and scream, and scream or else my head would explode.

Walking back from the tube one day I noticed in the distance a most incongruous scene: two men were fighting, or rather one large man was punching and kicking a much smaller man, when a tall girl ahead of me just threw herself at them, trying to pull the large man away from the other one. "Bless you!" I thought, and immediately rushed to join her, pulling at the tall man's belt from behind (I am just five foot) while she tried to separate the two men, the smaller one looking quite battered already. Of course they were both drunk, judging from their breaths, and possibly tired already. The big man gave up and staggered away. The small man looked at us and even said thank you, not believing his own eyes. After the tall girl left, an angry passer-by shouted at me: "What business is it of yours?" And I shouted back, at the top of my voice: "Is that the world you want to live in?!"

★

Two or three weeks later I received a letter from Odile. I remember it as a calm letter, without spite or condescension: was it because I depended on her this time, did my suffering bring me closer to her? She remembered no abuse, she replied, sorry she couldn't help me. I forget what she said about Couledoux, nothing significant.

I felt helpless at her lack of any memory, but from the professional literature I read on case histories, I see that it can often take about fifty years for such memories to come to the surface, particularly if the abuse took place in infancy. I am reminded of dead leaves lying half rotten at the bottom of the pond, slowly emerging as mere dark shapes on the surface.

I was in complete disarray. I asked Ella:

– Did I make it all up? At times I think I have, it is all so loose, so intangible. At other times it hits me in the face as if a tree was falling on me, and I haven't a single doubt. And why would I invent it all when it is so painful to even think about? I am not perverse... I often wish I were bad and mad as long as none of this had existed, but reading all those articles, the suffering of all those abused children, I feel I know all about it and it wrecks me. What Fred West did to these girls, it's just unbearable... It makes me want to be sick, and I want to vomit my life...

What did Mother mean when she said "that's how little girls are raped"? "We must forget..." What was it we had to forget? They *do* these things to little children? I had to keep pushing back the limits of horror. Every day more horror. I screamed inside. I didn't want to be part of this world. I knew in so many ways Odile was a parallel image of me, never protected either and now torn apart. I could still remember her shocking passivity in childhood, the hypnotic fascination she must have felt for the man who called all his ways with sex mere manifestations of love

232

instead of a twisted apprenticeship, and the later breaking through violence of her resistance to become what she was intended to be: a compliant prostitute. All these bruises on her poor young body... . Did she protest? Try to fight? Call for help? Try to run away? And now I wondered if she might have broken her foot unconsciously in order not to go to Romania? Was her fear of another catastrophe of the same kind stronger than her desire – her profound need – to help abandoned children?

I read again the leaflet Mother had sent me about the community where Odile was staying and was struck at the intensity of the religious fervour it expressed. It seemed at first extreme, but I was an outsider looking in: it was all-encompassing, filled every thought and every action, every minute of the day and night; a different way of being, and a demanding one; that community was a religious organisation which had the support of the bishop and the full consent of the local vicar; it aimed at promoting bonds between religious and lay people and also between the richest and poorest among them. '*The Virgin Mary is its guide*', it claimed, '*and its members are but instruments of her guidance in caring for children who receive no affection, food or education*.' It described itself as a complement of family life, and rather poignantly, as '*a haven of love for those unloved children*'.

I was irritated by the general tone, though: it reminded me so well of the language of those religious I knew at boarding school who, under the appearance of pious intent had very little love to give to the young girls our parents had put in their care. I had been outraged by their pettiness and hypocrisy; only the nurse-sister had been kind when I was suddenly taken ill with terrible pains from an ulcerated appendix and was rushed to hospital for an emergency operation, the nuns having refused to believe me and call my parents. Was there any love now?

What kind of nun was Odile? I feared she might be quite erratic in her conduct; Mother was doing enough delving herself, trying to stop her from being sent away again just when she thought Odile had returned to live in France and she could have a reasonably normal relationship with her younger daughter. She also seemed terrified of what could happen to Odile 'abroad', in countries 'where they rape women!' she had exclaimed with anguish on the telephone. I was at a loss to make her see sense but at the same time was repulsed by this drama. At her wit's end, she had written to the Mother Superior of a convent Odile visited after her arrival, begging her to take my sister in, but the Mother Superior had replied:

"That would be impossible, Madame, she is so difficult."

This had to be an understatement, I thought, judging from her conduct with both Mother and me; for there is also, more than perceptible under the anger and the pain, an unreason, a warping of normal or at least accepted manners of being, a distortion of logic and reasoning that didn't tally with the norm. She was very unwell, I feared.

"Do you know the latest?" Mother complains another time. "Your sister is accusing me now of harming her in the eyes of her Community, of having written to them about her, she says she senses a change of mood, a distance, and she blames *me* for it! As if I would ever do anything to harm her! It's insane, I don't know what to do, I don't know how to react with her, everything I do is wrong..."

Odile's rage at Mother suggested she might become a possible ally; maybe I could reach her? Her previous letter wasn't hostile at all, almost friendly for once; and she had broken her foot... So I wrote to invite her to stay with Sophie and me in London: would she like to come and visit for five or six days? She telephoned me immediately:

"How is your poor foot?" I asked cheerfully.

"We aren't going to chit-chat about silly things, I hope," she replied harshly. "So you want me to come?"

"Well, yes." I hesitated, alarmed at her tone of voice, "I thought you might like to come and stay with us for four or five days..."

"Ha! It was five or six days before, so next time it'll be three or four days?"

I took fright:

"Look, Odile, if that's the way you feel, maybe it'll be better if we postpone your visit until you feel a little calmer."

I could not cope with her hostility. I'd be good another time, if she let me...

Kentish Town was misbehaving, and as usual now it laid it at my door: the West Indian family next door – Sandra and her five children; Angus, her D.J. boyfriend and father of the youngest – were more than noisy and unruly. It was not just the din of two fridge-sized loudspeakers booming at all hours against my living-room wall ("Angus, could you play me some nice Marvin Gaye for a change?" I tried to humour him). It was the repeated late-nightly screams of Sandra being beaten, which I listened to with my Yugoslav au-pair girl, both of us sitting on the stairs, trying to make sense of the screams. We heard him chase her through the house as she tried to escape, the young girls yelling out and crying.

– Shall I call the police?

– But they won't do anything, it's a 'domestic'... Let's ring them anyway.

The police arrived promptly. We could not see them as the neighbours' front door was around the corner. I braced myself at the prospect of possible repercussions.

The next day, Sandra rang my bell to borrow the lawn-mower again and show me her weals, her bruised face.

"Sandra, does Angus know I call the police?"

"Yes, he does."

"Will it stop him?"

"I don't know…"

"Can't *you* go to the police?"

"No, I can't…"

"I will call the police again next time, Sandra, it's horrible for you and the children."

I was not afraid of Angus: very tall and thin with a face shaped like the steel of a spear and his matted hair tied up straight on top, he looked dramatic, not handsome but striking: right for a club DJ, I supposed. We had spoken a few times on the street and I had often shouted at him to turn the music down. One day I hammered at his door and he finally opened it.

"Angus, for Heaven's sake, turn the noise down! I live next door you know, I can't hear myself think!"

"That's my music, I have to practise."

"You don't have to practise that loud, that's bad behaviour, Angus, no wonder the world is in that state if people like you can't behave!"

"Don't tell me about the state of the world!" he yelled. "That's what I write about in my music!"

"Angus!!" I yelled back. "This is Kentish Town after all – THE WORLD STARTS HERE!" jabbing my finger at the ground between us.

He moved towards me, threatening:

"Don't you fucking tell me what to do, woman! No one fucking tells me what to do!"

He aimed at me, his finger turned up like a blade.

'Don't move,' I told myself coldly, 'or you've had it.' I was not afraid though, he would not touch me. His eyes glared but he stopped. We were quite close now. I did not move, steeled in calmness. Then he turned his back and

236

went home, put his music on again loudly but for a very short time.

I harboured a lot of anger, I knew, but I also felt very strong, fearless. For many months now I had intervened in local incidents. The first one was quite funny to begin with: as I was driving home, a drunk was standing on the road in front of a loaded bus and stroking its engine lovingly, his face ecstatic. The driver, head on his hand, waited for him to finish, mockingly patient. The sports car just in front of mine stopped in the middle of the road, the young muscle-man driver jumping out and throwing a punch at the beggar who flew backwards, hitting his head on the pavement and starting to bleed. I rushed to the driver and pulled his sleeve sharply:

"You idiot, what do you think you're doing? Are you completely mad?"

"Well," he muttered pathetically, "he were stopping the traffic, weren't he?"

"Is that a crime, then? Why don't you kill him while you're at it? You should be locked up, you imbecile!" A small crowd looked at me in disbelief.

An ambulance was called. I reported the incident to the police when I got home but they weren't interested: the tramp would have to report the incident himself.

The second time, a few months later, I was again driving back home after school when a group of boys caught my eye. They were marching a sad-looking fat boy towards the lock-up garages at the back of the supermarket. He knew his fate, seemed resigned to it, keeping his head down while they jeered at him. I promptly parked my car nearby as they entered one of the garages. As I rushed in, shouting at them to leave him alone, they ran away. The fat boy stood there without reaction, not even surprise.

"Are you all right?"

"Yeah…"

"How often does this happen to you?"

"Every day…"

"And you let them?"

"I can't do anything…" He looked worn out.

He lived in a nearby council block with his grandparents who had approached the headmaster of his school about the bullying, but nothing was done. I decided to drive him home in case the boys were still waiting for him.

"Don't let them do this to you, love, you've got to fight back, and tell people, you must…"

Afterwards, I stopped at the police station nearby to report the incident. They said they knew the garages, they'd keep an eye out.

The next time, I was queuing at the till in the High Street supermarket one evening when laughter and screams outside drew my attention to a scene on the pavement: a group of boys were literally spinning a tramp, pulling him about and cursing him. I instantly dumped my shopping at the till, rushed out and shouted, outraged:

"Will you stop doing this! Leave him alone! Stop this!"

"Who do you think you are, you fucking cow! Don't you try to mess with us! Fuck off, you bitch!"

There were three or four of them closing in on me threateningly, safe in their numbers. Stop it now, I said to myself, you have to stop doing this or you'll get knifed one of these days… I can't be the saviour of this world.

I told Ella all this, during our sessions. She nodded, and I saw what she understood. I told her about the terrifying dreams I used to have as a child and adolescent, when I was trying to run away from some awful danger, and ran and ran in terrible panic, only to realise that I was in fact running on the spot, never to escape.

I also told Ella what Sophie said to me at goodnight-kiss time:

"I am very attached to you, you know, Mummy."

And we laughed, as we could see what Sophie saw, that we were bound hands and feet in love, our knitted-together lives, and the pretty ribbons as well as the chains...

Chapter Twenty-five

This was no ordinary Pandora's box. It actually asked to be opened, whispering, suggesting, beseeching even. The prize was inside, a prize that burned and maimed at first touch – a necessary prize. This was forensic work too, requiring all the expertise I had, all the courage I could summon. It found me grieving, doleful, despondent, but thankfully also full of healthy anger. At once fearfully and compulsively, I read on child sexual abuse symptoms, dreading to find confirmation of mine – please someone tell me this isn't real.

– All right, yes, it is true that I fear losing control and have often felt powerless.

– I had nightmares and suffered flashbacks, and was amnesic about large parts of my childhood.

– I was a perfectionist in grooming, my appearance mustn't betray me.

– True also, suicidal thoughts were almost always with me.

– Yes, I used to be extremely passive, and would always put others' needs before my own.

– I could feel worthless and at times ate compulsively.

– I was impulsive (particularly when angry, and would now fly into a rage if someone tried to take advantage of me as, alas, I also trusted inappropriately).

– I was overprotective of children (in fact I was obsessed by their pain, always hearing danger in their screams).

– I was (shamefully) often seductive in ordinary situations as I tended to sexualise relationships with men. (I needed attention, and if I got it, felt mercifully chosen.)

– I was in my youth at times promiscuous (for few rewards as I was frigid until my late thirties and feeling numb during sex).

– I was attracted by abusive partners. (I can exclude Paul, but of course he chose me, I didn't choose him.)

– and, yes, I feared and disliked being touched unless it was my choice.

I was appalled. I felt like pleading guilty to some disgusting sin. I was this sad thing: a case history, a statistic, my whole being reduced to a list of symptoms. It still looked like me but maimed and warped as in a distorting mirror. It was me *after* the awfulness, which had left countless dents and scars, results of repeated cuts and wounds: a convalescence of sorts might only occur if I could read the meaning of those scars and attained a recovery secure enough to allow me to function in a plausible way; but I couldn't obliterate memories so deeply anchored in both body and soul, the pain of it eating at me daily in horror and grief. And it was transparent that many of these symptoms applied to Odile as well…

The lesson? I couldn't ignore the facts, so had to deal with them and try and move on. What did that visiting friend tell me after the death of baby Thomas? "We haven't been promised anything". So deal with it, girl. As they say. Could I cope? It wasn't as if I were the only one. But I don't know, it would be a lot easier if I were the only one.

Something had to be done, now. Couldn't people see that child abuse was increasing at an exponential rate? That one single abuser didn't just abuse one child but several if not many? Couldn't they see the destruction? Didn't they know that many of those abused would abuse in turn because they had been traumatized and were haunted by it, unless they happened to meet someone who could treat them with kindness and respect, showing them a different and healthy experience? That they abused, unconsciously, under a compulsion to regain for a moment the strength and power they lost when they were abused themselves – the ones who did not commit suicide or became drug addicts or prostitutes...

Old and not-so-old modes of educational 'culture' were also widely to blame, covering methods of child-rearing which thrived in British boarding schools, inculcating subservience to institutionalized violence and bullying, breaking the children's will and tolerating that young prepubescent boys, away from the normalizing influence of their families and estranged from mothers and girls, had their first sexual experiences with other boys in the prevalent and depraved atmosphere of sexual abuse that benefited some of their teachers. Later on, many would find a congenial place in Parliament and the ranks of the civil service and National Inquiries would be restrained and even sabotaged by their power.

Alice Miller – I read all her books (*The Drama of Being a Child, For Your Own Good*, etc) – understood and spoke about it. Why couldn't the papers say that most abusers had been abused themselves in the past? Because they couldn't blame it on EVIL, the dramatic device that rendered us hopeless – and sold newspapers of course. Because it would seem like an excuse, which it was not: it was an explanation. Damaged people did damage, that's how it was. But so many of those who did it seemed to do it just for fun; just because they could: was that what human nature was, or just this country where I sought refuge?

I looked at my Sophie, her sweetness, her grace, my lovely fun kids at school, and thought, aghast: how could anyone? – Kill them, kill them all.

When I returned to work at the end of my sabbatical, I knew that the frustration and distance I was experiencing meant that I had reached another stage in my development without yet being able to define my goal. I still couldn't 'do' goals, though I perceived that my decision to do a counselling course was at least pointing to a direction; qualifying as a counsellor seemed a possibility while working as a counsellor was still too unrealistic a project: how could I ever earn enough money to support myself, a child and a mortgage if I gave up teaching, when it takes years to build up a clientele? However, the fact that I could do that course in the evenings guaranteed a richer life – a better me. The future could cease to be the impasse it used to be if I was able find my way through the morass of nightmares that assailed me day and night and were wearing me down.

While my thoughts and words had been endlessly chaperoned in the childhood home, the truth forever in quarantine, I also knew that freedom began in the mind: I would have to start fighting 'my' demons – I should not claim ownership here because they possessed me most of the time: I was theirs, they were not mine. However, leaves that had remained for years, decades even, at the bottom of the pond were slowly lifted by some unseen current and rising to the surface. They had been blackened by mud, lack of light, and their shape was now uncertain, disintegrating at the edges. I barely recognised them. They were supposed to have been dead and were not, quite. I wept at almost everything.

A man who worked as a Father Christmas in one of New York department stores spoke on the radio of the sadness of some of the children he met. He took a little one on his lap, asking him what present he would like. The boy replied that it wouldn't be a proper Christmas: his father was dying in hospital and his best friend had Aids – then put his head on his shoulder and cried.

I heard the cries of all the children in the world, of those boys I read about in the newspaper, tied screaming to the rears of camels; in the Arabian desert, men enjoyed camel races but the animals were well used to the men's yells and shouts. They performed much better, ran much faster, if they were startled by the screams of a child bouncing on their rears. What adults will you make, young Saddam, young Adolf?

My desk was piling up with articles about children's suffering. I watched and taped all of Oprah Winfrey's programmes on child sex abuse. I reeled with pain: how to stop all this? How to stop so many lives being destroyed? I was filled with a terrible sense of urgency, I saw that sex abuse was increasing at an exponential rate, so many victims of a single man turning into possible abusers. I felt I was the only one who knew a tsunami was coming to swamp us all, it was becoming the only threat, the only pain. I sent for The United Nations Declaration on the Rights of the Child, I wanted to write to the Prime Minister to tell him to do something –or maybe to Norma, his wife, she could open the mail one Saturday morning and say: 'Look, John, I've got a really important letter I think you should read…' and he would read it of course, he would be convinced of the urgency of the matter; he would contact me and I would help him organise a Department for the Protection of Children with a minister and a large budget for a national campaign…

"You're not going to get out of teaching, I hope," said

Mother anxiously when I told her of my intention to do the counselling course.

"No, not at all," I replied, not lying yet since I was not even in a position to decide, "it's for me, it's interesting…" as I sealed my application in the envelope. "I've had to write a short biography."

"A what?"

"A biography, a résumé of my life."

"Ha! Your life!" she scoffed.

"That's right, Mum, are you telling me again that I don't exist?"

I have replied in apparent jest, quickly countering her words, and the light and playful tone I have adopted to fend her off has protected me against their nastiness. However, it has somehow also sheltered me against feeling my own anger properly since I recalled the conversation, astonished, only days later.

She had another blow for me: she let me know, just before she left for France, that she had ordered Jeremy's latest book and would try and find someone in Bordeaux to translate it for her. I seethed: she will *pay* someone to get close to him by reading his book, siding with him, showing me once more my own feelings don't matter but HE does. She was well aware of his cruelty towards to me, and that for all his graces when he saw her, he never visited or even rang when Sophie was ill, has never attended her school plays or met any of her teachers. She well knew this was painful to Sophie as well, but it seemed the 'special relationship' prevailed; she used that power against me and I raged.

She liked Paul too, justifiably this time – she liked all my men – and expressed her disapproval when on my next visit to Bordeaux with Sophie, I confirmed that I have left him.

"That man truly loved you," she said crossly, and added her sadness that I was no longer in a stable relationship, that

I was on my own again. She saw rightly that I was 'protected' by the mere fact of Paul's presence, and more deeply by his love, concern and commitment, which pacified me. I knew instinctively she also thought me unstable, as she did Odile when my sister changed jobs: well, gone were the days of the lifelong profession and the one and only miserable marriage… "It's the times we live in…" she reflected. Naturally I retorted I didn't need protecting, it was too tempting for me to assert my difference, or else my new status would give her an old power I was intent on denying her. But I knew I was not happy for long on my own: I have proved my endurance more than my independence, these lean ten years before Paul, and it was comforting to have his company – until exasperation kicked in.

"I get attached to your partners, I was very fond of Johan, you have to think of my feelings too… And at each one of your *failures*…" she added pointedly, and there was something else there, apart from what can pass for true concern on a good day, her choice of words told otherwise, something vengeful: I was not as clever as I thought, I might be a modern woman who gave herself airs, who claimed to be emancipated, but I also made a mess of my private life.

Well, I may have deprived her of Johan and then of Paul, but not of Jeremy, who always made sure to call when she visited at Christmas and for Sophie's birthday. It was unavoidable. It was even, infuriatingly, good: for Sophie who could feel at those times that she had more of a family, and for Mother too, who had the power of making Jeremy feel welcome and compensated for the light-hearted indifference I affected towards him; for what drew us together still operated at a deep and silent level. I couldn't be detached from the father of my child and knew I would never be free of him. I refused to play 'happy families' simply because it would be a lie; Mother would love it, though, just as she loved pretending when Odile and I were little that everything was orderly and harmonious. Well, Mussolini loved order too. I wanted to be true, fiercely, and my quest for truth gave me piercing sight: I could tell, as Jeremy wriggled and blushed in her presence like a shy little boy who was at last finding grace in a mother figure, that she might not recoil from him as she did from my father, she was only ten years older than him: other things were at play. I laughed internally although I was vaguely appalled, neither of them was remotely aware…

However, Jeremy surprised me one morning: coming to collect Sophie for the day, and sitting with me in the kitchen while she was getting ready upstairs, he blurted out:

"How do you live? How do you know how to?"

I was stunned. He looked grave, anxious, troubled. I replied hesitantly that I thought it was important to live a decent life – but had he given me some notice of his question I could have made a really good speech… . Besides, I reflected later, both bitter and amused, if your mum and dad don't show you how to live, perhaps you could look it up in a book or two? There was no shortage of books. Still, maybe it took him all these years to work out this was the right question to ask.

Sadly the product of a society where children were educated without being brought up, I could see Jeremy was lost, always was: separated from his family when he was exiled (his word) to boarding school at the age of eight, never watching his parents' connection and daily life, he never learnt about relationships between men and women, listened to their conversations or shared in the home activities, watched and discussed with them the conduct and lives of others. Crucially and most damaging of all, he had to unlearn the ability to show and receive affection since it wasn't available. The constant company of boys and men made girls and women seem like aliens, almost impossible to humanly engage and deal with, a foreign country difficult to interpret so easier to dismiss or scorn. So he and the other boys would bury their heads in their pillows at night, sobbing quietly in their large dormitories hoping no-one would hear, because they could be beaten. Emotions became shameful, to be hidden, first from others then from themselves too. They now lived such broken lives, in spite of their many talents.

As I suspected, Mother felt more entitled to interfere in my life now that I was on my own again. When, on her return to Bordeaux, she sent me another long peroration, I eventually found the strength to reply with what I hoped would be my last letter to her:

Dear Mum,

Two weeks after receiving your letter which made me literally ill by its endless criticisms and the right you think you have to meddle endlessly in my life, I have decided to write to you and you will read this to the end.

I do not ask for your opinion and your advice, and I DO NOT WANT THEM! Since Sophie's birth particularly, I have had nothing from you but blame. Maybe you aren't aware of this, so I think it is now my duty to tell you, not to enlighten you — as if it was possible! — but to protect myself.

Despite your criticisms and the illnesses I have suffered as a consequence, I have always tried to maintain with you the normal relationship of a daughter with her mother, and I therefore confided in you about things I felt it was natural to share with a mother and grandmother. What is sad — and I write this in despair — is that you always used it against me. Unfortunately for me I am stubborn in my feelings — some would call it loyal — and in spite of repeated health problems I persisted in maintaining these bonds. I only survived, each time we met, by taking tranquillisers.

Of course I was partly responsible for the situation since I was laying myself open to your judgement by confiding in you, as if you ever gave me any moral support! It was a long habit, learnt by heart in childhood, to put Mother's happiness before my own...

From now on, things must change: I have MY life and MY responsibilities and cannot to endanger my own health by maintaining such a destructive relationship with you. I am not ending our relationship. We shall see each other although I cannot say when. We shall speak on the telephone, but my dealings with you will be 'rationalised', Canadian fashion.

NEVER WRITE TO ME AGAIN: I cannot bear your letters. I need support in my life, not your moralising judgements and dramas. I have a duty to myself to make a success of my life, for my own sake and Sophie's. Think that if you had treated me with the friendship and discretion you reserve for your friends, we wouldn't have reached this stage. Children are not objects to be manipulated for one's own satisfaction. For my part, I have cried enough, even if I am still crying as I write this.

Hélène

Inevitably, that same week brought me back, like a boomerang, a letter from her which swelled the envelope threateningly. Curiously, she has sent it to me at work as if to give it more weight and urgency. And she has again, as is her custom, written on the envelope the word 'LETTER' which has always smacked of menace. I did not read it. I merely tore the side of the envelope enough to observe that, set out with bullet points, it contained a list of all the sacrifices she had made for me during her life and I consequently owed her for. Without another thought, I threw it in the nearest bin and carried on with my day.

The telephone still rang regularly and I rang her too, at dutiful times. My Sophie suffered though, increasingly the butt of her grandmother's moralising and scolding: she didn't write often enough, nor in the manner required, or without the awaited details; she was making Granny suffer, who loves her so much; granny cries, cannot sleep, and it is Sophie's fault; Sophie is a bad girl, must think of others, Granny's only happiness is a letter from her…

Sophie resented me for having somehow passed the buck as I must admit I was a lot happier without Mother's letters, although some news about old friends' deaths and the larger family were obviously designed to be passed on to me. Sophie increasingly cringed and protested: "I can't stand her letters!" and left them unopened for days – a family trait now. When she cried and protested that she didn't have to write to her grandmother, I told her she had a choice: she didn't have to write to her, this was true. On the other hand, Mother was the only granny she had, the only elder in our so-small family; so she would be depriving herself of that. And this granny, in spite of her tyrannical ways, loved her; but if it got too much, I'd understand: she was fourteen after all, she could decide. So, dutifully but now consciously, she would keep writing to her.

Being fourteen, Sophie was also fun, worked well at school, and dressed in an unmistakable fourteen-year-old way, with a near uniform of long skirts and Doc Martens. With her long blond hair she looked like a rustic princess, and she had me screaming with laughter some evenings at all the rude jokes she had learned in the school playground.

★

At the end of December, I received a note – it was never more – from Odile thanking me formally for my kind reply to her good wishes for Sophie's birthday… the previous August. "Congratulations on your brave Counselling studies," she continued. "I wish you an excellent year full of good things. Love to you both. Marie-Odile," her name as usual followed by a Christian cross. She had enclosed a photocopy of Martin Luther King's 'I have a dream…' speech. Nothing about herself. She knew I still dutifully visited Mother, but did she know I had told her never to write to me again? I doubted it, Mother would lose face, giving Odile more ammunition to hit her with, as she regularly complained of my sister's pious notes and aggressive criticisms: "…and she calls herself a religious!" she railed with mixed indignation and sorrow. "It certainly doesn't seem to make her happy!"

Although relieved at my sister's gentler notes to me, I still felt increasingly frustrated: they were rare and never graduated to anything like a letter: it was as if her life has been erased in a grand gesture of self-renunciation, all to the greater glory of God, I fumed: she might think herself holy but she didn't glow in the dark! She hadn't visited Mother in over two years now; distance was no longer an excuse since she lived only two hours away, leaving me as ever, responsible for filial duties I considered inescapable. *Plus ça change…*

I read from a library book on the training of young religious in their convents where a few nuns who have left and on occasion fled religious life, candidly recall it as a breaking of the will in order that nothing remains of their old ego: they were made to suffer constant undermining, belittling and public humiliation in order to become pliable to the will of God as expressed through their superiors. Only God had to matter: attaining closeness to Him required that they die to their old self and become a mere shell that only God's love shall fill.

Forbidden to speak to outsiders of what takes place in the convent and even less of what feelings animate them during their apprenticeship, the nuns' letters to their family were necessarily anodyne. But why had Odile not warned

Mother that this was the reason for her new style of writing, merely expressing good wishes, religious quotes and prayers? Didn't she know this would cause extreme anguish and worry? Wasn't there cruelty and possibly vengeance in the withdrawal of an explanation? Wasn't she forcing Mother to function in a void, without the chance of there ever being any elucidation? If she did, she was making sure that it spared her no pain.

So there was Odile, trying – instructed – to die to her old self, surrendering to a conditioning that made no room for her own needs: so parallel, so close to the way we had been brought up, by a mother whose own sad requirements dictated for us an existence of emotional bondage: there used to be no law but Mother's, now there would be no law but God's: the transition would have been easy, if equally painful. No wonder she had been so slave-like to 'that man'. Recalling Madame Niklaus's visits with her books on saints made me grateful for my own youthful dalliance with Jack London, although it later precipitated me towards Jeremy… Odile would have done better with his books, learning that conquest of any kind required clear vision, courage and a fighting spirit – if she wasn't totally broken.

There was to be no peace for her though, was there? Choices made from a warped education and reasoning were bound to create conflicts with the legitimate needs of a young self that yearns for love and protection and is never granted them. So she was 'difficult': aggressive, jealous, desperate, all expressions of her frustrations, and gave herself over to a religious pursuit which by its very nature was designed to increase those.

When Mother arrived for what would turn out to be her last visit, Sophie and I – myself suitably tranquillised in anticipation – were waiting at the airport and were stunned by the pathetic sight that came into view long after everyone else has disappeared: leaning on as much as pushing her caddy, her steps hesitant, that old woman shrouded in black from head to toe, was also, strangely, wearing dark glasses and unusually, no lipstick; a Tragic Widow figure. This was a terrific production, high drama indeed: we should be awed, overcome with pity, ready for repentance and to fulfil her every need. I was on my guard. She wasn't well, she said wearily, and although only in her seventies walked dragging her feet like a very old woman. It was difficult to totally dismiss her act; she must have felt very wretched and needy to even want to appear this way, but I could not ignore her desire to dominate. Indeed it wasn't long before Sophie warned me:

– She walks almost normally when you aren't in the room, Mummy, she only starts walking slowly when you come in…

When I enquired about Odile, Mother scoffed:

"Ha! Your sister! She now talks about your father as if he is a saint! She wants to know everything about him and nags me constantly for details of his life!"

She knew it was a terrain where we might meet: I was ready to commiserate on Odile's lack of communication, but other topics were out of bounds: I was guarded now about my life, studies, and Jeremy's visits and conduct. Naturally, not a word about the fact that she was no longer allowed to write to me. We were not officially at daggers drawn, as she replaced criticisms with sighs and shakings of her head; there were on both sides fleeting moments of gentleness – unless it was deliberate forgetting of all the sickness for the sake of a few moments' peace.

Apart from a skirt, she didn't wear black at all during her stay, nor when she finally returned to Bordeaux, I noted, and had also shunned her dark glasses, but she certainly made an impression on her arrival and I did not wish to feel unnecessarily guilty: I rang my Bordeaux cousin Chantal whom I considered a friend and on my visits often entertained with tales of my dealings with Mother. She herself visited her once a month, even at times inviting her to family occasions. I wanted to know the real facts about Mother's state of health. As it happened, Chantal declared Mother quite well, on the same medication as the previous two years – but she was going to ring me, she added, having been alarmed by a second call from my sister within a week (she had never received calls from Odile before) because my sister was "in a funny state, talking fast, and she rang up quickly without apparent reason". Without introduction, Odile had said: "*I am very cold, and my feet are completely wet, I don't know how long I can stay in that cabin in the middle of the fields.*" and then rung up without waiting for a reply. Chantal had no number to reach her on, did I? I didn't. Odile had rung again two days later '*with almost the same story, saying it was even colder in the woods and her shoes were soaking wet.*' Chantal was concerned: did I know what it was about? What a story!

I slept badly that night, trying, fighting almost, to remember something but to no avail. "*What a story!*" I had Chantal's words in my head. Then, just before morning, I remembered: I had lived something similar, or rather, I had written it. I was eleven or twelve at the time, and clearly remembered looking at myself in the mirror just after writing my first story, feeling I should look different after this first act of creation; my hair was almost down to my shoulders then, before it was required to be cut short by Mother's desire for distinction.

My story was about a young girl who was a vagrant. She had no family and trekked from village to village begging for food. People gave her food, but did not want her to remain in the village and kept telling her to go away. So she walked on, and it was the same in the next village, and the next…. . One day she found a dog: she was so happy, as it seemed to be a stray and took to her instantly. She had a companion now, life should be different. When they reached the next village, she found an abandoned wooden cabin in the fields where she thought they could live, they would be safe. However, when the village people saw that she had a dog, they killed it so she had to move on again. That was all.

Mother telephoned me later in a very agitated state, my sister was driving her crazy: Odile had called her, refusing to say where she was, except that it was very cold in the fields, her shoes were soaking wet and she didn't know where to go, then she rang off abruptly. Mother didn't mention Chantal but added that she would consult her parish priest, which I encouraged.

It seemed to me, from my more distant place of refuge, like a plot, a desire to cruelly alarm Mother and us all. If she wanted to be retrieved, she could just say where she was. This was attention-seeking. This was revenge. This was patently aggressive, for it was also obvious that she had access to a public telephone, so she wasn't in a wilderness.

Or else it was an extreme religious attempt to live as a hermit, to get closer to God through an act of deprivation, having renounced all comfort or safety (while complaining about it). The Christian religion had many stories of such saints and she wished to follow in their steps.

Or more likely this was the presenting symptom of her condition, and what she was living was simply an illustration of how she felt, the pain of abandonment she experienced had given her a way to alarm the world to her loneliness: this was only too real and it broke my heart as I recognized it; I remembered the story I wrote as a child; only Odile, in her anguished and God-haunted condition, was living it in her flesh and it illuminated me.

Chapter Twenty-six

I seemed to be the only one Odile hadn't rung about being cold and wet, alone in a field or a wood somewhere: she had restricted her calls to both Mother and Cousin Chantal who, living no more than two hours away from her, were the more capable of helping – without disclosing where she was she knew they would be the most affected by her calls. Here in London I could do nothing, and she must still have resented me for withdrawing my invitation: even if the bigger picture was evading me at this point – she was very unwell and needed not just shelter but treatment – I was haunted by her suffering and the similarities in our stories. She was my poor little sister, my little, difficult, angry and tormented sister. I wanted her taken care of. I wanted to see her safe. No-one should feel the way she did, ever, there was too much anguish, too much of a life destroyed. And I also wanted all of this to go away.

When I telephoned Chantal at the weekend, she spoke with exasperation: she had another call from my sister the night before, tried to be friendly and asked Odile why she was ringing *her,* since Mother obviously wanted to help, why wasn't she telling her or people close by? Because I consider you a friend, Odile had replied. Being a doctor as well as a cousin, Chantal might have appeared an obvious port of call to my sister in her need, but Chantal reminded her that they hardly knew each other since Odile had lived for so long in Canada, and pointed out that if she still refused to say where she could be reached in order to be helped, could she please stop calling her?

My heart sank. I couldn't blame Chantal, but this was yet another rejection for Odile to endure, confirming her in her conviction that she was and had always been unloved and abandoned by all: cruelly, the world was against her, for no reason that she could fathom. I confided in Chantal how much Odile's story was distressing me. Wishing to comfort me, Chantal then made the stunning comment that it was a relief that *I* at least was giving Mother a great deal of happiness in the way I ran my life and brought up my daughter, and by being so talented in all my enterprises (I recently had some poetry published). "She succeeds in everything she does," Mother cooed proudly last time they had spoken about me.

Did I live on a different planet? Astonished as I was, I made a point to inform Chantal that on the contrary, Mother had rarely spared me any blame, large or small, from childhood till now, and this had got a great deal worse after Sophie's birth. Whether it was about the way I looked, lived my life, my work, my choice of partners or friends, how I raised Sophie whom I was depriving of her father – this wonderful man – I had seldom found grace in her eyes. It was obvious that she would rather die than admit to the humiliation of two antagonistic daughters, proof of a failure of mothering she could not bear to face while feeling it in her bones: it was crucial for her to save face by pretending that her relationship with me was a success and that I too was a success: she was merely unlucky with Odile.

I was reeling with shock: Mother knew very well what she had been doing! The pretence, the dissembling, the double

257

game, it was all planned, deliberate. It was not just as if she had shown me disapproval and at times disdain out of some psychological weakness that was all the more systematic because it was unconscious (all mothers wish their children well, don't they?) but she had done so knowingly: I should be harmed by her treatment, this was what she wanted.

I knew irrevocably that I couldn't bear to hear her voice again, that ersatz of a loving and joyous tone she affected when speaking on the telephone, as if we were the most loving mother and daughter in the world. That had to stop, I had to live in truth. I could only live in truth.

The following morning, I had my telephone number changed.

Guilt? I can't admit to any feeling of guilt, no. I knew what it would do to her and would rather have avoided it, I just had to stop what she was doing to me. I had run out of strength. She had finally managed, over the years, to incrementally weaken the steel ties that had bound me to her, but it had left me with an awareness that I was being harmed, diminished, turned to impotency in my voluntary servitude. I had tirelessly fought that feeling out of what we carelessly call love at times, but love shouldn't hurt so much.

I was exhausted: bullied ruthlessly at work by the principal whom I was now told had a previous history of harassment: a secretary was paid off (she had made copies of every one of his insulting notes to her, it is all hush-hush). There were rumours, I was told again; people were talking; there had been complaints; parents had expressed concerns. For months I lived my life in anguish; like Odile breaking her foot and destabilized, I fell down the stairs and sprained my ankle. When I finally found the courage to check with my colleagues, the form teachers (they would be the first to know of any discontent), assured me that everything was fine, there haven't been any complaints at all, and I decided to let my principal know.

Jim, a man in his forties, cultivated an image of easy warmth and chumminess, but lied endlessly and carelessly to the teaching staff about his goals and decisions, boasting untrammelled adolescent ideals, eventually losing his early credibility. I could see through him and despised him, but he was six foot seven and I was five foot tall: the little girl in me was quite scared, although this time very angry. I was also warned by a couple of colleagues that the administration were trying to get rid of people who had tenure in order to employ staff on one-year contracts only, and two teachers were already leaving this year after some hassle, so it might be my turn and I was left to watch events unroll.

Under Jim's guidance, the administration now resorted to open harassment: Lower and High School administrators – not teachers – appeared in my classes unannounced (not Middle School, strangely), sat at the back discreetly, and I had to endure open sighs, shakings of the head, frowning, in front of puzzled pupils. Some of the latter were indeed removed from my classes without warning, and I later discovered that they had found a new desk in the classroom of the close colleague, Laina Hodge, who for years had seemed to want to ruin me: it was not difficult for her; she attended the American Church frequented by many parents every Sunday; all she had to do to inflame parental panic and keep a clear conscience was refuse to comment if they asked her questions ('I couldn't possibly... It would be wrong of me...')

Desperate, beyond anger but not completely helpless, I decided to seek legal advice, following which I wrote to the new headmistress and my principal to inform them that I would initiate a complaint procedure against the school for harassment unless they paid me compensation: I pointed out that I had witnesses and had also kept a journal. One day, there were eight of us at a meeting in which both the administration and I made our positions clear. Alone to face them, I would feel desperately vulnerable but for the advice of the Head of Academics who knew what was going on: "Take notes during the meeting," she advised me, "this will give you a countenance and show you are not intimidated." This worked, and strangely Jim remained silent throughout the meeting.

Three weeks after this, I gained compensation. Jim left the school too just a few weeks later, right in the middle of the school year, no doubt in possession of a good reference.

I had worked at that school for twenty years, for my sins. Twenty years that mirrored, physically and emotionally, the same twenty year-long regime of my airless childhood: the building was a kind of bunker separated from the world by walls that were almost all brick and no glass, the few narrow windows that existed being of smoked glass and impossible to open properly, emphasizing the blockhouse atmosphere; even the air we breathed was fed into the classrooms through noisy air vents. My first words to Ella as I had stood in front of her for my first therapy session had been:

"Ella, this school is my father and my mother. The same darkness, thickness of air, the same lack of human exchange and warmth; instead, endless rules and formalities, and the same isolation. How long, to leave childhood behind?"

"All right," she replied gently, "sit down and tell me about it."

This took me not just a long time but a long way too, in spite of more hurdles and ghouls from the past appearing, as I knew they did, uncalled for, sinister and out of nowhere. You cannot be prepared for these moments and you don't know how you are going to survive their assault, but if the truth is your goal, you will. You cannot brace yourself but have to go with it, trusting in the reactions of your body, that steady guardian of all your experiences. Among many over the years, this one flashed at me like gunshot: while I was doing the washing up that day, I dropped the plate I was drying, picked up another and this time threw it furiously onto the floor, and had to pull up a chair because I needed to sit down, breathless: there was this man who came to visit my parents during the war, I remembered his name clearly: Bernard Michelot, or Micheleau. He was in the Resistance and helped blow up trains carrying German ammunition; he was a very brave man and a friend of Dad's. When he visited, Father let him into his study and closed the door.

As if a film was being projected in front of my eyes I saw him in one of his later visits when I was ten or eleven, and dad calling me to come and say hello.

They were both sitting in my father's study when I appeared in the doorway where I froze, and my father, relaxed and laughing, was calling:

"Come in! Come and give a kiss to Bernard who used to bounce you on his lap when you were a little girl during the war!"

They looked at each other, convulsed with laughter. I stared at them. My father, extraordinarily, was laughing heartily, his face bright red. I had never seen him like this. His friend, a fat man with clammy skin, was shaking with laughter and his face had turned almost purple as he looked at me. I became aware of a fetid smell. Normally docile, I couldn't move. I didn't know why they were laughing. Then I ran away.

Remembering this made me feel quite faint and nauseous, and weak on my legs, as if bleeding slowly. I wanted to die. I wanted to be dead. Because this time, I understood. They were sharing a dirty joke, a dirty secret, about me.

Chapter Twenty-seven

The London summer of 2003 had me bathing in the glow of heat and the bliss of light. Mother had just died, and the journey I had to make shortly afterwards to Bordeaux, my birthplace, didn't take me out of my euphoria. I was to see to the funeral arrangements, the clearing of the room in the retirement home where she had spent the last two years of her life, and attend the reading of her will. Also, inevitably, meet Odile again. I dreaded meeting her again, attempting to temper that dread with hope.

I looked ahead to a very busy time. No-one in the family thought that Odile, even though she had entered religion, would want to take part in any of it in view of her conduct of recent years. Remembering my mother's words on one of my previous visits: "Your sister is mad but we must help her," I knew not to rely on much rationality and expecting kindness was a forlorn wish: could I rescue a sister for myself out of the remains of my family? I couldn't know what effect our mother's death would have on her, it was still too early. Besides, I might never know. Mother's rented property in Limoges was finally sold, no thanks to Odile. She was unaware our parents hadn't contracted joint ownership of their assets on their marriage, and that the Limoges property had later been bought by Mother alone and in her sole name. When it was discovered that Father had his name added to the deeds of that property with the connivance of a colleague, unknown to Mother until the recent sale and to her consternation, Odile saw there was an opportunity to obtain a share for herself. I assured Mother I had no claim in the so-called share and signed a letter to that effect: she should have the funds to pay for her retirement home, but Odile refused to comply: she took her own lawyer, declaring she would take Mother to court for despoiling her of Father's presumed inheritance.

The poor woman was shattered by this dual betrayal. I wrote Odile two long letters to explain what Father had done, our parents' marriage contract of which Mother had told me one tearful day when I was fifteen and she felt the need to confide. I begged Odile to sign away her supposed dues for Mother's sake, but these letters remained without reply. She only relented when Mother's lawyer countered by threatening to invoice her for her share of urgent repairs to the property, if it failed to sell because of her obstruction.

Mother, bedridden and sick, was hurt to the core. Her lawyers, outraged by what they saw as sheer vindictiveness, advised her strongly to sanction my sister's conduct and to amend her will accordingly, which she eventually did without explaining the reason. She must have thought Odile would understand, but it was a sin by omission which only increased my sister's sense of persecution: she was the unloved one, always had been.

Despite a vague hope that we might achieve some reconciliation, I knew that meeting Odile would be a trial as I vividly recalled our last moments of many years ago, in the taxi we shared to take her to the train station before driving me to the airport for my flight home to London. Mother had insisted on coming along to 'prolong our togetherness', but in part to conclude a conversation with Odile where my sister wouldn't give way:

"Promise you will call me the minute you arrive!"

"Certainly not."

"Oh please, you know how anxious I am; I won't be able to sleep if I don't know you've arrived safely!"

"I shall have arrived safely."

"But I will need to hear your voice!"

Odile had gone silent and Mother started to weep quietly next to me in the back of the taxi. Odile then turned to the driver next to her and pompously explained:

"She wants to inflict on me the sight of her tears." The driver knew better than to respond and Mother continued weeping. Wiping her eyes finally, she resorted to what I used to call at the time 'heavy artillery': she extended her open hand towards Odile and the tension went sky-high: would Odile comply by putting her own hand in hers as tradition as well as subjection dictated? I was mesmerized. I remembered my own fury and confusion when Mother did 'it' to me; my shame at giving in, my anger at being forced, and my guilt at wanting to turn down a 'gesture of love' or at least peace. She had started doing it to Sophie who stiffened, but of course, being sweet and careful not to hurt, she submitted herself to it.

Well, Odile didn't budge and I found myself admiring the clarity and purity of her anger. Weeping still, Mother finally withdrew her hand and I wouldn't see Odile again until after our mother's death, nearly ten years later – in a few days now.

★

Apprehensive, I looked back at my previous visit alone to Bordeaux three years previously, when I felt, throat tightened, that there would be no end to my life-long entrapment. Mother was still alive but, after a stroke, lying half-paralysed in her retirement home. It had been incredibly hard to let her back into my life as my own health had seriously depended on that recent nine-year estrangement; what aggravated my situation was that Mother had decided that we had now reconciled and all was perfect between us: I should therefore play the compliant daughter so that she in turn could act the loving and forgiving mother, another fantasy. The very idea of living a lie made me sick to my stomach. My reappearance at her hospital bedside with a bunch of flowers (bringing nothing would have seemed a rejection, but I knew she would see it as an appeal for forgiveness). Our first kiss was unavoidable and undeserved by us both, but my questions about her condition confirmed I would take charge of her care. As I wished her no harm while my soul yearned to be at the other end of the earth, I saw myself re-entering the sly world of falsehood so awkwardly managed in childhood.

It had been obvious to Marie-Chantal who had alerted me of Mother's accident (her carer had found her lying on the floor one morning, unable to get up), that I was the only daughter able and above all rational enough to conduct herself correctly and accomplish her duties. I knew I could do what was expected of me. Almost overcome with nausea, I opened once more the door of her apartment where I would be sleeping, on a wool mattress that stank of anti-moth ('like they made them in the old days, very expensive, you know'). I was back in the cage.

Having to clear it, find a buyer who would be free to act promptly enough and sell as well as possible her furniture and possessions, give away her clothes, sort through her files as well as personal papers, I was being constantly confronted by her insistent voice inside my head advising me what to do with this and that: "This is valuable, be careful, ask the auctioneer for a good estimate, I would be very upset to think this was almost given away…" It was easy to feel pity when she told me, forlorn, from her bed: "I no longer own anything…" Images came to me from my adolescence of her joy at finding in some village junk shop a decorative object, a bargain, for our country house in the hills, these objects were also moments of her life. I loved her then. Now I felt crowded and stifled by all these things, each vase, lamp, painting or piece of furniture making claims on me that I had to brace myself against.

I was determined to be organised, clear, efficient, although dealing with her personal papers was a cursed privilege. On opening the drawers of her antique bedroom chest, my very first thought made my heart leap: I might at long last find René-Jacques' letters, those precious memories of my childhood sweetheart. I was reminded that she had always found some pretext not to give them back to me and I preferred to believe her excuses than think she might have destroyed them. It wouldn't be the only time she had tried to deprive me of my life.

Mounds of papers and letters followed drawers packed full of clear plastic boxes ("so useful for storage"), about thirty of them, more boxes containing hundreds of elastic bands, paper clips, labels, postcards. Those had followed stacks of drab old Post office calendars going back nearly fifteen years, hung in turn in the utility room where she used to write her shopping lists as well as do her ironing. Why she had kept all of those, carefully arranged in chronological order, without any distinguishing sign that one year was any different from the next, had baffled me; did they mean: 'I have lived through this year, then that year, and then that…'? So what? It was all overwhelming and I couldn't wait for the amazing freedom to come.

No letters from René-Jacques. Finding them would have meant that they had a right to exist at least, even if she had wanted to deprive *me* of them, but not finding any trace of them forced me to face her enmity and this was incredibly hard to bear. I wanted to scream at her, curse her, ask her why she had wanted to deprive me of the only things I really valued, that spoke of my hopes, my love, and a future that had been taken away early. As I couldn't give the thought any space in me at that moment I had to put it aside; get busy, quickly, and what of those stacks of rectangular lined filing cards (held together by elastic bands) covered on both sides with her assiduous and elegant handwriting — now those promptly held my attention: they were numbered but not dated. Her voice rose strong and clear from all of them, and reading them was compulsive. There she was in this one, losing herself in conjectures about the reasons why my father had divorced his first wife — also a lawyer's daughter: she had never known. I concluded later that he had married her for a position in her father's practice which he would eventually inherit, the only way for him to advance his career and become a proper bourgeois. (I had read Balzac.)

The explanation he gave hadn't satisfied her: why would he have felt obliged to divorce his wife when he had '*discovered that her parents weren't married*'? since he was working for her father? None of it made real sense. Mother had persisted in questioning him and he kept refusing to give her a rational answer until one day he simply forbade her to question him any further. She was hurt and slighted at having no right to the truth. As she was an intelligent woman, I wondered if she ever envisaged he might have committed some dishonesty, possibly appropriating funds, for which he was forced out of the practice by his father-in-law and made to divorce: to avoid any scandal the police wouldn't have been involved, and he would have been 'let go' to find himself another rich wife. This made complete sense to me.

A rounder, almost child-like hand-writing later caught my eye: a recent and desperate letter from Odile – sent by recorded delivery, was solemnly accusing Mother of lying and persecuting her by trying to despoil her over the Limoges sale.

Mum, you are lying.

If you are so upset at the thought of seeing me in rags, accept your responsibilities and don't treat me as a scapegoat in your usual arbitrary and despotic way.

Accept the fact that I was conceived freely. Recognise that you and your husband's (my father) possessions were held jointly in your marriage contract. You were an adult and in full possession of your intellectual faculties.

Give equal parts to my sister and me, without any gifts to my niece Sophie.

Give me back what is due to me. Repent.

Do me justice.

It is not too late. Thank you.

Marie-Odile Dufresne

Then a cry of anguish, heart-breaking, covering a whole postcard sent on the last Mother's Day, only a month previously, which pleaded:

Mother's Day 2001. Alleluia!

HAPPY MOTHER'S DAY, MUM IN HEAVEN

Prayer for Mother's Day:

Father in Heaven, Jesus Saviour,

Thank you for the MOTHER who never abandons, never lies, never betrays, wears no mask and never pretends.

Thank you for THE MOTHER who heals the wounds of all her children who feel abandoned even when they are adults.

Thank You, MUM in Heaven for never repudiating your earthly children whom your Son gave you on the Cross.

Thank You, MUM in Heaven for healing, being patient, persevering and helping us to live our life, strong with FAITH, HOPE and LOVE.

Distraught at so much pain, I had to take a break. I opened a window to feel the cold air on my face and made myself some soothing tea. I wanted to run away, I wanted my home in London, my garden. I cannot remember much of what I went on to read: horribly, this time, Mother railed mostly about me, venting her rage at my refusal to repeat her sacrifices by remaining married to a weak and dishonest man; her outrage that I seemed to treat my own divorce lightly (I made a point of it, she would have loved to see me suffer openly.) and later kept my handy English name instead of taking back my maiden name as tradition dictated. I broke all the rules, paying no heed to conventions or her sacrifices, diminishing them.

What horrified me as I read those cards was her hostility. She had been imprisoned by custom and duty at every turn: I should have suffered her fate, I should have paid the price. I was making a mockery of her life, taking advantage of new freedoms that hadn't been there for her. But it was mostly the apparent ease with which I changed partners which outraged her the most: "Men? She dismisses them!" her tone pointing to me as an enemy, not seeing that I refused to suffer as she had because I was free. No reassurance anywhere, never any praise or appreciation. Nothing kind or loving, nothing. I threw all those cards in the bin and immediately took it downstairs for the next morning's refuse collection.

Weary, dizzy almost, I then knocked at the door of the upstairs neighbour who had befriended me, Stephanie, to invite her out for a coffee, and we chatted pleasantly for an hour or so in a nearby cafe, after which I went to bed.

Then at half past one, rushing to the bathroom, I was violently sick for a painful half hour. I wasn't ordinarily sick: my stomach had seemed to be turning itself upside down as I was vomiting shit, my own shit, and this I repeated every hour for half an hour each time until half past six, to my utter surprise and exhaustion: I thought it might kill me in its violence but strangely it didn't; I was amazed at my own endurance. At seven o'clock, hearing Stephanie's footsteps overhead, I went up the stairs and knocked on her door to tell her of my ordeal and beg her for some boiled rice which she soon brought down to me. I then had a shower, put my make-up on and got ready for the ten o'clock appointment with the lawyer, my first duty of the day. Having somehow purged myself of Mother, I felt strangely strong.

Later in the afternoon, at the Home, came the time to say goodbye as I was returning to London that day: standing at her bedside, having assured her that everything was now in order, I saw her watch me resignedly as she took in that I had finally accomplished my task. She knew I would have read her papers and didn't ask me to kiss her. I was very calm, in charge, keeping the tone light. She was expecting her lawyer's visit that afternoon, after my departure, but needed my advice one last time: before his death my father had extracted from her the promise that she would be buried with him in their small town graveyard in the Pyrénées; she couldn't refuse him then, resigning herself once more. "But now," she said plaintively, "after his last betrayal over Limoges, I no longer want to be with him." She wanted to be cremated in Bordeaux: would she be breaking a promise? A great deal less than he had betrayed her, I assured her, she had every right to make that decision. "I agree with you," she conceded.

I was finally ready to leave and might not see her again; I felt strangely empty of feeling as I looked at her, tapped her feet from the end of her bed, shaking my head slightly and sighing, and left her room without a word.

Back home in my London flat, I rapidly sank. Where was I in my life? Nowhere, it seemed. Worse still, the past had re-absorbed me, which was fatal: regular telephone calls to and from Mother kept me in an angry fog of bondage as if she was now living with me in this flat, with conversations about her health and thoughts. I was faking concern again, asking the right questions as if I had no other care but her condition; she faked normality in tone as if I had returned under her rule and her satisfaction burned me: there was no escape. There came a moment finally when I became incapable of calling her, my strength exhausted: I couldn't bear to hear her voice again. Alarmed at my silence, Madame Laville rang me:

'Tell her I'm unwell,' I said, 'I just can't do it.' I lay for hours on the couch, inert, staring at darkening clouds.

My Sophie was abroad, travelling the world with Adam after their university successes. I was alone, drifting; I couldn't breathe. I attempted suicide near Hampstead Heath in my car one night with an overdose, my last thought that this might at least kill Mother now – finding myself the next morning in hospital, dazed and unscathed. A friend came, then another, and I stirred back to an appearance of normality. Two weeks later, Mother died from the relentless summer heat of that summer of July 2003 and I was being summoned back to France to do my very last duties.

On my arrival in Bordeaux that simmeringly hot day, I immediately called the lawyer to warn her that my sister would be contacting her and was a 'difficult' person, but she took me aback: Odile had arrived two days previously, demanding sternly that Mother's assets be frozen immediately: "What do you want to freeze, Madame? Your mother's flat and possessions have already been sold and the proceeds are in her bank account."

The town was basking serenely in early July heat, the sunlight almost intolerable in its brightness, so different from the gentler English one – a raw, impudent light, the light I remembered. The day before the funeral felt absolutely magical. I had finalised the arrangements with the undertaker, the home, the vicar, the very few family members who would be coming as well as Mother's two young carers. Everything was settled and planned, I was almost free. Odile having forbidden the lawyer to communicate her contact details to anyone including me, I was alone on that shining summer Sunday. The cafés were buzzing with people chatting and drinking happily, seemingly forever at leisure.

A book of poems in my bag, I got a newspaper at a kiosk and went to the bakers to buy a magnificent ham and salad baguette, a slice of apple tart and some mineral water. Making for a bench in the Jardin Public with the best view of the pond, the waterfowl and the birds, I had a heady feeling of celebration. I watched the birds and the ducks in this park where long ago I was taken myself in a pram as a baby and where I could sit again now without equivocal feelings, curiously at peace. I savoured my sandwich and my apple tart, throwing crumbs to a dozen chirping sparrows hopping at my feet.

Too happy to read, I held the book of poems in my hand and watched the afternoon light soften. I later made my way back to the town centre to watch an old Rossellini film after which, sitting at a café terrace, I finally relished some strawberry ice-cream in the gentler afternoon sun.

When morning rose on another glowing day, I got dressed in black trousers and black blouse under a cream jacket. On the way to the Home where I was due to meet the undertakers and a friend of Mother's, I stopped at the florists to collect the pink roses I had ordered. The florist was clever with her arrangement and kindly with her words:

"...and how old was she?"

"Eighty-seven," I replied.

"Ah, isn't it wonderful to see people living to such a great age, it's progress, isn't it?"

"Not at all, Madame," I replied firmly, "believe me, there is nothing wonderful about it. My mother had been paralysed from the waist down for the last two years and had become doubly incontinent; it caused her terrible suffering."

She looked stunned and stood there, speechless. I thanked her as I paid, assuring her the roses were beautiful. Was I too blunt, giving reality its dues?

At the Home, a building of pale stone converted with care from a beautiful old church, I walked to the reception to announce my arrival. I avoided looking at the rows of vacant and not so vacant-looking old people who lined the walls facing the entrance, trying not to take in too much and stay on task.

The manageress did not ask me again if I wanted to go and see Mother, I had previously assured her I had no wish to do so. I had given her a condensed version of my family's story a few months beforehand and she was friendly with me.

I enquired about Odile: where was she? Had she arrived? My head full of assumptions, I had taken it for granted that she would be coming to meet me there. To my astonishment, I was informed of her many recent visits to Mother's room, to Mother's body. Odile had introduced herself as Madame Dufresne – our family name, since she never married. Everyone in the office had been surprised. Knowing there would be no visits, Mother had never mentioned her. In shame and embarrassment that her younger daughter didn't wish to see her, she only ever talked about her 'daughter from England' – myself.

On her arrival at the Home a few days beforehand, Odile – or Marie-Odile as she called herself since becoming a nun in Canada twenty years previously – had stood at the desk and declared sternly she wanted to be taken to Mother's room and be left alone there, *"as I have to talk to her"*. I imagined anger, sorrow, a lot of tears and recriminations. Typical of Odile to speak in this way, I thought, she had to spill out her internal drama regardless of circumstances. And while Mother was lying, stiff, hopefully peaceful and mercifully silent on her refrigerated bed, Odile had called on her every day, sat with her, talking to her, no doubt crying and maybe holding her hand, maybe asking why she was so little loved and protected. Poor little girl, my heart went out to her. I could imagine anything. I could understand everything.

She made no appearance at the Home: didn't she wish to see me at all? I gave my flowers to the undertakers and was driven to the church by my mother's friend. The sun shone again brightly on that Monday morning, swifts screaming shrill joy in the summer sky. We were to join two cousins and their wives outside the entrance, who greeted me with quiet affection. I explained my mother's last wishes, having learnt about those only two days before when discussing the arrangements with Madame Laville:

"But your mum doesn't want anyone at the crematorium! Didn't you know?" I didn't. She showed me the letter, hurriedly made photocopies for the undertakers and the relatives, my sister, myself. It would all be strangely short, almost casual, I felt. A dismissal; a throw-away funeral.

"Was it Odile who just walked into the church?" said Chantal.

"I didn't see her; maybe."

"A woman in a pale blue dress wearing a dark scarf on her head? She looked at us but walked straight in."

"I don't know," I replied. "She does wear a scarf."

As the undertakers hadn't yet arrived there was a little time and I slipped into the church. It seemed dark, I didn't notice her straightaway. Then, a very still figure sitting to the right of the aisle, almost hidden behind a thick pillar, claiming her separateness. I walked quickly towards her, anxious:

"Odile?"

She stood up abruptly, a stiff horizontal smile on her closed lips but not in her eyes – feverish, hostile without restraint – held her hand out to me formally. I took it, dumfounded – *doesn't she recognise me?* She shook my hand ironically, spat:

"Delighted."

"Odile, I'm your sister!"

"I know – " sardonic tone. "Ab-solutely delighted!" I was stunned.

"Are you well?"

"Yes – " aggressive – "wonderfully well, as you can see."

She was as frightening in her coldness as in her appearance: an old face – when she wasn't even sixty – with bitter lines and folds on dry skin, her burning eyes glaring at me through glasses that magnified them: the sun visors clipped to the glasses were lifted, giving her the look of an odd insect. Her hair was invisible, covered with a plain navy scarf tied at the nape and a large crucifix hung on her chest. I had hoped to be able to say: 'Can we see each other after mass and have a talk?' but she spat at me again:

"Thank you for inviting me, thank you very much!"

"But Odile, you never answered letters!" I replied clumsily.

"Oh, come on, stop pretending, like the rest of the family!"

This was hopeless. I turned away to leave, when she hissed:

"And thank you for helping me these last few years!"

★

Even after several months the scene is so clear in my mind: I have left her now; the music is starting to soar, the undertakers bring the coffin in slowly – it's my mother in there. I join the others, a very small group of eight on the left of the aisle. The old priest stands facing us, starts speaking. Iva, my mother's young carer who visited her every day these last nine years, is crying. I hold her arm, stroke her hand, she's the one grieving. Her flowers are on top of the coffin, she tells me, gratified. I can't see mine anywhere.

The priest makes a sign for me to come and read the piece from the Book of Wisdom I chose in his brochure the previous week, a text of quiet piety picked among heady ones from the Gospels. 'I'm not a Catholic,' I had said, 'I just want to do what's right for my mother,' but I also didn't want to read anything I could not believe in: I mattered too.

I face our small congregation and read slowly, I have forgotten about Odile. Iva is still crying. My mother is in that box on my left. This is a church. It will all be over soon. I am calm.

We come out into the sun and the still-rising heat and it's not yet eleven-thirty. The coffin is just being placed in the hearse. The undertakers come and shake my hand, and I thank them. I ask where my flowers were, and they say:

"Inside the coffin, with your mother."

I nod, but I want to scream. I do not want my flowers on her body. I don't want my flowers close to her body. My flowers are in her box. Part of me is in that box. I want to scream. I am very calm.

The priest comes to me and shakes my hand, I place my free hand on his. I smile, kiss my cousins goodbye, watch the hearse drive away without us. How odd. Odile is nowhere to be seen so I leave with Madame Laville.

I knew Odile and I would meet once more two days later for the reading of the will and dreaded the coming encounter: I was aware of Mother's decision in my favour (as a single parent, I had a daughter to bring up and this was being acknowledged) and feared a violent or at least dramatic reaction on Odile's part; obviously, she would feel vindicated in her old perception of herself as a victim, which no-one, including me, had the courage to challenge: she would have had an equal part were it not for her conduct towards Mother. But how could she ever change her view of herself if she remained ignorant of the reality? Who could have said to her: "You are a vindictive woman and your hatred is blinding you: this is the reason your mother's will was amended." And also: "You are a terribly wounded woman and your rage is confusing you, you need help in seeing the truth." If she had let me talk to her, I would have told her. Could the lawyer have been asked to tell her? I think not, but I am not sure, this is a family issue only. As things stand, the unsaid still has far too much power, and I regret not telling her; I didn't even envisage it at the time: all I could think of was wanting it all to be over.

The lawyer called the following day to warn me: my sister was asking for my consent to bring 'an adviser' with her for the reading of the will. I immediately thought of a member of the Church. It was assumed in the broader family that Odile had become the victim or come under the influence of a sect, the only possible reason for an attitude so at odds with the saintly behaviour automatically assigned to Catholic clergy. I knew myself, after my boarding-school experiences in a convent, that the reality was not so simple, and more recently the two lawyers assisting Mother had assured me: 'Nuns are the worst.' This puzzled everyone a great deal.

I agreed to my sister's request, it might shed some light on her entourage – the people who wanted to lay their hands on her inheritance. I asked to bring Madame Laville, whom I had become very fond of: as an ex-Post-Mistress and a woman of generous character, she had for years helped Mother with her financial affairs and she would be able to answer any questions as well as hopefully act as a buffer.

Odile appeared on her own. Madame Laville and I were sitting in the waiting room as she entered, a pale and tense figure: so much pain, I thought woefully, looking at her face. She stared at me and without a word sat at the opposite end of the room. I walked towards her:

"Odile, would you like to meet Madame Laville, who used to help Mum with all her papers?"

She sprung off her seat, looked at me furiously:

"Ah, no! This is certainly not the time!" and stormed out into the stairwell.

When the lawyer, a tall, authoritative woman, finally asked us into her office, I made sure to have Madame Laville sit between Odile and me, afraid she might attack me physically when she heard Mother's wishes. Meanwhile she was ignoring me, which gave me the opportunity to observe her sad, hard face and watch her frequently interrupt the proceedings with sarcastic and hostile questions, obviously irritating to the lawyer. She demanded (*'I demand,'* she kept saying peremptorily) photocopies of every single sheet of paper on the desk. Irritated, the lawyer had to keep calling her secretary in for more copies to be made. When the moment came for the reading of the will, Odile fell silent. Then she said – and anguish had replaced anger in her voice:

"This was my worst fear, I have been disinherited," she moaned.

"You haven't been disinherited, Madame, since your mother is leaving you a third of her estate."

Odile regained her hostility, leant forward on her seat and shouted:

"I wish to tell you that I totally disagree with my mother's decision!"

She suddenly looked haggard, her stiffness threatened.

"And so, what do you intend to do, Madame?" the lawyer replied firmly. If you are trying to say there is anything wrong with this will, I can assure you I know my job, and if I ever did anything irregular, I would be struck off! This will is only a year old and your mother's wishes were taken down by me in front of two witnesses. So if you want to take it any further, you will have to take *me* to court, and I can promise you it will cost *you* a lot of money!"

Dumbfounded, Odile changed her tone immediately, and meekly asked if she could have an appointment with her the following day after consulting her own lawyer. She was given a time for the afternoon. By then, I thought with relief, I would be flying back home to my wonderful London garden. Good.

This is an autumn of incomparable grace. My landscape of fourteen trees is this morning animated by an impish wind that sends the last few leaves in capricious horizontal showers. The ash on my left, His Royal Goldness, stands its ground proudly, tries to hang on to its last corn-coloured leaves which the wind picks out in reluctant drifts. They all seem to land in my garden, a gracious gift. In a couple of days I shall rake them all up in soft hills and bag them up in black plastic, my part of the deal to ensure the grass can breathe. I shall have fun throwing pieces of bread among them, watching squirrels discover them as they play. Two of them from the new litter already fool around on the grass this November morning as if tickled by the gusty wind on their young fur. One of them comes to explore the orangery at the French windows, stretching above the bottom of the frame, all round eyes and mischief. I sit still. The cat dozing on the armchair barely lifts his head.

High above, a rush of white and grey clouds announce the mood of the day, with sound effects now, as the wind hisses and whistles all around me. The single propeller blades of the sycamore keys nose-dive seed-end first, making a slight opening in the ground, ready for opportune fertility. The leaf stems that hit the glass roof, before the hurried slide of the leaves themselves, land sharply with little taps. Tap, tap–tap.

On the desk that stands along the glass wall where I sometimes work lies a fading photograph of Odile as a little child. All blond curls and bursting with laughter, she is sitting on a garden chair, arms defiantly crossed on her chest. She wears a smocked dress; no doubt I had the same one, it was then in good taste to dress sisters alike, they looked so cute. She was fun then and I think I liked her as I remember agreeing with Mum that we were lucky to have her to make us laugh. What is uppermost in my mind, though, is my annoyance and frustration at watching her being so spoilt, often at my expense. ("Give it to her, she is little, she doesn't understand; you are the elder, you must set a good example.") There was no choice, it seems, but to behave perfectly at all times. I remember at times itching to hit her, but she would start screaming before I was able to do it, Mother would come running, shouting: "What have you done to her?" and I would be scolded for something I hadn't even had a chance to do. I have this symbolic image in my mind, Paula Rego style, of my mother as a huge little girl pulling behind her two little wooden toy-daughters on wheels. She plays her role to the hilt, cuddling and admonishing in turns, fulfilled by her powerful mission to be A MOTHER.

Looking at old photographs of Odile and me, I feel no conviction now that we were together in heart and spirit; we were neither friends nor accomplices. She looked at me with suspicion (whose side was I on?), envy and hostility. Very few were the times when we had a heart to heart – only when loneliness was too much, times too severe or pain too great, and we would whisper to each other our questions and feelings, what to make of life, how to survive. Father was aloof, which in itself made him powerful. Mother was omnipresent and in her way formidable, although her frequent protestations and tears behind closed doors in my father's study defined her for us as a victim. So we were on her side, hated Father for making her cry. I wished him dead, quite simply.

Postscript

Mother died in 2003, and I have remained without news of Odile. Jeremy died a few years ago year aged eighty-eight, un-mourned by our daughter and myself or any of his other children, merely leaving sad traces.

René-Jacques on the other hand, or at least his memory and the frustration and outrage of not having been allowed to keep his letters, has followed me throughout my life. He even has a posthumous role in my first play, *The Deal*, in a scene where I confront Mother about not returning his letters. I was so exercised writing this scene that I tried to contact his sister Anne-Rose afterwards, in their old French town, Tulle —a shot in the dark, well over fifty years later — pleading with her to send me some photographs of René-Jacques nearer the time he died and we had briefly met again; did she by chance find any letters from me? All I am left with is a photograph where he is, aged about fourteen, looking at me mischievously and beaming his wonderful smile; it now lives in a small copper frame near my desk.

About a month later, to my surprise, Anne-Rose rang me: she remembered me, she said, she had even lent her brother the money for his train fare to come and see me that Sunday as he was always broke. She and René-Jacques were very close, they even had a secret language to communicate as their parents always insisted on reading everything they wrote: "Daddy was very strict," she kept saying. I pressed her: was he bullied by his father? "Oh, we all were," she replied, "but him particularly: he didn't want to become a surgeon like Dad, he wanted to do his own thing, and Dad never left him alone because he wasn't getting the grades." He never told me he had problems with his father, I remarked. I remembered the blissful day we had when he visited me: the whole day together, walking on the boulevard and later kissing on a bench, being close again: maybe that's all he wanted that day, to be happy, without the intrusion of familiar pain. I had developed a deep hatred of Vespas after he died, I added, and cursed each one I saw for killing him. "Oh, but he didn't die in a Vespa accident," she interrupted urgently, "that was the official explanation you see, there couldn't be any scandal, Dad was a pillar of society in our small town, very important, very proper. No-one knew what he was really like." But what happened, then? I begged, burning and dreading to know what happened?

"Well, that day after school, René-Jacques came home, took our father's gun out of the cupboard and went up to his room. Mum was alone in the house and heard a shot and rushed to see. He had put the gun to his heart and fired, there was blood everywhere and he was dead." "Oh no, I cried, I can't bear to hear what you are saying, I can't bear it... But why? For what reason?"

"We don't really know; he didn't leave a note. Daddy was very strict, you see. There was nothing any of us could do." I was stunned, wrecked: my sweet boy had killed himself; eighteen years old; so beautiful, so full of life, so gifted and giving. I wanted to howl. I stopped breathing then caught my breath in sobs.

He was being taken from me again, even more painfully this time, because of his own pain and need to put an end to it. Was it because of his grades? Had he failed, consciously or unconsciously, in order to be true to himself, the only way to stand up to his father's terrorism? Still, there was no issue: his father didn't accept disobedience. René-Jacques being his own man, living his own life, was simply not allowed.

It is only three years since my conversation with Anne-Rose and I am shaking again writing this. So, what happened then? I asked. "Nothing," she replied, "we never talked about him again, Dad forbade it. Now Dad is dead, there are photos of René-Jacques everywhere, you can imagine, even though I only come here once a year to visit old friends. This is where he lived and I still miss him, we were so close."

"I can't bear to know this," I moaned, "it is so painful and so new, as if he died yesterday and I've lost him again. I feel so shocked, and it must have been so terrible for you and your mum, what did you do?"

"There was nothing we could do. The Vespa accident, you see, that was the official version. Tulle is a small town and Dad knew the right people; he knew how to avoid a scandal."

I thought of his mother at home running upstairs after the shot, finding her son's body and having to clean all the blood herself, having to cope through her despair.

"Could we meet?" I managed to ask. "I could come to Paris and meet you. I could show you the photo I have of him, the only one I have, he must be about fourteen I think, in the garden of the villa my parents rented in le Pyla for August. And you could show me more recent photos of him, when he was grown up? Would you meet me?"

"I would like to very much if I could, Hélène, but I have to go into hospital for a big operation the day after tomorrow. I have been very ill with cancer for a long time, you see, and this is supposed to be my last chance, even though I don't believe it myself. So I don't think it will happen, I am really sorry."

"You have no idea how much I regret it," I replied. We said our goodbyes, and I was left bereft again. I feel I know that Anne-Rose died following her operation, she would have contacted me otherwise.

There are no neat endings to life stories like this, and mine continued for a long time almost in the same way. Thanks to my therapy though, there was more of myself in me: I was much more alert, stronger, and becoming able to act. At other times I felt haunted, lost, defeated when faced with more and more stories of child abuse; I was being constantly re-traumatised; I was sinking, trapped, feeling 'it' would never stop.

A few years earlier, in another house next door, horrendous cries early one Sunday morning through my bedroom wall, a little boy screaming high-pitched screams because he is being raped by Daddy: "No! No! Don't do that, Daddy! No!" I tell myself improbable stories for two weeks, trying as if to save my own life to believe in other scenarios, then realizing my denial and facing it, calling the NSPCC, then the police. Too late. Then being threatened with death by the father. Then the police again, since I am fighting back…

Finally one day, the godchild I adore, a sixteen-year-old, is subjected to advances by her father and I feel capable of murder, top of my list the man who destroyed my sister, but of course it is easier to kill myself: so one day I attempt again to put an end to the pain that doesn't leave me, and fail.

Yet I have surfaced. There is this new flat with a garden that affords me such healing that I often feel a joy that seems like happiness; more than death, life is a surprise. After more work on myself and the merciless acknowledgement of what sexual abuse at such young age did to me, which I detail in the Prologue, I was able to achieve complete catharsis at age seventy-nine, and become, a little late, the person I should always have been. My daughter is happily married with two lovely and well-loved children. I am also investing myself in writing. I can even look ahead, with a project for a campaign: THE PROMISE, which I detail further on.

Conclusion

One of the great benefits of age is that one has seen so much, lived so much, that the multiplicity of lives and choices eventually makes our own legitimate and therefore possible: fear has been removed, if not obstacles.

My mother used to say I was a quiet little girl. I am sure I was, sitting nicely with a book, but I certainly do not feel quiet now. I feel I have prevaricated long enough. It is a great relief to me that speaking and acting have now become unavoidable.

I wish action could have come in one big leap, racing over steps and obstacles, ignoring or at least making small work of the slow and arduous trail between the halfway houses of whim, wish, desire, decision, and action. Acting is what proper grown-ups do, those who are equipped with self-worth, clarity and confidence, the result of a well-nurtured childhood. Mine being as it was, I could so easily have failed completely if it hadn't been for a nagging impulse, born of need and at times anger, to put things right before it became too late, to even out the past, establish order or at least clarity in what would have otherwise remained incomprehensible chaos.

Being a docile child was deemed a virtue at the time – it still is – and incitements to be obedient under pain of making Mother suffer and Father upset created in the early years a compulsion that became the inevitable language of being. Thank goodness for being allowed to read, and my adolescent hormones that gave me a separate sense of myself. Eventually leaving home for university, my cravings for attention and love merging with panic at being isolated led me to becoming on occasion the prey of others' whims, and mine. It was evidently worse for my sister: having no sense of self-worth and safety she would become a ready victim. Sadly remaining at home while I was given the opportunity to rage at the hypocrisies and neuroses of our Catholic religion by being sent away to a convent school, she became doubly the victim of our upbringing and Mother's need.

This state of being, often due to emotional abuse, is called in psychology: *'learned helplessness'*, a term which is self-explanatory; it causes long-term suffering and is the source of multiple failures if not consciously faced and challenged, usually in therapy, by a stubborn desire to free oneself, in order to develop and later hopefully thrive.

I can thank Monsieur Coutant above all others, the philosophy teacher who saw that I could and needed to use my brain. I was able later to publish poetry and write two plays, as well as a book telling of my search for love in my sixties. I could have done so much more if my brain had not been poisoned and warped at the start of my life.

Now, at a snail's pace, I am able to conclude this story: the long-awaited and shattering public acknowledgement of child abuse, sexual and otherwise, is a painful and useful prompt; it has ravaged me at each of its revelations, but now with a view to action which is the true healer.

This book cannot be enough because it isn't just my story: life need not be so harsh if, quite simply, you have been valued and protected as a child. In this modern, 'advanced' society of ours, millions of children live the despair of abandonment and abuse, this is our own indictment.

It is undeniable that the society I have been living in for over fifty years has changed considerably since I left France and arrived in England: seeing young fathers able to express easy affection to their small children has often moved me to tears, and young mothers, when they are not too absorbed by their iPads, seem also to find parenthood a joyful and rewarding experience. Both invest themselves to a large extent in their children's lives and education.

Of course you cannot make loving your children compulsory but it strikes me that you can help it along by making people more aware of their duties and responsibilities in new ways.

I don't mind being presumptuous by launching an idea: if popular, it could become a fad, a fashion; if people come to see its benefits it could become a custom: there are already laws, customs and rituals that form part of the commitment of a marriage ceremony, religious or civil: vows are made publicly in front of witnesses, we know and understand their legal and affective content.

By law, in Britain, the child's birth has to be declared at the local town hall, the name entered of at least its mother if the father is unknown. This public duty is executed easily, much too easily: it feels like an errand at the post office, there is no declaration, no intimation that a lifelong commitment had been entered into, how profound it is, or that there is any joy in it.

This, to my mind, is what needs changing.

If this story has moved you, please leave an honest review on amazon or Waterstones etc. Feedback would be so much appreciated.

THE PROMISE

THE PROMISE can also be found on the author's website – www.helenepascal-thomas.co.uk – in a reader-friendly format.

CHILDREN AND SOCIETY

All societies and religions of the world have always had ceremonies that celebrate the major steps of our lives, which change according to our understanding of priorities at the time. But in view of shocking recent revelations of widespread sexual abuse in homes and institutions in the last decades, our priorities must now be focused on children.

The State passes laws for the proper development of each child, providing education and health care, supporting the family in its duty to take care of the child until the age of eighteen.

The status of children in their family has been discussed throughout history, but it was always assumed that the child belonged to its parents, owing them respect and obedience, stating that they were their property.

Helena Kennedy, QC reminds us in her book: *Eve Was Framed*, that: 'The common law upon which our legal system is based developed in the Middle Ages when, drawing on the Roman Law traditions, women and children were placed under the jurisdiction of the paternal power, the head of the household, and were deemed to be his property.'

A new law for the benefit of children

As the child has come to be considered as a human being and less of an appendage, it seemed timely, after centuries of status quo and in view of the ill-treatment and exploitation of children throughout the world, **to re-assess the law** and **grant human rights to the child** to put a stop to shocking and widespread suffering.

This topic has been debated and fought over between couples, families and societies and in more recent times in parliaments which is why the wisdom of nations, in the form of the **United Nations**, has formulated the **Convention on the Rights of the Child (UNCRC 1989).**

New legislation in this area redrafted the deal between parents and children and some did see the new law as a contradiction: *this child is your child and yet you may not own them?*

The UNCRC is an international human rights treaty which sets out the civil, political, economic, social, health and cultural rights of children. The Convention (CRC) defines a child as a human being under the age of eighteen, unless the age of majority is attained earlier under national legislation. Nations that ratify this Convention are bound to it by international law, while compliance is monitored by the UN Committee on the Rights of the Child.

Most countries (197) are party to it, and it includes every member of the UN, except for the United States, **all others having ratified it** over time apart from South Sudan, Somalia and the United States, mostly for religious and labour law reasons and the fact that each of the American States has its own laws.

Compliance, however, is a different story and progress is slow, as 90% of the world's population live in countries where corporal punishment and other physical violence against children is still legal, and it is to be deplored that **England and Northern Ireland are still refusing to ratify the law on corporal punishment.**

In England, section 58 of the Children Act (2004), provides for 'reasonable punishment' of children. Similarly, **in Northern Ireland**, article 2 of The Law Reform (Miscellaneous Provisions) Northern Ireland Order allows 'reasonable punishment'. (Wales and Scotland have agreed to comply with the Children Act.)

There are concerns that section 58 of the Children Act 2004 continues to breach Article 19 UNCRC by failing to provide children with equal protection under the law on common assault.

We should ponder on the reasons: why is physical violence on the child still so prized in these countries by so many adults who would call the same 'common assault' on other adults, and pay a price? Considering the child is at its weakest physical and emotional stage, is it not a 'privilege' too far, and too close to cruelty?

Opponents have argued that the Convention is anti-family and that ratifying it would undermine the freedom of parents to raise and discipline their children: this, to my mind, comes from a standpoint of ownership and everything in me cries out against this notion. I am only too aware of the crimes perpetrated to this day in families where this stands for the law of the household and the psychological, emotional and sexual abuse that too often follow.

We cannot pretend to be uninformed of the often-dire conditions in which many children are born and forced to grow up nowadays, when our claims to be enlightened in our knowledge and progressive in our ways could make us think that we are at last treating our children as we should.

It is enough to read the newspapers at random over a period of years to get a broad and distressing view of all our failings:

- "ENGLISH CHILDREN ARE AMONG THE LEAST HAPPY." (*The Times*, 13/05/15)

- "BRITAIN HAS THE MOST CHILD DEATHS IN THE EU." (The *Independent*, 27/03/13)

- "BABIES BORN POOR IN BRITAIN WILL BE NO HEALTHIER THAN THOSE IN LIBERIA." (*The Times*, 2015)

- "ONE IN THREE CHILDREN HAS SUFFERED VIOLENT ATTACK." (*The Times* 1/01/15)

- "U.N. TELLS UK TO BAN CHILD SMACKING AT HOME." (*The Times*, 27/07/15)

- "TRAFFICKING OF CHILDREN RISES FOR THE SECOND YEAR RUNNING." The *Observer*, 1/09/13)

- "WE IMPRISON MORE CHILDREN AND YOUNG PEOPLE IN THE UK THAN MOST OTHER COUNTRIES IN EUROPE. THIS IS IN BREACH OF THE UN CONVENTION ON THE RIGHTS OF THE CHILD." (Sir Al Aynsley-Green, Children's Commissioner for England)

- "SEX ABUSE FILE SHUT UNTIL 2056." (*Sunday Times*, 29/03/15)

- "CHILD MENTAL HEALTH SERVICES FROZEN OR CUT BY THREE QUARTERS." (*The Times*, 28/07/15)

- "VATICAN PAPERS REVEAL THAT INCEST IS THE SIN MOST CONFESSED TO." (Hellmut Karle, on BBC Radio 4 in interview with Brian Redhead in the 1980s or 1990s. After checking with the author by letter, he couldn't be sure of the exact date.)

It is widely agreed that the State *is currently failing* in its duty to keep our children safe. Some of our laws are far from making child protection a priority, and when they do, they are rarely implemented: in Great Britain, our place in international comparison leagues is often extremely poor: *the reasons why should be faced and addressed.*

At a time in the social history of this country when we are overwhelmed with stories of lack of care in so many institutions, widespread neglect and physical and sexual abuse, in spite of the role of well-meaning officials appointed by successive governments, there still remains a reluctance to recognise that children's problems are everybody's business and reflect on us all.

As I sought to give more updates, I found online on The *Independent* of 23 January 2019 an article by Lizzie Dearden, the Home Affairs correspondent, titled:

CHILD CRUELTY AND NEGLECT OFFENCES DOUBLE OVER THE PAST FIVE YEARS IN UK, POLICE FIGURES SHOW.

SEPARATE DATA SHOWS RECORDED CHILD SEXUAL ABUSE HAS RISEN BY 206% SINCE 2013.

Government spending on children at risk of abuse slashed by 26%.

and I think: as a species, **what are we**? And as individuals in in a 'civilised' society: **who are we**? These facts and figures are damning and call for more individual involvement in the cause of children, as it is shockingly obvious that **any child is in danger from the moment it is born**, **mostly from its parents and would-be carers,** first in their general ignorance that a child is nowadays born with rights. As usual, the solution for this is in our own hands, individually and globally.

To my mind, the obstacles are many:

* – ignorance, hence the prime importance of education, at all times of life.

* – assumption that the parents own their children and know best.

* – a tradition of laissez-faire.

* – resistance: a powerful and common instinct to stay with the status quo, not question difficult subjects, and protect oneself.

* – criminal intent, unconscious or deliberate: power over the child is used for private, psychological, emotional, sexual or financial gratification. By all accounts, this is frequent.

* – and, secretly, we do not wish our children to be aware of the danger they run in some of their parents' hands, because we are ashamed that some of us, and we as a species, are capable of such things. Cowardly, we choose to do nothing.

Then the State itself is responsible when it seems to tolerate this law-breaking. When it is seen to default through the scandals revealed, public opposition may force a government to conduct an Independent Inquiry into whatever has caused this lapse.

The Inquiry

This is what has happened in 2015 through the Independent Inquiry into Child Sexual Abuse in England and Wales, in families and institutions, following the greatest scandals of abuse of children in schools, children's homes, churches and charities ever to be known.

This Inquiry, initiated in 2015 by then Prime Minister Theresa May, which gave its conclusions this year, on 21/10/22, was conducted by Prof. Alexis Jay, **took over seven years**, cost **£186.6 million** and heard from more than **7, 300 victims and survivors** of abuse through **15 investigations**, with **men accounting for 89%** of abusers. Last year, **girls accounted for 59%** of children at risk.

10,431 allegations of child abuse were made to the police, resulting in more than 100 convictions. A conservative estimate is that 15% of girls and 5% of boys experience some form of sexual abuse before the age of 16 (half a million children per year).

Alleged abuse at schools was most common, followed by children's homes and religious institutions.

The Main Recommendations

- **– The Inquiry says children have faced 'limitless' cruelty and that the problem remains 'endemic', permeating all sections of society,** but as a Statutory Inquiry, it could not determine criminal liability of named individuals or organisations.

- **– The Inquiry recommends the mandatory requirement** for people working with children, in both paid and voluntary roles, **to report allegations of abuse, but only if they are the victim or witnesses of it; this includes priests told in confession;** (reports from a neighbour 'should be ignored', providing a huge loophole). Some other countries have such laws, the UK should too.

- – The Inquiry recommends the creation of child protection authorities in England and Wales, in the form of a cabinet-level minister. This used to exist under New Labour.

- – The Inquiry recommends a requirement for the registration of all care staff in residential care, young offenders' institutions and secure training centres. *(Children in care homes are four times as likely as other children to be victims of abuse.)*

- – The Inquiry recommends a compensation scheme for all victims of historical abuse in England and Wales.

- – The Inquiry recommends a ban on 'pain compliance techniques' for detained children.

- – The Inquiry recommends that internet search engines block all known child sexual abuse images from being uploaded.

- – The Inquiry recommends that all social media apps strengthen their age verification processes. The huge recent rise in reports of online abuse so far suggests that the overall position is getting worse rather than better. The Online Safety Bill, preventing social media child abuse, is presently going through parliament. (Dec 2022)

The government intends to consider the recommendations made in the final report, then decide whether to accept them and legislate if necessary and give its reply in six months' time; the government's reply should therefore be made public in August 2023.

★★★

From my own experiences in life, readings and study, a twenty-seven-year career as a secondary school teacher, and further study, qualification and work as a counsellor, I can see that the obstacles to progress are many. Among them, a few stand out:

- – Imbalance of power between abuser and victim.

- – Tendency to disbelieve the victim. *(The Rotherham and Rochdale scandals provide good examples.)*

- – Refusal of this recent Inquiry to consider the testimony of neighbours *(in my experience, neighbours know a great deal)* which stands out as a major loophole.

- – Child protection professionals have no minimal training expectation on child sexual abuse, some having no training in it at all.

- – Permissive institutional failures: no recommendation of sanctions for social media companies and search engines that fail to block child abuse images or check the age of users.

- – Requiring people to go to the police is sometimes a disincentive given the chronic failures of the criminal justice system in relation to women and girls revealed in several recent scandals (2021/2022) where policemen themselves were the abusers.

- – We are not generally aware of the potential for harm of most of us and refuse to acknowledge the abuse that takes place within families, as it is a terrible realisation.

★★★

As a result, I thought of a ritual: The PROMISE, to be a major part of the registration of the child and/or religious ceremonies chosen by parents/adopters/carers, and also: staff of all and any establishment dealing with children (nurseries, schools, play and **youth centres, hospitals, libraries, sports and dance venues, holiday centres,** etc. **The Promise should expressly represent the wish and commitment of the person(s) responsible for the child who would sign it and fulfil those requirements to** *respect* **and** *protect* **the child according to the International Convention of Children's Rights.**

THE PROMISE

The Promise is:

1. **Greeting babies, children,** those born to us as well as those we adopt or foster, promising them our love and care, but also, solemnly, respect and protection in a form of words which is signed and legally binding.

2. **The equivalent of marriage vows** but made to the child by its parents or carers in their own words (at any age but preferably soon after birth/adoption or fostering). It would be a public acknowledgement of the duties of protection and nurture that we have to the human being who is at the mercy of our goodwill and capabilities.

3. **A specific meaning of the word 'respect'** when it comes to the child's body which should never be hit or touched sexually by any adult. It also comes with the acknowledgement that a child's feelings should be dealt with thoughtfully as harsh words have a deep and long-term effect. Children learn respect from the way they are treated by adults and are then able to reciprocate the feeling as they grow up.

4. **A joyful affair,** a celebration. And it would spread the knowledge of the true place of the child among us.

Many will wonder: '*Why should I make an official promise to care for my child when I know I can be a perfectly good parent without going through this palaver?*' and they may well be right. This was and is a common reaction when discussing the comparative benefits of marriage and partnership and it is obvious that a public promise to be faithful or to remain together 'till death do us part' doesn't necessarily stop lies, betrayal, or simply failure.

Still, few if any who made these vows can have regretted making them at the time. *The significance of such moments of intensity lies in the fact that they anchor us deeply in ourselves and the unfolding of our lives.* More than a step, they are a milestone of which we are aware at the time and can never look back upon later without feelings of sadness, disappointment and failure if they haven't held good: it *was* important, and we know that something of great value at the time hasn't materialized or lasted.

It is in this context that we must look at the place we make for children in our societies. Some religions may well celebrate and confirm the role the new child will play in their midst but there is, I believe, a need for a public promise of the nurturing role we shall have to play at least until this child is an adult; of our joy at its arrival and the recognition of our duty in its essential forms:

CARE, PROTECTION, RESPECT

(Sadly, we cannot legislate for **Love**, the necessary bonus.)

The PROMISE would have value as a commitment, and there is value in example: in the end, each one of us creates a world in our own image, and as Barack Obama said recently: '*What we do echoes through generations.*'

TOWARDS FURTHER SOLUTIONS

At a time in the social history of this country when we are overwhelmed with stories of lack of care in families and institutions, widespread neglect and physical and sexual abuse, in spite of the role of well-meaning officials appointed by successive governments, there remains a reluctance to recognize that children's problems are everybody's responsibility and reflect on us all.

— This could begin to be remedied by an addition to the registration process, when the new parents would be given a copy of the UN Declaration on the Rights of the Child, required to read it, then sign it, committing them to its conclusions and the duties they infer.

This new duty of commitment should be extended to every group and institution that deals with children and their welfare, state-funded or private, lay or religious, and signed by every individual involved.

— All social work training must be required to include Child Sexual Abuse. Safeguarding recommendations must be improved and implemented. Budgets must be increased.

— The mandatory reporting of all allegations of child sexual abuse must be legally binding, and subject to sanctions.

— In view of peer-on-peer sexual abuse, frequent in schools and universities, children and young people must be taught how to deal with it, helped to report it, and when at school discuss their difficulties in assemblies, small groups, or privately.

— School children should be given a copy of their rights as defined in the Convention of the Rights of the Child (an easy-to-read copy is available, as shown in this book and also on my website: __www.helenepascal-thomas.co.uk__) and asked to discuss them.

— They should also be asked to PROMISE to respect and protect each other.

We must spread the information that child abuse is the rot that affects society in all its forms, as it disempowers and confuses the victim, is a major factor in increasing crime, putting stress on the judicial system, increasing suicides and mental illness, increasing demand for more hospitals and treatments, increasing financial demands on care in the community as well as the public purse.

The psychiatrist, researcher and writer Bessel van der Kolk says in his book:

The Body Keeps the Score

Mind, Brain and Body in the transformation of trauma.

"Child abuse and neglect is the single most preventable cause of mental illness, the single most common cause of drug and alcohol abuse, and a significant contributor to leading causes of death such as diabetes, heart disease, cancer, stroke, and suicide."

I could not recommend this book more.

At a time when members of the present Parliament are letting other people's children go to school hungry, it is high time for us all to act.

By acting, or not acting, each of us decides the fate of children who so far have been so ignored or damaged. **Ideas matter, and your voices, added to mine, could create a huge wave that would bring about the changes children need so much.**

We can all dream, but in some cases, thanks to new laws, the media and the goodwill of many people, results can be attained that can change attitude and society. So WHO is going to do something about this, IF NOT US, NOW? I shall do all I can myself and ask you to support me in this campaign.

Helene Pascal-Thomas.
November 2022.

References

Alice Miller: *The Drama of Being a Child / of the Gifted Child. Thou Shalt Not Be Aware*
For Your Own Good (Virago Press)
The Body Never Lies (W W Norton & Co)
Judith Lewis Herman: *Trauma and Recovery* (Basic Books)
John Bowlby: *Loss / Sadness & Depression* (Penguin)
J M Masson: *The Assault on Truth* (Penguin)
Hellmut Karle: *The Filthy Lie* (Penguin)
Morton Schatzman: *Soul Murder: Persecution in the Family.*
J Konrad Stettbacher: *Making Sense of Suffering* (Dutton)
Claire Burke Draucker: *Counselling Survivors of Childhood Sexual Abuse* (Sage)
Karen Armstrong: *Through the Narrow Gate* (Flamingo)
Alex Renton: *Stiff Upper Lip* (W&N)
Bessel van der KOLK: *The Body Keeps the Score* (Penguin)

DECLARATION OF THE
RIGHTS OF THE CHILD

*Adopted by UN General Assembly Resolution 1386 (XIV)
of 10 December 1959*

WHEREAS the peoples of the United Nations have, in the Charter, reaffirmed their faith in fundamental human rights and in the dignity and worth of the human person, and have determined to promote social progress and better standards of life in larger freedom,

WHEREAS the United Nations has, in the Universal Declaration of Human Rights, proclaimed that everyone is entitled to all the rights and freedoms set forth therein, without distinction of any kind, such as race, colour, sex, language, religion, political or other opinion, national or social origin, property, birth or other status,

WHEREAS the child, by reason of his physical and mental immaturity, needs special safeguards and care, including appropriate legal protection, before as well as after birth,

WHEREAS the need for such special safeguards has been stated in the Geneva Declaration of the Rights of the Child of 1924, and recognized in the Universal Declaration of Human Rights and in the statutes of specialized agencies and international organizations concerned with the welfare of children,

WHEREAS mankind owes to the child the best it has to give,

Now, therefore, Proclaims

THIS DECLARATION OF THE RIGHTS OF THE CHILD to the end that he may have a happy childhood and enjoy for his own good and for the good of society the rights and freedoms herein set forth, and calls upon parents, upon men and women as individuals, and upon voluntary organizations, local authorities and national Governments to recognize these rights and strive for their observance by legislative and other measures progressively taken in accordance with the following principles:

1. The child shall enjoy all the rights set forth in this Declaration. Every child, without any exception whatsoever, shall be entitled to these rights, without distinction or discrimination on account of race, colour, sex, language, religion, political or other opinion, national or social origin, property, birth or other status, whether of himself or of his family.

2. The child shall enjoy special protection, and shall be given opportunities and facilities, by law and by other means, to enable him to develop physically, mentally, morally, spiritually and socially in a healthy and normal manner and in conditions of freedom and dignity. In the enactment of laws for this purpose, the best interests of the child shall be the paramount consideration.

3. The child shall be entitled from his birth to a name and a nationality.

4. The child shall enjoy the benefits of social security. He shall be entitled to grow and develop in health; to this end, special care and protection shall be provided

both to him and to his mother, including adequate pre-natal and post-natal care. The child shall have the right to adequate nutrition, housing, recreation and medical services.

5. The child who is physically, mentally or socially handicapped shall be given the special treatment, education and care required by his particular condition.

6. The child, for the full and harmonious development of his personality, needs love and understanding. He shall, wherever possible, grow up in the care and under the responsibility of his parents, and, in any case, in an atmosphere of affection and of moral and material security; a child of tender years shall not, save in exceptional circumstances, be separated from his mother. Society and the public authorities shall have the duty to extend particular care to children without a family and to those without adequate means of support. Payment of State and other assistance towards the maintenance of children of large families is desirable.

7. The child is entitled to receive education, which shall be free and compulsory, at least in the elementary stages. He shall be given an education which will promote his general culture and enable him, on a basis of equal opportunity, to develop his abilities, his individual judgement, and his sense of moral and social responsibility, and to become a useful member of society.

The best interests of the child shall be the guiding principle of those responsible for his education and guidance; that responsibility lies in the first place with his parents.

The child shall have full opportunity for play

and recreation, which should be directed to the same purposes as education; society and the public authorities shall endeavour to promote the enjoyment of this right.

8. The child shall in all circumstances be among the first to receive protection and relief.

9. The child shall be protected against all forms of neglect, cruelty and exploitation. He shall not be the subject of traffic, in any form.

   The child shall not be admitted to employment before an appropriate minimum age; he shall in no case be caused or permitted to engage in any occupation or employment which would prejudice his health or education, or interfere with his physical, mental or moral development.

10. The child shall be protected from practices which may foster racial, religious and any other form of discrimination. He shall be brought up in a spirit of understanding, tolerance, friendship among peoples, peace and universal brotherhood, and in full consciousness that his energy and talents should be devoted to the service of his fellow men.

Overleaf is the Children's Version. This may look a little drab, but look online and you will see UNICEF have a great child-friendly version; also PLAN INTERNATIONAL have a lovely poster, both great ideas for the classroom!

THE UNITED NATIONS CONVENTION ON THE RIGHTS OF THE CHILD

– The Children's Version

The United Nations Convention on the Rights of the Child is an important agreement by countries who have promised to protect children's rights. The Convention on the Rights of the Child explains who children are, all their rights, and the responsibilities of governments. All the rights are connected, they are all equally important and they cannot be taken away from children. This text is supported by the Committee on the Rights of the Child.

1. Everyone under the age of 18 has all the rights in the Convention.
2. The Convention applies to every child without discrimination, whatever their ethnicity, sex, religion, language, abilities or any other status, whatever they think or say, whatever their family background.

3. The best interests of the child must be a top priority in all decisions and actions that affect children.

4. Governments must ensure every child can enjoy their rights by passing laws to promote and protect children's rights.

5. Governments must respect the rights and responsibilities of parents and carers to provide guidance and direction to their child

6. Every child has the right to life. Governments must do all they can to ensure children survive and develop to their full potential.

7. Every child has the right to be registered at birth, to have a name and nationality, and, as far as possible, to know and be cared for by their parents.

8. Every child has the right to an identity. Governments must respect and protect that right, and prevent the child's name, nationality or family relationships from being changed unlawfully.

9. Children must not be separated from their parents unless it is in their best interests (for example, if a parent is hurting or neglecting a child). Children whose parents have separated have the right to stay in contact with both parents, unless this could cause them harm.

10. If a child's parents live apart in different countries, the child has the right to visit and keep in contact with both of them.

11. Governments must do everything they can to stop children being taken out of their own country illegally by their parents or other relatives, or being prevented from returning home.

12. Every child has the right to express their views, feelings and wishes including during immigration proceedings.

13. Every child must be free to express their thoughts and opinions and to access all kinds of information, within the law.

14. Every child has the right to think and believe what they choose and also to practise their religion.

15. Every child has the right to meet with other children and to join groups and organisations, as long as this does not harm other people.

16. Every child has the right to privacy. The law should protect the child's private, family and home life and reputation.

17. Every child has the right to reliable information from a variety of sources, and governments should encourage the media to provide information that children can understand and is not harmful.

18. Both parents share responsibility for bringing up their child and governments must create support services to help them.

19. Governments must do all they can to ensure that children are protected from all forms of violence, abuse, neglect and bad treatment by their parents or anyone else who looks after them.

20. If a child cannot be looked after by their immediate family, the government must give them special protection and assistance Including continuous care that respects the child's culture, language and religion.

21. Children who cannot be looked after by their own family should be looked after properly by people who respect the child's religion, language and culture etc

22. Refugee children separated from their parents should be reunited with them and have the same rights as children born in that country

23. A child with a disability has the right to live an independent, full and decent life with dignity and play an active part in the community with the support they need.

24. Children have the right to the best possible health care with good quality health care, clean water, nutritious food, and a clean environment and education on health and well-being. Richer countries must help poorer countries achieve this.

25. If a child has been placed away from home for care or protection (for example, with a foster family or in hospital), they have the right to a regular review of their treatment

26. Every child has the right to benefit from social security. Governments must provide money or other support for children from poorer families.

27. Every child has the right to food, clothing and a safe place to live so they can develop in the best possible way. Governments must help families who cannot afford to provide this.

28. Every child has the right to an education. Primary education must be free and different forms of secondary education must be available to every child. Children should be encouraged to attend school to their highest level and discipline in school should respect dignity and never use violence.

29. Education must develop every child's personality, talents and abilities to the full. It must encourage the child's respect for human rights, as well as respect for their parents, their own and other cultures, and the environment.

30. Every child has the right to learn and use the language, customs and religion even if these are not shared by the majority of the people in the country where they live.

31. Every child has the right to relax, play and take part in a wide range of cultural and artistic activities.

32. Governments must protect children from economic exploitation and work that is dangerous or might harm their health, development or education. They must set a minimum

age for children to work and ensure that work conditions are safe and pay appropriate.

33. Governments must protect children from the illegal use of drugs and from being involved in the production or distribution of drugs.

34. Governments must protect children from all forms of sexual abuse and exploitation.

35. Governments must protect children from being abducted, sold or moved illegally to a different place in or outside their country for the purpose of exploitation

36. Governments must protect children from all other forms of exploitation, for example the exploitation of children for political activities, by the media or for medical research.

37. Children accused of breaking the law must not be tortured, sentenced to the death penalty or suffer other cruel or degrading treatment or punishment. Children should be arrested, detained or imprisoned only as a last resort and for the shortest time possible. They must be treated with respect and care, and be able to keep in contact with their family. Children must not be put in prison with adults.

38. No child under the age of 15 should take part in war or join the armed forces. Children affected by war and armed conflicts should be protected.

39. Children who have experienced neglect, abuse, exploitation, torture or who are victims of war must receive special support to help them recover their health, dignity, self-respect and social life.

40. A child accused or guilty of breaking the law must be treated with dignity and respect. They have the right to legal assistance and a fair trial that takes account of their age. Governments must set a minimum age for children to be tried in a criminal court in a justice system that

aids their reintegration into society .Prison should be the last resort.

41. If a country has laws and standards that go further than the present Convention, then the country must keep these laws.

42. Governments must actively work to make sure children and adults know about the Convention. The Convention has 54 articles in total.

43–54 are about how adults and governments must work together to make sure all children can enjoy all their rights.

Acknowledgements

I would like to express my gratitude to my friends Fran Markotic for her sensitive feedback and advice, and Gabi Braun for her dedicated help over the years. Also Lesley Robb for her help, and keeping me on the straight and narrow.

I also owe countless thanks to my mentor and friend Neil Arksey for his professional advice, critical judgement and his frequent prompting to 'go deeper': he took me further.

Helene Pascal-Thomas, November 2022